Choice, complexity and ignorance

Choice, complexity and ignorance

AN ENQUIRY INTO ECONOMIC THEORY AND

THE PRACTICE OF DECISION-MAKING

BRIAN J. LOASBY

Professor of Management Economics
University of Stirling

CAMBRIDGE UNIVERSITY PRESS

CAMBRIDGE

LONDON · NEW YORK · MELBOURNE

Published by the Syndics of the Cambridge University Press
The Pitt Building, Trumpington Street, Cambridge CB2 1RP
Bentley House, 200 Euston Road, London NW1 2DB
32 East 57th Street, New York, NY 10022, USA
296 Beaconsfield Parade, Middle Park, Melbourne 3206, Australia

First published 1976

Printed in Great Britain by
Western Printing Services Ltd
Bristol

Library of Congress Cataloguing in Publication Data
Loasby, Brian J.
Choice, complexity, and ignorance.
Includes bibliographical references and index
1. Managerial economics.   2. Decision-making.
I. Title
HD58.5.L622   658.4'03   75-22558
ISBN 0 521 21065 8

Contents

Contents

Foreword

> Speaking and writing is an ever renewed struggle to be
> both apposite and intelligible, and every word that is
> finally uttered is a confession of our incapability to do
> better.
>
> M. Polanyi (1958, p. 207)

The scope of this book is defined, not by a single specialism, but
by a general theme: the implications, for economic theory and
practical decision-making, of complexity and partial ignorance.
This theme is developed in relation to a number of specialist
topics in, for example, organisational behaviour, theories of competition, macroeconomics, and research management; but the
treatment is designed to appeal to all kinds of economists, even
when – indeed especially when – it is not ostensibly concerned
with the reader's own speciality. Nor is it addressed to economists
alone. Substantial parts deal, directly or indirectly, with issues of
practical importance to managers, or with questions, such as the
appraisal of theories and the uses of abstraction, which are
relevant to scientists and philosophers of science. Such diversity
of application is intended to demonstrate the unifying power of
the theme.

The book is constructed primarily from other people's ideas;
they are better than my own. I have tried to weave together
strands of thought from organisation theory, the philosophy of
science, and managerial practice, as well as a variety of strands
from economics, and have often expressed these thoughts in their
author's own words. Where it has seemed necessary to be critical,
I have directed my criticism only at those whose reputations are
securely founded. I have re-used some previously-published
material of my own: major parts of Chapters 5 and 6 are adapted
from 'An Analysis of Decision Processes', published in *R & D
Management*, 4: 149–55, and most of Chapter 11 is recognisably

descended from 'Hypothesis and paradigm in the theory of the firm', published in the *Economic Journal*, 81: 863–85. I am grateful for permission to reproduce this material.

The first drafts of this book were written during the tenure of a Visiting Fellowship at the Oxford Centre for Management Studies in the first half of 1974, and I much appreciate the hospitality extended to me by the Director, Bob Tricker, and Fellows of the Centre. Professor Shackle has been extremely generous with advice and encouragement, and Dr Alan Coddington a welcome source of ideas. Since I am unable to cite any publications by him, I would like especially to acknowledge my debt to David Clarke, a former colleague at the University of Bristol, who first showed me, in the days before Cyert and March, how an economist might approach the study of organisational behaviour. His own concept of the decision cycle I regard as a major contribution in that approach.

Yet this book is above all a product of the University of Stirling. That the new University should take an especial interest in the relationships between economics, the natural sciences, and problem-solving was a firm belief of its first Principal, Dr Tom Cottrell, who, together with Duncan Davies, of I.C.I., coined for this interest the name of technological economics. The development of this interest has brought me into contact with many professional scientists, and in particular with Frank Bradbury, Professor of Industrial Science, and Charles Suckling, Honorary Visiting Professor and now Chairman of I.C.I. Paints Division. I have learnt a great deal from these contacts, and not least about economics. In addition to reading and commenting on earlier drafts, Professors Bradbury and Suckling have discussed with me many of the topics in these pages, and are jointly responsible for one of its central ideas, that sterile debates about 'realism' should give way to analysis in terms of abstraction and sufficiency.

That the Economics Department at Stirling has provided an intellectually stimulating environment, free from intra-discipline disputes or demarcations, must stand to the credit of its founding Professor, Andrew Bain. Like other members of the Department, I have benefited greatly from the free interchange of views between, as well as within, the conventional subdivisions of the subject. Though to omit any name may be invidious, I must make especial mention, in addition to Andrew Bain, of Paul Hare, Peter Jackson, Richard Shaw, Clive Sutton, and Alastair and David Ulph. Paul Hare read the greater part of two successive drafts, and Peter Jackson, Richard Shaw and Alastair Ulph all read and commented on the whole of the penultimate draft; the final version is much improved as a result. For the absence of other improvements that the reader would like to see, I must take responsibility.

Finally, every choice imposes its opportunity costs; and the opportunity costs of authorship are borne predominantly by the author's family. For acceptance of these costs, a line in a foreword is slight recompense.

18 June 1975 B.J.L.

I

Knowledge and ignorance

> Now my suspicion is that the universe is not only queerer
> than we suppose, but queerer than we can suppose...I
> suspect that there are more things in heaven and earth
> than are dreamed of, in any philosophy.
>
> J. B. S. Haldane (1927)

Choice, and the implication of choice, within complex systems
provide the basic subject-matter of economics. Sometimes the
emphasis is on individual choice, sometimes on the ways in which
the economic system responds to and regulates such choices.
Cutting across this distinction is that between positive and
normative study, between the attempt to explain or predict, and
the attempt to prescribe. Though such a characterisation of
economics may not satisfy everyone, it will, no doubt, be regarded
as quite harmless. Yet its implications are deep and disturbing. To
explore these implications is the purpose of this book.

The consequences of complexity

We may begin by looking more carefully at the significance of
complexity. The individual choices which economists study are set
in an environment conditioned by the choices of other individuals. Isolated choice is not their concern; when economists refer,
as from time to time they do, to the economic problems of
Robinson Crusoe, it is not because these problems are of intrinsic
interest to them, but because they permit a useful preliminary
clarification of some basic principles. Economics is a systems
study.

Economists study systems from two points of view: that of the
overall behaviour of the system and that of the decision-maker
within it. Now it is a characteristic of both points of view that
visibility is limited. Even Robinson Crusoe had to operate within

a complex natural system, the future states of which could not be predicted with confidence; how much more difficult then to predict the future states of a system which is driven in part by the acts of other decision-makers similarly placed. Choice within a complex system cannot be fully informed; neither can the study of a complex system from the outside. Partial ignorance is intrinsic to the problems of choice which economists claim to investigate. Indeed, if one accepts Popper's (1969, p. 342) view that 'the main task of the theoretical social sciences. . .is to trace the unintended social repercussions of intentional human actions', then partial ignorance becomes, not merely an inevitable feature of economic analysis, but the essential condition of its existence as a subject.

For the unavoidable ignorance of both analyst and decision-maker there are two major causes. One is the extent of the complexity of the phenomena around them, the complete analysis of which seems to require handling on a scale far more extensive, and also far more detailed, than either can manage. The other is the very limited human ability to cope with such analysis. The problem appears to lie less in the brain's ability to receive or to store data than in its processing ability; and computers seem to share the human preference for the simple processing of streams of data rather than the performance of intricate operations on smaller quantities. Thus potentially dangerous simplifications are unavoidable. In both economics and organisation theory, interdependencies (or external effects), by threatening the adequacy of any subsystem study, present well-known obstacles both to the effective analysis of behaviour and to the prescription of effective action.

There can be little doubt that in many fields our understanding is improving; but the very prospect of improvement, of learning tomorrow something which we do not know today, emphasises the incompleteness of our present knowledge. What has not yet been discovered cannot be part of that present knowledge. From a logical standpoint, historical determinism and the perfect knowledge of equilibrium theory are equally absurd. That is not the last possible word on either, but only the latter will be considered further in this book.

The impossibility of foreseeing future knowledge and the

impossibility of making full use even of present knowledge are both facts of human life. What Simon has labelled 'bounded rationality' is part of the human condition. Bounded rationality is natural rationality; it is the assumption of infinite capacity to handle infinite quantities of data which is artificial.

The consequent difficulties pervade both the subject-matter of economics and the method of analysis. There appear to be more relevant interdependencies than the analyst can handle, yet much of the data which he believes important is not available, and some can never be available. Thus he must simplify, assume and guess. If his aim is to hold a mirror up to nature, it will be a distorting mirror at best. We may therefore reasonably ask on what principles the analyst should make his choices, and what are likely to be the merits and limitations of the resulting work.

The subject of the analyst's study, the decision-maker faced with complexity and partial ignorance, is in a similar plight. He too must find some means to simplify, assume and guess, and the way in which he does this may be expected to have some effect on the choices he makes. Indeed, the systematic effects of these difficulties will turn out to be of critical significance in the analysis of competition and of macrotheory. Thus the questions which form the subject-matter of economics are closely analogous to the questions of methodology raised by the very attempt to theorise about this subject-matter. This book attempts to consider both.

It would be wrong, however, to imagine that the difficulties resulting from complexity and ignorance are to be found only in the study of decision-making: all human analysis is necessarily selective. Thus the situation of the economist is less distinctive than Shackle (1972, p. 259) has claimed. 'Analysis is the intellectual process appropriate to a problem assumed to be already fully stated and ready made. But the economist's task is utterly different. He must begin by posing his own problem, and that is a task of selection and composition...The problems of economics, the questions to be attempted, await their setting by the candidate himself.' It is perhaps true that some questions about natural phenomena appear to pose themselves more readily than questions about economic or social phenomena – though we should remember that scientists, like wise examination candidates, are careful not to attempt certain questions. But if scientists do indeed worry less than economists, or decision-makers, about what problems they should concern themselves with, it is because they have more useful, and more generally agreed, criteria for defining problems. Some such criteria are essential, if we are to avoid being over-whelmed by more data than we can handle.

A structure must be imposed before anything can be done: an interpretative framework is needed to convert data into informa-tion. There must be room for enquiry, but that room must be limited. At any one time, many things must be taken for granted in order that a few may be investigated. As Simon (1965, pp. 97–8) observes,

People (and rats) find the most interest in situations that are neither completely strange nor entirely known – where there is novelty to be explored, but where similarities and programs remembered from past experience help guide the exploration. Nor does creativity flourish in completely unstructured situations. The almost unanimous testimony of creative artists and scientists is that the first task is to impose limits on the situation if the limits are not already given. The pleasure that the good professional experiences in his work is not simply a pleasure in handling difficult matters; it is a pleasure in using skilfully a well-stocked kit of well-designed tools to handle problems that are com-prehensible in their deep structure but unfamiliar in their detail.

In the face of complexity, selection and simplification are essen-tial. But the methods of selection and simplification are not unam-biguously determined. The set of problems in a subject area is not uniquely defined by the subject-matter itself; nor is the set of problems to be tackled by any organisation at a given time. In both cases, there may be working agreement on the definition of current problems; but other definitions are possible, and may even be better. For both analyst and decision-maker, the way in which they define their problems may have profound consequences, as we shall see.

The paradox of choice

It is not only complexity and bounded rationality which are sources of trouble; the economist's difficulties are rooted in the very concept of choice. To be worth studying, choice must be meaningful; and, as Shackle has repeatedly pointed out, this implies, first, that choice is genuine, and, second, that choice matters. It is, of course, not necessary that all – or even most – choices should be genuine or should matter; but the principle is essential.

To be genuine, choice must be neither random nor predetermined. There must be some grounds for choosing, but they must be inadequate; there must be some possibility of predicting the consequences of choice, but none of perfect prediction. If knowledge is perfect, and the logic of choice complete and compelling, then choice disappears; nothing is left but stimulus and response. Yet there must be some knowledge, and some logic, for economists are concerned with reasoned choice. Whether seen from the point of view of the decision-maker or from that of the outside analyst, the theory of choice must be incomplete. Both must strive to make it more complete; but their triumph would be a disaster – just as the attainment of final scientific knowledge would destroy science. Scientists, economists, and decision-makers are all pursuing a goal which it would be fatal to attain.

Choice must also make a difference. If all roads lead to Rome, the choice of route is of no consequence to anyone interested only in the destination – though it is of interest to anyone concerned about the itinerary or the time of arrival. But if choice can affect future events, and choice is genuine, then the future cannot be predicted. Choice and determinacy are incompatible, as Shackle has striven to emphasise. If choice is real, the future cannot be certain; if the future is certain, there can be no choice.

Among the economists who emphasise the predictive function of economic theory, Machlup (1967, 1974) has recognised that choice must be meaningless, and has argued both that decisions are fully determined by the competitive situation and that the competitive situation makes decisions ineffective. He does not seem entirely clear that these two arguments are partly contradictory, nor that only one is necessary. What is certain is that choice must be excluded from positive economics, which is concerned with 'typical responses to typical stimuli' (Machlup, 1974, p. 276).

In confronting the paradox of choice, the economist is not alone. The philosophers of science face a similar problem: they wish to explain how scientific progress is possible; yet there can be no way to guarantee progress. There can be no universally applicable rules of induction or of deduction, for that would allow us to find the answers to scientific problems which are at present insoluble. As Popper has recognised, the logic of scientific discovery must be incomplete.

Choice and purpose

It has become fashionable in economics to draw a clear distinction between positive and normative analysis – between a study of what is and recommendations for action. But though these two modes can be distinguished, it is often impossible to keep them apart. Positive analysis often has a normative purpose, and not only in economics; for just as economists study the causes of inflation in order to advocate remedies, so philosophers of science study the means by which science progresses in order to advise scientists how that progress may be maintained.

But the link between the positive and normative modes is even closer. Choice is a normative activity; thus positive economists are offering a theory of normative behaviour, and positive analysis must include a discussion of the purposes of those whose decisions are being analysed. As Chamberlain (1968, p. 109) observes, 'purpose...cannot be viewed as simply an application of a purpose-free theory. It is an ingredient and hence a potential modifier of theory.' Even economists like Machlup, who are compelled by their zeal for positive purity to deny the reality of choice, postulate the maximisation of profits; and profit maximisation is a normative concept. Moreover, since the analysis of choice leads to conclusions about the consequences of choice, it can hardly avoid passing judgement on the effectiveness of the chosen action in achieving its intended purposes. That is why positive economics is so often advocated as a means to policy recommendations, and why policy recommendations appear to flow automatically from positive analysis. Because of these close interactions, although positive and normative elements will be distinguished, there will be no general distinction in this book between positive and normative modes of analysis.

The idea of purpose reinforces the logical necessity of partial ignorance, for purposive action is intended to make the future different in some respects from what it would be without such action, and thus, in Chamberlain's (1968, p. 34) words, 'to make it something other than predictable'. The future is not perfectly predictable by the analyst, because he cannot be certain what the decision-maker will do; and it cannot be perfectly predicted by the decision-maker, because he cannot be certain what other decision-makers will do – nor, indeed, how the natural environment will evolve. By this route too, we reach the conclusion that economics, as a subject, rests on the presumption of partial ignorance.

Risk, uncertainty and ignorance

In the following chapters we shall consider how the explicit recognition of choice amidst complexity and partial ignorance affects economic analysis. What must be said immediately is that the standard treatment of decision-making under uncertainty is not an adequate framework for this discussion. That treatment proceeds by modifying a theory based on the assumption of perfect knowledge in ways which purport to take into account the admitted fact that knowledge is normally somewhat less than perfect. However, this approach does not in practice allow analysts to stray very far from perfection.

There are two stages of modification. In the first stage, known as the analysis of risk, the decision-maker is assumed to be equipped, not with precise knowledge of the outcome of every available choice, but with a complete listing of the set of all possible outcomes (sometimes boldly described as a complete listing of the set of all possible states of the world) relevant to each choice, and also with a probability distribution fully defined over that set. On the basis of this information, he can calculate, not only every possible outcome of each choice, but also the expected value (defined as the probability-weighted average) of each. The weightings may be adjusted, in ways described, for example, by Lindley (1971) and Raiffa (1968), to reflect the decision-maker's attitude to risk. Thus it is only necessary to substitute these expected values for the known values of the simple model, and everything can proceed as before.

In this stage, both the set of outcomes and the probability distribution applied to that set are regarded as pure, or objective, knowledge. This is crucial, for otherwise the decision-maker may not share the analyst's definition of the situation, and not behave as the latter's model predicts. Now the notion of an objective probability distribution carries a strong (but unstated) implication about the nature of the world, namely that it generates all the necessary (and quite unambiguous) frequency distributions from a stable population of events. The mere statement of this implication is enough to show its implausibility as a general proposition.

Even if such a world existed, its existence could never be proved, for as Popper (1972, p. 169) emphasises, 'every predictive estimate of frequencies, including one which we may get from statistical extrapolation – and certainly all those that refer to infinite empirical sequences – will always be pure conjecture since it will always go far beyond anything which we are entitled to affirm on the basis of observations'. Popper's argument derives from Hume's observation that experience can provide no assurance of the future. Any hypothesis, however well attested up to the present, remains potentially falsifiable. It is thus not clear what precisely can be objective about a probability distribution defined over future states or events.

The need for such unscientifically perfect knowledge can be avoided by introducing the second-stage modification, known (misleadingly) as the analysis of uncertainty, in which the decision-maker is presumed not to know the relevant probability distributions, though he must still possess a complete list of outcomes.

This second-stage modification can lead to awkward problems. Even the state of risk produces uniquely optimal decisions only if the expected value criterion is accepted; and the state of uncertainty necessarily allows for a variety of possible criteria, depending both on the decision-maker's attitude to risk and the way in which he may choose to deal with the absence of a probability distribution. These criteria, such as optimism (aim for the best possible outcome), pessimism (assume that the worst will happen, and make that choice which minimises the damage), and minimum regret (in effect, minimise the opportunity costs) may, not surprisingly, lead to contradictory solutions.

For the management scientist, these difficulties are not fatal: the decision-maker, having heard all the arguments, may be allowed to make up his own mind. But for the economist who wishes to analyse system behaviour, this is not good enough, for unless he can predict the decision-maker's criterion, he cannot predict his choice. The most favoured escape from such embarrassing indeterminacy is to postulate, and advocate, the use of subjective probabilities, thus converting the problem into a form equivalent to a state of risk. Much of the content of decision theory consists of a variety of devices by which the trick may be done. Even this does not wholly resolve the analyst's problem, for he must still somehow predict the decision-maker's subjective assessment. However, the use of subjective probabilities is believed to be adequate for enquiries into the existence, uniqueness, and stability of equilibrium, even though it does not allow one to describe its content.

Thus the search for determinate solutions permits no greater departure from perfect knowledge than to subjectively perfect risk. Even the very limited amount of uncertainty allowed by the definition has to be conjured away. Yet this definition itself implies a remarkably complete knowledge; for, like risk, it requires a complete listing of all relevant outcomes, and also a full listing of all possible courses of action. In general, such listings are not available. When someone says he is uncertain, what he usually means is not just that he doesn't know the chances of various outcomes, but that he doesn't know what outcomes are possible. He may well be far from sure even of the structure of the problem that he faces. This normal state of partial ignorance is simply not defined in the theory of decision-making under uncertainty, in which 'uncertainty' acquires an esoteric meaning. This meaning serves to hide from the layman the fact that the economist, faced with a very awkward problem, has succeeded, as so often, not in solving it, but in denying the legitimacy of its existence.

Because of the prevalence of this device among economists, and management scientists, much use will continue to be made in this book of the term 'partial ignorance'; the adjective will sometimes be omitted when it is clear that 'ignorance' is not meant to infer a total absence of any relevant knowledge. Any reader who is neither an economist nor a management scientist may freely substitute the word 'uncertainty', in its everyday sense; economists and management scientists are forbidden to do so.

As will be argued in Chapter 11, theorists are not necessarily to be blamed for declining to tackle problems which they do not know how to solve, though the manner of their exclusion is liable to mislead even the moderately wary. In its insistence on a framework which cannot accept ignorance, general equilibrium theory is very specific: as is argued in Chapter 9, it is a far less general theory than that proposed by Keynes. The equilibrium may be general, the theory is not. This book aims to be more general in its treatment of both the methods and content of theory, by exploring some of the implications of partial ignorance.

Although imperfect information and partial ignorance may appear to be alternative definitions of a single reality, they define different viewpoints; and different viewpoints give different views. The view obtainable from the viewpoint just discussed is inadequate for our purpose; far too much is concealed. Therefore little use will be made of the standard economic analysis of imperfect information. We shall find a variety of devices (decision theory being one) which allow ignorance to masquerade as knowledge so that choices may be made; and we shall consider the circumstances and consequences of their use, including their influences on the information employed. We shall also find a number of very important means by which choice may be avoided, means which are themselves major determinants of economic structure and behaviour. We shall also consider the corresponding difficulties facing the analyst, and their implications for his choice of model, and for the usefulness of the models so chosen.

Preview

Some of the following chapters are addressed to problems of economic theorising, and some to the analysis of the decision-maker's situation and behaviour. Some deal with both, for one of the uses of economic theory is to advise decision-makers. Yet the basic justification for thus intermingling questions of methodology with substantive issues is the belief that, because of the effects of complexity and ignorance, they share a common structure. This is also the justification for the intermingling of abstract formal argument and practical examples from industry and innovative science. The eventual aim, in the traditions of science, is to reveal unity in diversity.

Though this book aims to integrate rather than to separate, it may nevertheless conveniently be divided into three sections. The first, comprising the present chapter and the two that follow, is concerned primarily with questions of method, and in particular with the relationship between method and subject-matter. In the next chapter we consider the adequacy of the positive and axiomatic prescriptions for the conduct of economic analysis, and then, in the third chapter, take a more extended look at the problems of understanding and predicting complex behaviour, and at the dangers entailed by the simplifications and distortions which are inevitable if these problems are to be tackled at all.

The main theme of the next five chapters is the firm as an organisation. A detailed analysis in Chapter 4 of the logical place of the firm in economic theory leads to the conclusion that there is a need for economists to study decision-making as a process, and the following two chapters suggest how this study might proceed, and what it might achieve. (These two chapters contain fewer references to conventional economics than any others in the book.) Chapters 7 and 8 examine the topics of organisational objectives and organisational behaviour respectively, in both instances offering a critique of the usual treatment (explicit or implied) of these issues by economists. It is not the intention of this group of chapters to provide a full exposition of the economics of organisational behaviour. Their purpose is to investigate the foundations of an alternative method of analysis and to provide evidence both of its logical structure and of its possible use: to show what this alternative looks like, and what it can do.

The final section draws on ideas developed in both previous sections to explore some major issues in conventional economics, and with their aid reaches some unconventional conclusions – about macrotheory in Chapter 9 and imperfect and monopolistic competition in Chapter 10. Chapter 11 is, in effect, an investigation of the question: 'Why does the economists' theory of choice not help economists to choose between conflicting theories?' Finally, Chapter 12 attempts to summarise some of the earlier discussion, to make a partial appraisal of the state of economics, and to make some suggestions for its future development.

As will rapidly become apparent, this book is heavily dependent on general equilibrium theory; and that is not only true in the sense in which the police are heavily dependent on crime. The development of that theory has emphasised – indeed, as will be argued, over-emphasised – the virtue of a carefully-specified axiom set as a basis of strict logical argument; and the attempt in the following pages to expose, examine, and clarify the axiomatic bases of various models owes much to the spirit of general equilibrium theorising. Furthermore, since general equilibrium models are so explicit about their own axioms, they provide an obvious starting-point for the generation of alternative theories by the variation of those axioms.

Because the intention is to warn of the dangers inherent in any single mode of theorising, and also to advocate greater use of an undeveloped mode, it is inevitable that the treatment of presently dominant modes will be mainly critical; and the greatest weight of criticism will be directed against general equilibrium theory. The intention is not to undermine that theory, but to examine its scope, implications, and limitations, topics which general equilibrium theorists seem reluctant to discuss. Materials for the defence of general equilibrium theory will be found in the following chapters, but there will be no attempt at a balanced assessment. For this book is not simply about general equilibrium theory, nor indeed simply about organisational behaviour, or about any other particular economic field; it is about the problems involved in the attempt to deal with the questions of choice and change within complex systems, which are the central issues of economics. As we shall see, its scope is not even restricted to economics, for many of these problems are encountered in the practice of both pure and applied science, and in managerial decision-making. They are among the fundamental problems of human existence.

2

Logic, evidence and belief

> Science is a system of beliefs to which we are committed. Such a system cannot be accounted for either from experience as seen within a different system, or by reason without any experience.
>
> M. Polanyi (1958, p. 171)

For most economists, no doubt, Archibald's (1971, p. 14) declaration that 'personal belief is immaterial to the status of a theory' is a simple statement of scientific principle. Since it is not difficult to find instances in which the attitudes of distinguished economists to important theories appear, in part, to reflect their beliefs, this declaration is not only a principle, but also a programme. In fact there are two programmes, each aiming to cleanse economics of subjectivity and fallacy, and to establish the subject in full scientific rigour. The first programme, that of the positive economists, relies on the clear formulation and careful testing of specific hypotheses, in an attempt to provide an equivalent to the experimental method of the natural scientists; the second, or axiomatic school, seeks to emulate the mathematicians by the careful construction of watertight logical systems from a brief but comprehensive axiom set.

The first programme is currently the favourite among macroeconomists, while the second appears to dominate microtheory. Lancaster's (1969, p. 2) distinction between these two subject-areas helps to explain why.

Microeconomics remains primarily concerned with economics in general...Thus simplification in microeconomics will often be of the kind that rejects some special relationship that holds only for one time and one place, and concentrates on features common to many times and many places...simplification in macroeconomics is likely to take an opposite course...rejecting general possibilities in favour of known behaviour here and now...The difference in outlook has made macroeconomics more empirically oriented than micro-economics.

To the investigation of circumstances which are both particular and observable the careful testing of particular hypotheses seems obviously more appropriate than a chain of reasoning based on general axioms; for the study of general classes of phenomena the opposite is true. Positive economics tends to sacrifice the general for the specific; axiomatic economics does the reverse.

But Lancaster's argument implies that neither approach guarantees complete truth. In a typically sardonic passage (which incidentally reminds us that the assimilation of method to subject area is not complete) Clower (1969, p. 21) complains that 'monetary specialists. . .have tended to turn either to econo-metric study of observed behaviour (measurement with so little theory that it really does not matter) or to consciously academic exercises in the dynamics of monetary growth (theory with so little reality that it does not matter either)'. Nor can failure to decide between competing doctrines (for example in the long-running capital controversy) always be attributed to a failure to use the proffered tools, of either sort. There are some formidable difficulties in the way of the complete exclusion of personal belief from the assessment of an economic theory (or indeed of a scientific theory, as Polanyi (1958) has argued). Otherwise there must surely be some objective criterion which would be decisive in rejecting one or other of these distinctive research pro-grammes. To see what these difficulties are, let us look at these approaches a little more closely; and since they appear so dif-ferent, let us take them in turn.

Positive economics

The typical Keynesian model is an exercise in institutional adhocery: its performance depends crucially on some piece of specific irrationality (such as wage rigidity or a money illusion) for which no theoretical justification is offered, and which indeed conflicts with the fundamental axioms of behaviour offered by any general equilibrium theorist. The standard models of imper-fect competition similarly imply a pattern of consumer preference which is clearly irrational when judged by those fundamental axioms. (The premises of both theories will be examined in some detail in Chapters 9 and 10.) If the quality of one's conclusions depends on the quality of one's inputs, then it must be dangerous to erect a rational structure on a foundation of unanalysed special assumptions; and it is made no less dangerous by the elaboration of a mathematical model which, intentionally or not, diverts attention from the quality of that foundation. The special relationships of which Lancaster writes may be quite wrongly specified. Measurement without theory is liable to produce the wrong measurement.

Such failings are not confined to economists. After several years of study, the highway planners of Washington, D.C. were in 1965 still basing their plans for 1980 on calculations derived from a traffic census of 1955; bemused by the multifarious possibilities of manipulating the data which they already had, the planners made no attempt to question its adequacy, let alone to improve its quality by the simple expedient of further surveys (Arthur D. Little, Inc., 1966).

Friedman (1953, pp. 7–9, 21–2) has boldly claimed these theoretical defects as virtues; he not only asserts that 'the only relevant test of the *validity* of a hypothesis is comparison of its predictions with experience', but even commends the use of demonstrably false hypotheses provided that the predictions derived from them appear to be borne out. Perhaps, after all, it is good scientific practice to explain the Swedish birthrate by the migration of storks. It has not always been so. If Galileo had accepted the advice of contemporary Friedmanites, he would have been spared his troubles with the Roman Church, which was perfectly ready to acknowledge, and indeed to make use of, the predictive success of Copernican theory; but for Galileo the structure of a theory mattered as much as its predictions. Even for those who believe that truth is an irrelevant criterion for the assessment of theories, this insistence on judgement solely by results appears a little excessive: it seems neither necessary nor sensible to wait until 1980 before evaluating the quality of Washington highway planning. But if all such objections are to be dismissed, and the testing of predictions is to be the only means by which hypotheses are to be judged, then the method of testing needs careful examination. And this it does not get.

The positive economists' attitude to evidence has been scrutinised by Coddington (1972), many of whose comments are reflected in the following paragraphs. On one point the positive economists are adamant. The only relevant evidence is that provided by external observation. The paradox this entails is clearly displayed by Machlup (1946, pp. 535–7), who argues simultaneously that decisions depend on decision-makers' own subjective assessments and that subjective assessments are not a fit subject for scientific enquiry. Thus positive economists manage to combine the presumptions of the action research school of sociologists (that action can be explained only in terms of the actor's definition of the situation) with the practice of the strictest behavioural school of psychologists.

Of course, the trick is easy in conditions of perfect knowledge, for then, by definition, internal and external views coincide; but this is an expedient much more congenial (not to say indispensable) to axiomatic theorists than to hard-headed pragmatists. So in practice, though actions are supposed to follow from beliefs, beliefs have to be inferred from actions. No wonder Friedman admits that they may well be pseudo-beliefs. In fact the creed of positive economics repudiates any attempt to distinguish between real and pseudo-beliefs. It should therefore be no surprise that its treatment of expectations is so cavalier. The rejection of subjective evidence compels the acceptance of subjective hypotheses.

Contrary to the assertions of Friedman and Machlup, the deliberate exclusion of available subjective evidence is thoroughly unscientific. The first-person viewpoint is excluded from natural science by necessity: as Coddington (1972, p. 12) observes, 'the physical scientist. . .cannot consider, as a basis for inquiry, the electron's own understanding of what it is doing'. Some natural scientists, at least, regard this exclusion not as a virtue but as a serious, if unavoidable, handicap. A group of biologists studying the behaviour of larvae feeding on potato plants had no doubt that they could do much better if they were able to administer questionnaires to their subjects, and were astonished that economists should wilfully deny themselves the use of such evidence. Harrod (1972, p. 398) is being very properly scientific in recommending that 'the account by operators of what they usually actually do should be given greater weight than the theory concerning what they ought to do'.

Subjective evidence must naturally be used with caution; but so must the statistical evidence which the positive economists commend. To treat statistics as facts is much too naïve. Quite apart from observational error, misreporting and misrepresentation, all of which may present serious difficulties, the basis of classification is not always beyond dispute. Classification problems occur in the natural sciences too: the group of biologists just mentioned found it quite impossible to agree on a working definition of the 'top' of potato plants, the stems of which drooped to the ground: was it the highest part of the plant, or its furthest extremity? The answer depends upon the theory of larval behaviour which the data so classified were to be used to test. Here is one situation in which subjective evidence would have been very helpful.

The report of the Economic Development Committee for Mechanical Engineering on ventilating, air conditioning and refrigeration equipment (1970) provides an example of a classification impasse in the economist's field:

The programme of work originally outlined for the study of demand for ventilating, air conditioning and refrigeration equipment could not be completed. It proved to be impossible to obtain industry agreement on the definition for different systems or products that should be used as a basis of the study. It was also found that the various product definitions proposed after consultation with leading authorities in the industry were incompatible with the sales records of the 15 manufacturers consulted before work was discontinued. Even on the basis of providing total sales data alone without product breakdown no meaningful quantitative results could be obtained. Accordingly work on the study was halted.

To read this distressing tale, supplemented by some republished United Nations data, the public was invited to pay £10.

However it is rare to find such a public admission of defeat. Economists and statisticians are very clever at devising schemes of classification. Indeed, Shackle (1972, p. 39) claims that 'economics is the supremely ingenious device for eliciting scalar quantity from vast heterogeneous assemblies of qualitatively incommensurable things'. The trick may be done in various ways, and it is not always a matter of indifference which is chosen. Mrs Robinson is of course perfectly correct in asserting that capital is not a homogeneous factor of production; yet she habitually treats labour as a homogeneous factor on grounds as flimsy as those which she scorns when used by the neoclassicals in defence of capital. No doubt it is easier for a typist to move from a car firm to a drug company than it is to convert a steel press to the production of medicines; but a fairground generator may be adapted to drive a lathe in far less time than it takes to convert a showman into a skilled machinist. To treat either capital or labour as homogeneous is pretence; whether either is a useful pretence depends upon our purposes. The value of such pretences, more politely called abstractions, is discussed in the next chapter. But economists of great power and distinction really ought not to base their arguments on a system of classification which those arguments are needed to justify.

Classification depends on theory, for phenomena can be grouped only by choosing among possible criteria. Things which are similar are, as Popper (1972, pp. 420–1) points out, 'always similar *in certain respects*'; thus 'similarity, and with it repetition, always presuppose the adoption of *a point of view*'. Shackle (1972, p. 118) makes the point very clearly. 'There are no such things as "objective" facts, only judgements (of similarity, association, separateness, etc.); measurements (a classificatory operation), selection (according to criteria provided by personal background, sensitiveness, "ear"). The role of theory is to be an illuminant. . .it will not do to mistake theories for realities. But without the illumination there is nothing to be seen.' What comes as a surprise is to find Friedman (1953, p. 54) saying virtually the same thing. 'Known facts cannot be set on one side, a theory to apply "closely to reality" on the other. A theory is the way we perceive "facts", and we cannot perceive "facts" without a theory.' But if these theory-laden facts are the sole means by which theory is judged, are we not in some difficulty?

Even in the natural sciences, the form of an experiment may determine the result, and that form depends on theory. For example, an apparently well-conducted double-blind experiment demonstrated no significant difference between chloroform and the new anaesthetic halothane, which is now generally agreed to be far superior; the experimental design achieved the desired conditions of ceteris paribus by excluding just those factors which differentiated their performance (Bradbury, McCarthy & Suckling, 1972a). The experimental design reflected a theoretically-based presumption of similarity, and that presumption generated evidence in its own support.

It is impossible to test one hypothesis without assuming the truth of many more. The validity and reliability of the means of measurement depend on critical assumptions, which may, of course, themselves be separately tested – but only by making a fresh set of assumptions. This process may continue, every assumption in turn being converted into a hypothesis and subjected to test, until, perhaps, the original hypothesis is required as an assumption. There is no definable end to the process of testing hypotheses.

Thus not even negative results are definitive, a truth of which Popper (1972, p. 50) is well aware. 'In point of fact, no conclusive disproof of a theory can ever be produced; for it is always possible to say that the experimental results are not reliable, or that the discrepancies which are asserted to exist between the experimental results and the theory are only apparent and that they will disappear with the advance of our understanding.' And such arguments are used, if the results are theoretically inconvenient. Commenting on an elaborate experiment which recorded the arrival of neutrinos from the sun at a rate of one every two days instead of 5–10 a day predicted by current theory, an expert theoretical physicist admitted that these results, if confirmed, would be very disturbing; but he was confident that, with better equipment, the missing neutrinos would be found. The standard of evidence required for acceptance, as well as for rejection, depends on theory; the evidence for the existence of the omega-minus particle is apparently rather weaker than the evidence for extra-sensory perception, yet most scientists are readier to believe in the former than the latter.

Experimental scientists have long recognised that, in the words quoted by Lakatos (1970, p. 152), 'the number of false facts, afloat in the world infinitely exceeds that of the false theories'. Such attitudes are not perverse; they are properly scientific. As

Polanyi (1958, p. 138) observes, 'very little inherent certainty will suffice to secure the highest scientific value to an alleged fact, if only it fits in with a great scientific generalisation, while the most stubborn facts will be set aside if there is no place for them in the established framework of science'.

The importance of theory in determining the acceptability of evidence may be simply illustrated in two examples from pharmacology. The use of chloroform entailed a known risk of liver damage; and the assumed similarity of halothane aroused fears that it carried a similar risk. Evidence of liver damage in patients anaesthetised with halothane was therefore sought – and, being sought, was found. To the proponents of halothane, this evidence cast doubt not on the drug's virtues but on the experimental design which produced the evidence; and more detailed research showed that the incidence of liver damage among patients exposed to halothane was actually less than in other patients.

But such a response to unwelcome evidence may be mistaken, and even disastrous. The manufacturers of thalidomide had some reason to discount reports of deformed births, for these reports were in conflict with their test results. The effects on human offspring cannot be found in any of the experimental animals then in normal use for such tests; but in this instance it was the accepted doctrine of drug testing that was found to be in error. So too may extra-sensory perception eventually win more scientific support than the omega-minus particle. But it cannot do so without a change in the theoretical determination of what is to be acceptable evidence.

The difficulties of the economist wishing to test hypotheses are apparently greater than those of the natural scientist. (It will be argued in the following chapter that the differences depend largely on the uses to which the hypothesis is to be put.) The economist is typically in the position of trying to evaluate a hypothesis about laboratory behaviour on the basis of evidence derived from a far more complex full-scale plant; in addition to extracting and using the evidence, he therefore has to decide how far discrepancies are due to weaknesses in the hypothesis under test and how far they are determined by a failure to achieve the conditions to which it was intended to apply.

One might expect, in view of all these difficulties, that the advocates of positive economics would be particularly concerned to give us guidance on the selection, use, and interpretation of evidence. But if we did expect such advice, we should be disappointed. Indeed, by talking variously of 'facts', 'evidence', 'experience', and 'observation', with no suggestion that these are different categories, and may conflict, advocates such as Friedman and Lipsey appear not to recognise that there is a problem at all. It is fair to add that, with frequent warnings about the uncertain status even of experimental evidence, Popper himself seems to give us all aid short of actual help. The difficulty is made worse by the commendable willingness of positive economists, following their pragmatic principles, to use a variety of different models in different situations; for this suggests that the choice of an appropriate hypothesis for prediction requires a knowledge of motivations and expectations, which have been castigated as unacceptable data. Thus the insistence on judgement by results seems to be incompatible with the insistence on objectivity.

In practice, if the acceptability of evidence is not allowed to rest on sound logic, then it must rest on belief. The failure to expel belief as a determinant of acceptability is not simply a failure of application; as has been shown, the basis of the approach is dogmatic. Those who reject theory for pragmatism are liable to find themselves unwitting adherents of bad theory.

Axiomatic economics

The attempt to provide a rigorous theoretical basis for economics has been the prime intellectual enterprise within the subject in recent years. Its very difficulty and the highly abstract methods employed by its practitioners have ensured at least one major success: microtheory has become intellectually highly respectable, now that it is axiomatic. 'Modern microeconomics', as Lancaster (1969, p. 2) observes, 'is "general equilibrium" economics...It is not the study of individual components (consumers, firms) *in themselves*, but of individual components *and how they fit together*.' 'Partial equilibrium' and 'Marshallian' have, by contrast, become terms of such contempt that when Arrow (1971, p. 9) wishes to be complimentary to E. H. Chamberlin it

is natural for him to assert that in developing the theory of monopolistic competition 'Chamberlin's purpose was certainly the
incorporation of monopoly into a general equilibrium system'.
Chamberlin's purpose is thus to be found, not in his determined
efforts to cast his analysis in terms of large and small groups, but
in his ultimate failure to do so.

Whereas positive economists insist that propositions must be
judged by the evidence, axiomatic economists require them to be
formally and rigorously proved. It may therefore appear remarkable how little attention axiomatic theorists pay to the credibility
of the premises from which they argue. The adequacy and
elegance of their axiom sets are discussed at length, their credibility hardly at all.

One reason, no doubt, is that the structural axioms which are
required to prove the existence of Pareto optimal equilibria are
known to be violated by all existing market systems; and indeed
such violations are regularly used to demonstrate that no existing
market system can be expected to achieve Pareto optimality. But
the use of incredible axioms for this purpose appears to have
concealed from theorists the rather obvious fact that the remaining axioms, relating to consumer preference and the possibilities
of production and exchange, are no more believable. Pareto optimality is excluded by the fundamental conditions of human existence. But that is not at all the kind of conclusion that axiomatic
theorists like to draw, because it appears to cast doubts, not on
our institutional arrangements, but on their theoretical methods.

A second reason for ignoring the credibility of the theoretical
base appears to be a widespread impression that work on simpli-
fying the set of axioms needed to produce the desired results is
work in the direction of realism. But there is no general reason
why the minimal assumptions should necessarily be the most
plausible. Consumer theory provides a clear example. No one
would now deny that not only cardinal utility but the concept of
utility itself, in its old connotations, is superfluous to an austere
model; for such a model the notion of a complete set of preference
orderings is much simpler, and perfectly adequate as a primitive
concept. But it can hardly be called more realistic. For consumers to construct such a set by the method of paired comparisons
would be impossibly time-consuming; the use of some simple

preference criterion, such as cardinal utility, appears far more credible. Preference functions do not logically require the old-fashioned concept of utility; but it is much easier to believe in them if one is allowed to believe in utility as well. If we are to axiomatise preference functions, so be it; but we had better not attempt to justify our procedure on any considerations of realism.

Consumer theory also provides a striking example of the extent to which the search for minimal assumptions may impede the development of analysis. Lancaster (1966, p. 132) has complained that 'the theory of consumer behaviour in deterministic situations . . .has been shorn of all irrelevant postulates so that it now stands as an example of how to extract the minimum of results from the minimum of assumptions'. The effects of the slightest variation in the set of available products are beyond its compass; revealed preference cannot predict what has not yet been revealed. Well might Dennis Robertson (1951, p. 121) ask: 'Was it worthwhile to go to such mountainous trouble to formalise in non-mental terms the behaviour of beings whom we have every reason to suppose to be equipped with minds?' For the concept of 'preferences for goods' which has replaced consumer satisfactions leaves consumer theory incapable of handling many of the most important issues of marketing or of competitive behaviour; and even Lancaster's (1966) discovery that goods have attributes repairs only part of the damage. But axiomatic and positive economists are, unfortunately, at one in their odd and unscientific attachment to 'objectivity'. The first-person viewpoint is excluded from a value theory which is essentially subjective.

We may have doubts about the value of conclusions derived from such unlikely origins. However, the credibility of the axiom set is not nearly so crucial as has been implied in the preceding paragraphs. Since general equilibrium theory is a form of abstract mathematical reasoning, its choice of axioms can be defended on the grounds used by Whitehead & Russell (1910, p. v).

The chief reason in favour of any theory on the principles of mathematics must always be inductive, i.e. it must lie in the fact that the theory in question enables us to deduce ordinary mathematics. In mathematics, the greatest degree of self-evidence is usually not to be found quite at the beginning, but at some later point; hence the early deductions, until they reach this point, give reasons rather for believing the premises because true consequences follow from them, than for believing the consequences because they follow from the premises.

Thus it is not unreasonable to require of an axiom set that it be spare and elegant, rather than plausible – provided that it leads to empirically plausible results. If the results are not plausible, then the axiom set is open to question, and implausibility may be a clue to the cause of failure.

But Whitehead & Russell's argument does imply that theory cannot be judged simply on the quality of its logic, which is the outstanding characteristic of general equilibrium theory. As Clower (1965, p. 124) observes, 'the danger in using this instrument to think about practical problems is that, having schooled ourselves so thoroughly in the virtues of elegant simplicity, we may refuse to recognise the crucial relevance of complications that do not fit our theoretical preconceptions'. Though Clower was referring to general equilibrium theory, his warning applies to any strict formal model, and not only in economics.

Hahn's (1973a and b) recent spirited defence of general equilibrium theory is thoroughly ambiguous on the importance of realism in economic models: though he makes bold claims for the power of the Arrow–Debreu system, he concedes without question the need for 'a conceptual apparatus which is much more nearly descriptive' (1973a, p. 329). Had he properly understood the purpose of abstract theorising, he would have realised that no such concession was necessary; he would also have been rather more guarded in his claims. For he argues that general equilibrium theory already provides precise criteria by which to judge the proposition that a market system (or indeed any other, though this he does not mention) is efficient, and it also provides at least the basis of an explanation of how a market economy works. But Hahn does not explain how the same model can serve two such different purposes. As noted earlier, it is difficult enough to evaluate a hypothesis about laboratory behaviour on the basis of evidence derived from a full-scale plant; to attempt simultaneously to use the hypothesis under test to redesign the plant is surely a little dangerous – particularly when we are pretty sure that the hypothesis does not refer to any plant which could actually be made to work.

Hahn appears to be arguing that when a description of an economic system is compared with a general equilibrium model, a double comparison is possible. If the description conflicts with the model, as it does, then the model must be rejected as a model of that economic system; but, if the model has Pareto optimal properties, then the economic system must be simultaneously rejected as failing the criteria for an ideal system. The validity of Pareto optimality is assumed to be beyond test. It is immanent in general equilibrium.

We may pass lightly over the rarely questioned value judgements implied in the acceptance of the Pareto criterion, in order to emphasise that for any conceivable economic system such optima are not merely impossible to attain; outside the formal models, they are impossible to define. The recommendation to achieve a Pareto efficient allocation is a special case of the admonition 'Be ye perfect, as your Father in Heaven is perfect.' Since the Pareto efficiency test is a matter of theology, we might charitably apply to all economic systems the undeniable truth that 'all have sinned, and fallen short of the Glory of God'. General equilibrium theorists writing on welfare economics have an unfortunate tendency to Pharisaism, when the attitude of the publican would be much more becoming.

How are we to evaluate general equilibrium models as explanations of what happens, as distinct from prescriptions for what cannot? The list of situations to which the logical structure formally applies is, to put it mildly, somewhat restricted: it is an economy without groups, except those which behave exclusively as teams – therefore with no firms, or even families, as we know them – and not only free from any of the problems of macroeconomics but free from any kind of unexpected change. It is not therefore surprising to find some eminent (and some less eminent) economists urging us to pitch the whole apparatus over the side in order to get on with real problems. That is not the view taken in this book. Hahn urges us to have patience; more realistic models will emerge in time. Where they disagree, both parties are right: work is needed on both general equilibrium and very different types of model. Where they agree, on the need for realism, they are unfortunately both wrong.

Unrealism is by no means a peculiarity of general equilibrium models; it is just more obvious than usual and (to their credit) more readily admitted by the model-builders in their more reflective moments. As was argued in the previous chapter, to build any model requires a selection of variables to be included (and therefore of variables to be excluded), their specification, and the form of the relationships between them. None of these choices need match reality; it is often more convenient if they do not. Every model is an argument by analogy: all models are 'as if' models. Friedman's billiard player is perhaps the best-acknowledged example, but there is one far more striking, if only we recognise it, in the concept of equilibrium itself. As defined in our usual models, it could not possibly exist. Equilibrium models cannot explain, because they specify no causal process. Coddington's (1972, p. 8) comment that, 'Strictly, the whole apparatus of microeconomic theory is no longer interpreted as a logic of choice but only as an apparent logic of choice-like acts', though directed at the positive economists, applies even more forcefully to axiomatic theory. Yet the stricture is less severe than Coddington implies. No model which purports to explain can be accepted on the basis of logic alone, nor (fortunately) on the realism of the axioms to which that logic is applied. There must be a pragmatic test. This was Friedman's essential insight.

Thus the attempt to establish propositions about actual – or potential – economic systems by logical rigour cannot succeed. Just as the acceptability of evidence depends on logic, so the acceptability of logic depends on evidence. Logic itself cannot tell us what unreality we should be bothered about. Modern theorists are inclined, for example, to take great pride in having abolished the theoretical necessity for variables to be continuously differentiable; but some chemists and engineers who rely on continuity as an essential fiction in their daily work are not particularly impressed by this achievement. General equilibrium theory is social science fiction, and thus requires the willing suspension of disbelief.

Conclusion

It should not be surprising that both of these endeavours, the positive and the axiomatic, to exclude belief should in the end be doomed to failure. That is not to say that the attempt was not worth making. It was, and will continue to be. The mutual interdependence of logic and evidence, properly exploited, fosters scientific progress. But progress requires belief: that is, willingness to accept, and build on, some ideas which cannot be conclusively established by either evidence or logic.

The world is so complex that no one can begin to understand it all. Indeed, as Churchman (1965, p. 32) observes,

The more we want to know about a particular thing, the more we have to assume about the whole world. If a man is satisfied to experience Nature in a gross way, he can be modest about his beliefs. *The more he wants to learn about Nature in a precise manner, the more he must be willing to extend his power to believe.*

Thus some kind of belief system is essential for life, and even for that part of life which is the subject-matter of a single discipline. Nothing can be explored unless much is unquestioned; and the greater the precision of detail, the greater the need for belief.

In economics, orthodoxy often means believing impossible things. 'Alice laughed. "There's no use trying," she said. "One can't believe impossible things." "I daresay you haven't had much practice," said the Queen. "When I was your age, I always did it for half-an-hour a day. Why, sometimes I've believed as many as six impossible things before breakfast." ' No one can be a competent economist, in the present state of the subject, without at least attaining the White Queen's standard. Moreover it may be a very useful ability. For if one is used to believing the impossible there should be no difficulty in believing the merely unproven; and willingness to believe the unproven is a condition of further progress, as Popper (1972, p. 38), often regarded as the chief proponent of subjecting all theories to stringent tests, observes. 'I am inclined to think that scientific discovery is impossible without faith in ideas which are of a purely speculative kind, and sometimes even quite hazy; a faith which is completely unwarranted from the point of view of science, and which, to that extent, is "metaphysical".'

There is no better example of such unwarranted faith than Newton's reluctant acceptance of the clearly absurd notion of force acting at a distance as the essential explanation (in Friedman's sense) of gravity: such occult planetary influences seemed far more akin to astrology than to mechanics. Archibald is wrong: indeed his very statement that belief is immaterial to the status of a theory is itself a matter of belief. Though logic and evidence are essentials of scientific enquiry, neither separately nor together are they sufficient. In the face of complexity and ignorance, some portion of belief is also required; and in the generation of new ideas, the need for belief, and particularly personal belief, becomes paramount (though never to the exclusion of logic or evidence).

Since we have observed a theological tendency in economic theory earlier, it is perhaps better to follow Popper in talking not of belief but of faith. Much of Hahn's inaugural lecture is a rebuke to those of little faith. The major churches are not altogether in agreement on what is the true faith: the High Churchmen of axiomatic economics emphasise the necessity of public and formal ritual, and the select status of the priest in his mathematical vestments; while the positivist Low Church is a priesthood of all believers, sceptical of vain ceremonies and relying for divine guidance on the personal revelation of the correlation coefficient. But in the house of economics there are many mansions. What is clear is that none can be entered without some dependence, in St Paul's words, on 'the substance of things hoped for, the evidence of things not seen'.

3

Abstraction, sufficiency and ignorance

Economics has veritably turned imprecision itself into a
science: economics, the science of the quantification of
the unquantifiable and the aggregation of the incompatible.

G. L. S. Shackle (1972, p. 360)

Natural science is an artificial activity.
E. G. Edwards (Vice-Chancellor, University of Bradford)

Neither evidence nor logic can be relied upon to establish beyond
all question the validity of a scientific proposition; for, in relation
to the phenomena being studied, both the hypothesis and the data
by which it is judged must be selective, and therefore incomplete.
Selection and omission are particularly necessary with respect to
the myriad of possible interrelations between the immediate
object of investigation and other phenomena. No man is an
island, nor is any thing. Now the study of interdependencies is the
very heart of economics, for, logically as well as historically, its
development as a discipline derives from the increasing extent and
complexity of the division of labour between individuals, between
organisations, between regions, and between countries. Economics
may indeed claim to be the best developed, as it was the earliest
explicitly recognised, systems study.

All system descriptions are patterns imposed on the set of
phenomena to be described or investigated; and the choice of
description presents a dilemma. The greater the degree of complexity that is essayed, the more intractable becomes the problem
of specifying – let alone analysing – the system, and the greater
the chance that the information obtainable will be inadequate or
inaccurate. But if we seek to avoid these difficulties by keeping our
description simple, then is it not possible that the degree of
misrepresentation thus implied will make both description and
analysis worthless?

There appears to be an almost universal preference for the second danger. Even in economics, where the proliferation of multi-level interdependencies is the essential basis on which the subject has been built, very drastic simplifications are the rule. Highly complex subsystems, such as firms or even whole sectors of an economy, containing within themselves many layers of complexity, are regularly treated as simple elements, while components of a complex system are analysed as isolated units.

Now the incentive to such a high degree of abstraction is plain. It conforms to natural rationality, which, as previously observed, is primarily adapted to performing a series of simple operations on (if necessary) large quantities of data, and which responds best to challenges which are bounded by a fairly simple structure. But is such abstraction compatible with an effective study of complex systems? By what right do we claim validity for any highly simplified description or analysis of what we are sure are highly complex relationships? If the universe is queerer than we can suppose, how can we hope to understand even part of it?

This chapter is an attempt to provide a partial answer to these questions. It is an answer which relies partly on evidence (our methods work – sometimes), partly on logic (there is a plausible argument that they should often work), and partly on a faith that we live in the kind of world in which we may expect them often to work. The answer cannot be complete, because simplified analysis is indeed sometimes not valid; and we shall try to explain why, and to suggest what might be (and sometimes is) done about it.

Decomposable systems

Whether it is sensible to consider no more than one (or perhaps two) levels of a multi-level system seems to depend on the extent to which the complete system is decomposable, to use Simon's (1969) expressive term. To what extent, on the one hand, is the functioning of detailed components independent of the external environment, and, on the other, to what extent is the response of a system to its environment apparently independent of its internal structure? To take a simple example, can one reasonably predict the behaviour of a thermostatically-controlled heating or cooling system without reference to the conditions in which it is to work, or assume that the temperature within a building or a vehicle will be effectively controlled without considering the particular means by which this is to be done? The answer is that within fairly wide limits we can do both, once it has been established, on the basis of our own or someone else's experience, what these limits are. Provided that we then remain within them, the efficiency of a subsystem is independent of its environment, while only its aggregate output is relevant to the analysis of overall system behaviour. The system is decomposable. For the study of the critical limits, or of what lies beyond, however, decomposition is not appropriate.

Simon argues that existing complex systems are likely to be highly decomposable. His principal reason is that complex systems are much more likely to emerge from subsystems which are themselves stable over a range of environments than are systems composed directly from basic elements, and without such stable intermediate levels. The advantages of decomposability are emphasised by the parable of the two watchmakers, Tempus and Hora. Each produced high quality watches, containing about 1,000 parts; but whereas Tempus constructed each watch directly from these parts, Hora's watches contained ten major assemblies, each made up of about ten subassemblies, which in turn each comprised about ten basic parts. Any complete assembly or subassembly could be safely laid aside, as of course could a complete watch, but any that was not yet complete would fall apart if put down. Assuming that each craftsman was equally skilful, and equally liable to be interrupted, Simon then demonstrates the enormously greater productivity of the second method (Simon, 1969, pp. 90–2).

Thus, if there are obstacles to the development of complex systems, those which are made up of stable subsystems would, other things being equal, have much the greater chance of emergence; therefore, after a lengthy period of Darwinian evolution, one would expect a very high proportion of the complex systems currently in existence to be composed of subsystems which were independently stable. Almost all the watches in the world would be made by Hora's methods. We might also expect to find (and indeed we do find) similar subsystems combined in very different ways, and complex systems composed of very different subsystems showing similar aggregate behaviour. This degree of independence between system levels justifies the practice of studying them independently. A decomposable world lends itself to a decomposed structure of analysis.

Though Simon's parable concerns an artifact, his direct inferences are to natural systems. He supports his logic by the evidence of scientific development, which has proceeded from matter to molecules, thence to atoms, and only then to elementary particles (if indeed they prove to be truly elementary).

This skyhook-skyscraper construction of science from the roof down to the yet unconstructed foundations was possible because the behaviour of the system at each level depended on only a very approximate, simplified, abstracted characterisation of the system at the level next beneath. This is lucky, else the safety of bridges and airplanes might depend on the correctness of the 'Eightfold Way' of looking at elementary particles. (Simon, 1969, p. 17.)

In the last sentence, Simon implies that, since artifacts are produced according to our understanding of natural phenomena, the decomposability of the natural is thereby inherited by the artificial. He believes that successful social systems are highly decomposable too.

The argument that complex systems are likely to be highly decomposable is plausible, and very consoling. It is always a comfort to be told that the way we have been doing things (in this case almost the only way that we know of doing things) is a reasonable way. However, as Simon himself points out, two cautions are necessary. First, since we habitually treat complex systems as decomposable, it may be that decomposable systems are the only kind of complex system which we are capable of recognising. The effects of the models which we use on our perception of the world will be discussed in Chapters 6 and 11; for the present we will concentrate on other problems. Second, decomposability, especially of artifacts, may apply only to a particular set of circumstances: temperature control systems can cope with only a specified temperature range, and even within that range may not work very well in a sandstorm or when drenched with sea-water.

The circumstances in which the assumption of decomposability breaks down are worth further investigation. Decomposability is of significance primarily in conditions of change – either random or systematic. If watchmakers were never interrupted, the methods of Tempus might be just as good as those of Hora; the differences between them, being of no apparent significance, might not even be noticed. There are, it is true, other possible advantages. For example, the physical difficulty of keeping up to a thousand components together might prove an encumbrance to Tempus. Moreover, the study of an unchanging system, and the solution of a timeless, though complex, problem are both easier, and may sometimes only be possible, if they can be resolved into components for quasi-independent analysis. Such advantages are almost entirely neglected in this book.

Decomposability matters above all because it facilitates adaptation. A completely decomposable system, as defined by Simon, would be fully adaptable to any change in its environment. The assumption of complete decomposability is an assumption of complete adaptability. Adaptability may result from isolation, or from a multitude of alternative linkages, as in many biological and social systems. Complete decomposability is a guarantee of success; Friedman's billiard player never misses a shot. But such an assumption cannot be generally true. Even natural systems are not completely decomposable; for if they were, each would be equally fit to survive. But, as we know, history is littered with the record of extinct animals, technologies, and political and social systems. Whether a system is sufficiently decomposable must depend on the particular characteristics of the environment to which it is subjected. The effects of environmental changes are most obvious in the case of artificial systems; thus, with the development of the jet engine, the safety of aeroplanes suddenly became dependent on an understanding of metal fatigue, and the wreckage of Comet airliners demonstrated the interdependencies between components of different system levels, which had hitherto been safely neglected.

However, the distinction which Simon makes between natural and artificial phenomena, based on differing degrees of dependence on their environment (especially the task objective of their human designers) seems misplaced. Simon (1969, pp. ix–x) contrasts the 'necessity' of the subservience of natural phenomena to natural laws with the 'contingency' of artificial phenomena which, 'given different circumstances, might be quite other than they are'. But given different circumstances, natural phenomena might be quite different also. Without observing those different circumstances, we cannot know – although we may be able to surmise. It is not difficult to think of erstwhile natural laws which have been found to be contingent on particular classes of environment: the phenomena explained by Newtonian physics might stand as good examples of systems which might be quite other than they are. The prospect of as yet undiscovered limits to the adaptability of familiar natural systems gives scope to the imaginations of science fiction writers, many of whose hypotheses we have no present means of testing.

Thus abstractions from complexity are safest in familiar situations. Simon's advice (1969, p. 16) on the exploitation of the decomposability of complex systems, though sound enough, is less helpful that it appears at first sight. 'The more we are willing to abstract from the detail of a set of phenomena, the easier it becomes to simulate the phenomena. Moreover, we do not have to know, or guess at, all the internal structure of the system, but only that part of it that is crucial to the abstraction.' The question left unasked is: how do we know what is crucial? The answer must be that we can never be absolutely certain. We can reasonably be confident if we are dealing with phenomena already well understood, and consciously remaining within the limits of our understanding. In such instances the abstraction is perhaps not very likely to yield significant new information, though it may lead to much better control. But it is the nature of knowledge that every trial in different circumstances is capable, in principle, of confuting the hypothesis under test; therefore every new use of an accepted abstraction is a test of the continued usefulness of that abstraction, and not simply a new source of information about the phenomena abstracted from.

With both natural and artificial systems, any extrapolation is a venture into the incompletely known. We may cross a critical boundary unawares. In general, the degree of confidence with which we may reasonably assume decomposability is likely to depend upon the degree of novelty in the application. The assumption of decomposability based on past evolutionary success is available to newly-designed systems only in proportion to their lack of novelty. Too often we know little and care less about the bounds of decomposability. Indeed, the structure of organisations and the boundaries of academic disciplines are often designed on the assumption that such inconvenient questions have been settled for ever – even, on occasion, when they have just been revised from an earlier arrangement once thought to be definitive. As will be seen later, there are quite respectable reasons for making such assumptions. But the use of decomposed analysis to study change must always be subject to unexpected error.

The chance of unexpected error is increased by another factor. The process of model-building, in whatever field, goes beyond the decomposition of complexity. It involves the transformation of a set of phenomena into a form which is amenable to treatment by the techniques available. Transformation implies distortion; those who like to talk of mapping problems onto techniques may be reminded of the difficulty of mapping the globe (let alone the heavens) onto a flat sheet of paper. That the form of model may depend on the available techniques, and that differences in their technical equipment may cause different people to formulate a given problem in very different ways, have implications which will be taken up later. What should be emphasised at the moment is that the decomposability of a system does not imply that the set of models used to analyse it should themselves form a decomposable system – which is certainly good news for economists – and, even more important, that decomposability of the set of analytical models does not imply that the system being modelled is itself decomposable.

One must be careful in making inferences from a model to the phenomena being modelled, whether they be natural or artificial; but of course this is far from being true only of inferences about decomposability. Experiments, like logical arguments, take the form of conditional statements; and our real interest is usually in circumstances in which those conditions are not fulfilled. The remainder of this chapter is concerned with the legitimacy of such inferences, from both experimental and theoretical models. Let us begin with the former.

Experimental models

Experimental science is the art of being precisely wrong. It is a highly skilled and immensely valuable art. Precision is rightly much valued, but since, as has been explained, a precise model necessitates distortion, the price of precision is error. The experimenter creates an artificial situation in the laboratory, by scrupulously excluding many influences which affect the comparable real-world phenomenon; to the analysis of this invented problem (which, unlike conceptual models, does involve some physical reality) he then applies a formidable scientific apparatus. According to his motivations and interest, he may, or may not, then use the results as a basis for the exploration of similar phenomena outside the laboratory. If he does, he will discover that the predictive power of experimental science for this purpose, though great, is limited. Experimental science is more like a searchlight than a floodlight.

Economists are liable to misunderstand the significance of the experimental method in the natural sciences. Shackle (1972, p. 31) asserts that 'The controlled experiment is possible because the channels of possible interference are known and can be blocked, even if the possible sources of such interference are not known. But in the study of conduct, policy and history, who can tell what influences may approach by what roads?' But it is not possible to be sure that the channels of possible interference have been blocked in the experimental situation, for (despite Simon's assurance) it is impossible to be certain what is relevant. What is more important is that the channels often cannot be blocked in the situation which the experiment is designed to model, and thus, in so far as the results depend on blocking these channels, the very success of the blockade invalidates the application of the experimental results. This critical point is entirely overlooked by Lancaster (1969, p. 6), when he consoles economists for their limited ability to experiment by observing that 'even if we could, we might doubt whether human beings will behave the same way in experimental situations as they would do in ordinary life'. We might indeed, for in this respect we would expect human beings to behave like insecticides, drugs, or chemical processes.

The precise nature of the experimental method emerges very clearly when one examines the use of science in industry, where the object is the production not of pure knowledge but of knowledge required for the development of working processes and useful products. Development from the laboratory to full-scale production is not simple. The vast majority of laboratory successes are commercial failures. Often this is because of the exclusion of economic variables; but much more often it is due to the very exclusions which were the conditions of initial experimental success. The virtue of the controlled experiment is also its limitation.

The price of precision is error. What the price is can be seen by the cost of development following success in the laboratory – including the cost of those products and processes which have to be discarded along the way. But the reward for well-chosen error is precision; and the size of that reward may be measured by the development costs saved because one is able to reject so many possibilities on the basis of knowledge cheaply gained by an efficient experimental procedure.

Science students, and even some industrial researchers, are inclined to regard the laboratory as the real situation, and development as the process of making the world fit the model – annoying and expensive details, but not really what science is about. Indeed, the pervasiveness of this attitude, in a diluted form, is shown by the prevalence of the phrase 'scale-up problems'. In fact, the chemist, in particular, far from being plagued with scale-up problems, actually enjoys a very valuable scale-down facility (Bradbury, 1973). The problems arise from the distortions inevitably involved in small-scale experimentation. They are scale-down problems. The manufacturers of aero-engines appear to be relatively free from such problems, since it is necessary to build a full-scale prototype at an early stage. It is an expensive freedom. Even after accepting the drastic limitation on the number of alternatives which can be tried, the costs of development are enormous, and at least contribute to explaining the contrast between the aircraft industry's heavy dependence on government support and the absence of such support for the chemical industry.

Models are abstractions from reality. They are not replicas of it. There appears to be a widespread feeling that approximation to reality is always a virtue; but that feeling is quite wrong. A perfectly realistic model would be indistinguishable from reality, and apart from testing to destruction, what then would be its use for investigation? One uses a model precisely in order to escape from reality into something more tractable, but nevertheless useful, from which it should be possible to work back to reality. Rationality operates not on reality, but on abstractions. What is required is an abstraction which is good enough; and what is good enough depends on the problem, or more generally, on the stage reached in the attempt to solve it. Reality, as such, is no adequate criterion. Thus it is much more helpful to talk of 'sufficiency' than of 'realism'. One may abstract from detail, or from externalities; one may use a mathematical model, a rule of thumb, or a practical test. What matters is that the method chosen should be sufficient for its purpose; and its acceptability can be judged only in relation to that purpose.

Theory and experiment

Recognition that experiments are abstractions helps to clarify the relationship between theoretical and experimental approaches to problems. In the solution of complex problems, and certainly in the development of new products, they complement each other: theory guides experiment, and experiment extends theory. But at any one stage they may be alternatives. Pharmacologists have no adequate general theory which would enable them confidently to predict biological activity from a drug's chemical structure; they do, however, have a variety of fairly effective experimental methods. Economists, though less well equipped with experimental techniques, do have some moderately well-developed theories which purport to infer behaviour from structure – indeed almost all economic theory is concerned to elicit such inferences in one way or another. Economics is more a child of mathematics than of experimental science; and economic models are often quite a good substitute for experiment.

Indeed, it may be argued that the weakness of economics lies not in its limited scope for closely-controlled experiment, but in the absence of an equivalent to the small-scale experimental plant. Except in certain well-defined circumstances, industrial chemists would not dream of going straight from the laboratory to full-scale production, without trying out some of the critical stages in some detail first (thus incidentally demonstrating the limitations of the laboratory experiments); but economists frequently have no choice but to proceed directly from theories which are as abstract as the chemist's experiments to practical policy recommendations. The lack of such an intermediate stage is one of the major obstacles to the successful use of cost-benefit analysis. Of course, experimental plants are themselves not infallible predictors, as is shown by the cost and difficulty of commissioning full-scale plant, and the occasional failure to make a plant work at all.

Where theory and experiment are alternatives, the choice between them depends on their relative cost and relative effectiveness, and these not only vary from problem to problem, but may change with changing circumstances. The advent of the computer has produced a notable increase in the amount of economic work which is almost theory-free; meanwhile the apparently increasing odds against success by trial and error, and increasing concern over toxicity (especially long-term toxicity) which is likely to be neither cheap nor easy to evaluate by experimental methods, already appears to be giving an impetus to more theoretical approaches to pharmacological problems.

Beyond the bounds of rationality

We have seen that there are two general ways in which the conceptual or experimental models used in natural science, social science, or problem-solving differ from the reality which they are used to explore: they may assume a decomposability which does not exist, or they may be mis-specifications even of the system levels which they purport to represent. The recognition that such limitations are inevitable is the basis for Simon's concept of bounded rationality. Problems have to be force-fitted into artificial categories; and the more complex the problem the more artificial are likely to be the categories, whether of theory or experiment. 'More artificial' does not, of course, imply 'less useful'; but let us see what it does imply.

There is always something beyond the system as comprehended, and its exclusion is the price of comprehension. Abstraction always introduces ignorance – a willingness (reluctant maybe) to ignore the effects of the interactions left unexplored and of the distortions deliberately (or unwittingly) introduced. It is impossible to reduce this ignorance without substituting another model designed to deal with it – until the model is confronted with the situation it is intended to represent. If this is a stable situation (such as a well-established production process) it is then possible, by repeated trial and error, to develop a model in which predictive precision does not have to be paid for by ignorance of its applicability to that stable situation. The effective use of such a model is quite compatible with a rather poor understanding of the behaviour of the system being modelled, requiring only the assumption that the system is decomposable under the conditions of interest.

However, even when tested and modified in the way just discussed, the model introduces potential ignorance; ignorance of the consequences of change in the process being modelled. Such potential ignorance may be perfectly acceptable – and it is a basic theme of this book that some ignorance must be accepted – but its presence should not be forgotten. At least as much as any other kind of model, the pragmatic model is contingent on its situation; given different circumstances, the system being modelled might be quite other than it is. The more closely adapted to particular circumstances is the model being used, the less likely we are to understand the form and limits of its contingency.

Thus precision not only implies error; it implies unknown error, even unpredictable error – from which we may be safe provided that we avoid any change of circumstances. Both the chances and the extent of error are likely to be increasing functions of the degree of abstraction. As Simon observes, the success of science (particularly the extent to which higher-level systems have been successfully explained before the behaviour of component systems was understood) has rested on the high degree of decomposability in the phenomena studied. As a result of this long history of success, classic scientific method (the closely controlled experiment to test a highly-specific hypothesis) is based on the implicit premise of decomposability. As the double-blind experiment with halothane and chloroform shows, the results can be quite misleading if the system is not truly decomposable – and nothing in the method will indicate when it is not. The validity of the premise of decomposability on which such a model is based can be tested only by using a different model.

The insufficiency of abstraction

Models are concept-forming; and that may be helpful, or restrictive: in Shackle's (1972, p. 51) words, 'understanding consists in the recognition of familiarity'; but the recognition, and the understanding, may be false. As we proceed down the learning curve, it is not always easy to appreciate precisely what is the skill being learnt, and within what limits it may be transferred. Major innovations are very likely to violate the bounds of decomposability, including, very often, the bounds within which the critical invention is made.

The problem of extrapolation from past experience is particularly obvious when one is using an explicitly unrealistic model, such as Friedman's billiard player, who is an infallible mathematician. But extrapolation is a problem with every model which omits or distorts some aspect of reality – which means every model. 'In general it is only by the use of artificial experimental isolation that we can predict physical events. . .We are very far from being able to predict, even in physics, the precise results of a *concrete* situation, such as a thunderstorm, or a fire.' (Popper, 1957, p. 139.) 'Try it and see' is the only certain test – and even then only if we can be sure what it is that we see.

The limitations of abstraction point up the difference between prediction and explanation. As Marshall (1920, p. 773) says, the task in each case is to 'select the right facts, group them rightly, and make them serviceable for suggestions in thought and guidance in practice. . .the explanation of the past and the prediction of the future are not different operations, but the same worked in opposite directions, the one from effect to cause, the other from cause to effect.' The difference, as Shackle (1972, p. 345) comments, is that in the task of explanation the known sequel is available as a guide to selection among the antecedent circumstances, whereas the selection of antecedent circumstances for prediction has to be based on some other criterion.

Any principle of abstraction embodies its own selection criteria: the extreme case is the fully-programmed decision. Whatever may be true of education in general, the study of a well-defined discipline consists largely of the acquisition of programmes. A fully-specified programme provides for all listed possibilities, and ignores all those which are not listed. It is highly efficient; but it is not always effective. Decision theory provides a classic case. Lindley (1971, p. v) explains that

there is essentially only one way to reach a decision sensibly. First, the uncertainties present in the situation must be quantified in terms of values called probabilities. Secondly, the various consequences of the courses of action must be similarly described in terms of utilities. Thirdly, that decision must be taken which is expected – on the basis of the calculated probabilities – to give the greatest utility. The force of 'must', used in three places there, is simply that any deviation from the precepts is liable to lead the decision-maker into procedures which are demonstrably absurd – or as we shall say, incoherent.

Let us take chess, as a familiar example of a decision situation. Chess is a finite, two-person, zero-sum game. In principle, it is possible to exhibit every possible sequence of moves on a gigantic decision tree. Two-person, zero-sum finite games which are symmetrical yield a value of zero for every trial if both players always choose their optimal strategies. Though chess is not symmetrical, it may also have the same property (it can easily be made symmetrical by randomising the right to the opening move). But whether it does or does not is a question of rather little relevance to the chess-player, since there is no way for him to make use of it. It is indeed precisely with reference to chess that Simon (1972, p. 167) has demonstrated that 'the optimal decision in the approximated world is not necessarily even a good decision in the real world'; a detailed consideration of a small number of moves selected by informal judgement is more effective than an attempt to evaluate every possible move. Deviation from the precepts of decision theory leads to incoherence in terms of the abstraction which they define: but the precepts themselves are incoherent even in the artificially-simplified circumstances of a game of chess. One may be able to optimise a model; one cannot optimise a situation.

Rigour and ignorance

Models, whether conceptual or experimental, can be invaluable if their limitations are recognised; but one of the dangers in their use is that they leave us ignorant of our own ignorance. They not only tell us nothing about the effects of what is excluded; they are liable to prevent any recognition that what is excluded may have some effect. A survey of the problems of project development notes that 'difficulties arising when projects move from the drawing board to the practical scale are usually under-estimated. The error is particularly great when disciplines outside the person's own experience are required, as is increasingly the case with advanced technology projects today. He may dismiss these other disciplines as "mere engineering detail".' (Fishlock, 1973, p. 15.)

Emphasis on scientific rigour, as usually understood, may aggravate this difficulty. We have referred earlier to the conclusion, on the basis of standard scientific testing, that halothane was indistinguishable in its effects from chloroform. Fire tests provide another striking example of the occasional perversity of good scientific practice. In an investigation of the relationship between fire tests and fire safety, Hanlon (1973, p. 178), claims that 'the overriding problem with most fire tests is that in an attempt to make them scientific, precise, and reproducible, they have been divorced too far from reality'. Because of this search for scientific rigour, 'they test only one set of conditions – a particular sample size at one temperature in only one orientation, with no other objects nearby'; and as a consequence 146 people died in a French nightclub fire to which an approved 'self-extinguishing' urethane foam made a substantial contribution. It will be recalled that fires were chosen by Popper as an example of the limitations of prediction in physics. The search for rigour may conceal critical areas of ignorance.

The flight from ignorance is characteristic of both experimental and theoretical study. The scientist makes for the laboratory, the economist for statistics or mathematical theory. We know of the advantages of roundabout methods of production, including the production of knowledge. It is now a familiar economic proposition that the most efficient method of achieving a desired higher level of output incorporating a changed pattern of production may require the use of a growth path on which some other pattern of production is employed. There may be a comparable turnpike theorem of problem solving, so that the quickest way of proceeding from problem to solution may be to use a solution path which neither originates at the perceived problem, nor attains the desired solution. In applying the original turnpike theorem to growth problems, it is recognised that optimal growth requires us not only to join the turnpike, but also to leave it again. Scientists and economists faced with problems are ready enough to make for the familiar turnpike, but liable to pay no attention to the exit signs; they appear sometimes so bemused by the smoothness and speed of their journey that they forgot their destination. The conditions for the solution of the model are investigated with great care; the conditions for its application are often ignored. Academic rigour does not always facilitate the solution of problems.

General equilibrium theory: the neglect of rigour

General equilibrium theory provides some very clear examples of this failing. 'Microeconomics is primarily concerned with behavior at equilibrium...and economists have virtually no theory of how individual decision-makers behave out of equilibrium.' Taken literally, that statement by Lancaster (1969, p. 3) means, quite simply, that economists have virtually no theory of how individual decision-makers behave, a sad commentary on the state of what some of its practitioners call the logic of choice. In practice, economists normally employ a simple and comprehensive theory of non-equilibrium behaviour: an economy out of equilibrium always moves towards equilibrium – except when it doesn't. In the former case one uses microtheory, in the latter, the techniques of macroeconomics. These latter techniques, as is fairly well recognised, imply the abandonment of some of the foundations of general equilibrium theory; what is less well realised is that the use of equilibrium theory to explain behaviour out of equilibrium, though preserving the illusion of full theoretical rigour, is a course of breathtaking audacity.

A simple and well-known statement of the comparative equilibrium method has been given by Machlup (1967, p. 8).

Let us again pose four typical questions and see which of them we might expect to answer with the aid of price theory. (1) What will be the prices of cotton textiles? (2) What prices will the X Corporation charge? (3) How will the prices of cotton textiles be affected by an increase in wage rates? (4) How will the X Corporation change its prices when wage rates are increased?

Machlup's claim that 'conventional price theory is not equipped to answer any but the third question' is quite false: the formal theory is designed to answer the first two, and those alone. The solution of all equilibrium models rests on given data: there is provision for alternative solutions for different data; but no provision within the model for a response to any data which is not included in the original specification.

The use of the comparative equilibrium method of analysing change has no theoretical basis whatever. Indeed, it involves a fundamental inconsistency. For the method to work, it is necessary to assume that the change was totally unexpected: otherwise the initial position would have been different from that predicted by our analytical method. But if unexpected changes take place, can full adjustment to any set of given data be regarded as truly full adjustment? Thus the type of equilibrium model employed is inconsistent with the concept of comparative equilibrium as a means of analysing change. There is also a problem here for welfare economists, for what precisely is optimal about an equilibrium which ignores the (admitted) possibility of unforeseen change?

Thus the use of comparative equilibrium methods implies a total abandonment of the rigour on which general equilibrium theorists pride themselves. Application of the model destroys the purity of its logic: that purity can be preserved only by total abstinence. Presented with Machlup's list, general equilibrium theorists will maintain that questions about the effects of change are not properly posed general equilibrium questions; yet such theorists do not in practice forgo the use of their theory to analyse problems of change. Machlup is in rather better case, since he is too sensible to attempt a defence of the usefulness of conventional price theory on formal grounds; however his attempts to justify its use by the compelling logic of the situation have now (1974) confined it to predicting the directions in which a competitive industry will respond to specific changes which are generally known to have occurred. Such restriction in scope is in practice unacceptable, even to Machlup.

None of these criticisms denies the usefulness of this device of comparing artificial states. Thermodynamic equilibrium models are used in a similar way. But it should be acknowledged that the validity of the comparative equilibrium method lies in the simple Friedmanesque justification that it (often) works, especially in retrospect: it does not lie in the quality of the theory. Unfortunately, the method offers no way of warning us when its predictions are likely to fail.

A simple justification by works (rather than by faith) is, however, not adequate when a model is used not to explain, but to judge. It is in the field of welfare economics that the failure to relate the model back to reality is most marked. The most eminent of economists are very careless about leaving the turnpike. Here, for example, is Hahn (1973a, p. 324) extolling the achievements of general equilibrium theory. 'When the claim is made – and the claim is as old as Adam Smith – that a myriad of self-seeking agents left to themselves will lead to a coherent and efficient disposition of economic resources, Arrow and Debreu show what the world would have to look like if the claim is to be true.' That is an astonishing statement. It is, of course, perfectly correct that, in Arrow's (1971, p. 3) words, 'the best developed part of the theory relates to only a single question: the statement of a set of conditions, as weak as possible, which insure that a competitive equilibrium exists and is Pareto efficient'; but that is not at all the same thing. The point is not just that no economist of repute has ever suggested anarchy as an ideal political system, nor even that Adam Smith was looking for the best possible system, not an unattainable level of perfection. It is that equilibrium and Pareto efficiency are defined in relation to a model which is inescapably ignorant of some prominent features of any actual economy. It is far from clear that, as defined, they are relevant to such an economy, or even have any discernible meaning in it.

Arrow and Debreu provide 'the most potent avenue of falsification of the claims' of the advocates of market systems only in the sense that the double-blind experiment falsified the claim that halothane was a better anaesthetic than chloroform. Hahn's assertion that general equilibrium theorists have made 'precise an economic tradition which is two hundred years old' demonstrates that he has very little idea what that tradition is. He notes that general equilibrium theory 'is strong on equilibrium and very weak on how it comes about' without recognising that what is now regarded as the relative weakness on equilibrium of earlier writers was at least partly due to their greater concern with processes of change and of growth. General equilibrium theory belongs in a different tradition. In considering the claim that is 'as old as Adam Smith' we might do better to turn, not to Arrow and Debreu, but to Marshall and Keynes.

Hahn's (1973b) Cambridge inaugural lecture, though notable for its adumbration of a research programme which demonstrates the continued theoretical potential of the axiomatic method, shows a similar unquestioning faith in the virtues of rigour and precision, leading to some further extraordinary arguments. The most extraordinary of all is that by which Hahn purports to show that the Arrow–Debreu construction offers a quick way of disposing of the claim that the allocation of exhaustible resources may be left to the market (pp. 14–15). Hahn asserts that anyone making such a claim must be assuming an Arrow–Debreu equilibrium for the economy. On what compulsion must he? All that is necessary is to argue that the market will not do worse than the best available alternative. To assume an Arrow–Debreu equilibrium would indeed be rather foolish, for 'the inadequate treatment of time and uncertainty by the construction' makes it quite inappropriate for considering a problem in which these are essential elements. Hahn's position appears to be that the impossibility of formulating a proposition in a general equilibrium mode is sufficient to discredit that proposition. One must conclude that such theorists 'do not understand what they are claiming to be the case when they claim' that general equilibrium theory permits definitive judgements on such matters.

That is not to say that general equilibrium theory is irrelevant to the questions which Hahn lists. The double-blind experiment is not irrelevant to our understanding of halothane, for it demonstrates the importance of changing the system of administering anaesthetics, and not just the anaesthetic agent: it demonstrates the error of assuming that the anaesthetic system is decomposable.

But to make policy judgements on the basis of general equilibrium models necessarily involves the abandonment of that formal rigour which is the theorists' chief pride. Is the formal model a sufficiently good representation of the underlying situation – not just of the market structure – for its conclusions to carry over into recommendations on exchange rate policy or foreign aid? The rigour of the theory cannot itself provide the answer to that question, as Hahn assumes. The price of precision is error; and the greater Hahn's insistence on the virtues of precision, the greater the errors into which he falls.

A great deal of argument is required to establish to what extent the conclusions of the mathematical analysis can be sensibly applied; but usually no argument at all is offered. After noting that it is possible to specify the conditions for Pareto efficiency, Arrow (1971, p. 3) immediately concludes: 'Thus the denial of any of these hypotheses is presumably a sufficient condition for considering resort to non-market channels of resource allocation.' That (in two senses) is his presumption. Later in the same article he asserts that 'markets for many forms of risk-bearing and for most future transactions do not exist and their absence is surely suggestive of inefficiency' (p. 18). But the relevance of this criterion of efficiency has been established only for specified general equilibrium systems; to demonstrate that the existence of such markets is desirable in an economy where, for example, unpredictable events occur, people grow old and change their preferences, and markets use up real resources, requires a great deal of effort, and cannot, in principle, be accomplished beyond all possibility of refutation. Indeed, it may be easier to argue the other way, for Hurwicz (1972, p. 299) has observed that when the allocation mechanism (be it market or other) itself is a significant consumer of resources, the attempt to reach optimal solutions may itself be non-optimal.

Having failed to establish that the results of the formal analysis apply to the system being studied, theorists are very liable to recommend alternative methods of resource allocation. The specification of these alternative methods is of a standard that would be universally derided in a general equilibrium model. There is rarely much consideration of how they might work, or whether there is any reason to expect them to get anywhere near Pareto optimality, even assuming that Pareto optimality is desirable. If the motivations and structure of a market system do not produce these results, one is entitled to ask what alternative structure might do so with the same motivations, and why such a structure might come into existence; yet such questions are barely considered. Which of the available imperfect methods of resource-allocation is to be preferred is a question of great importance, which general equilibrium theorists make no attempt to answer.

Iain Macleod once remarked that Enoch Powell's logic ran straight and true as a railway track, but that he preferred to get off before the train crashed into the buffers (Fisher, 1973, p. 65). The logicians of general equilibrium theory are liable to become so exhilarated by the power of their analysis that they approach their destination much too fast, and the resulting violent collisions with reality have on occasions wrecked even such famous trains of thought as the Golden Arrow. One of the most spectacular crashes resulted from Arrow's (1962) attempt to pronounce on the allocation of resources for research. As usually displayed, the wreckage is accompanied by a detailed Inspector's Report by Demsetz (1969).

The report draws attention to three major types of defect. First, the argument is conducted by comparing the existing situation (as perceived) with an ideal, not surprisingly to the disadvantage of the former; 'thereafter a deduced discrepancy between the ideal and the real is sufficient to call forth perfection by incantation'. Government, for example, is invoked to overcome the asserted tendency for market systems to be risk-averse, with no recognition that governments are 'very averse to the risk of being voted out of office'. Second, Arrow assumes throughout that optimal arrangements have no costs: thus, for example, the possibility that a market may fail to exist because its cost would outweigh its benefits is not admitted. Demsetz calls this the fallacy of the free lunch: welfare theorists consume many of them. Third, many of the reasons adduced for the inadequacies of the market system are facts of life, with which any system would have to cope. Among these Demsetz cites indivisibilities, and the likelihood that insurance will reduce the incentive to avoid the contingencies insured against; he might well have added, as an obstacle to the existence of some of the markets deemed necessary for Pareto optimality, the unfortunate failure of our world to supply a complete list of all possible states of nature. Many of Arrow's conclusions about the desirability of government-supported research may be sound; but they do not follow at all simply from his argument. The greatest weakness not noticed by Demsetz is the assumption that invention – the generation of new knowledge – is equivalent to innovation; the innovative process by its nature does not fit easily into the general equilibrium framework.

Unfortunately, despite its thoroughness and explicit recommendations, this report does not seem to have been very effective, for similar unfortunate accidents continue to occur. Indeed, Inspectors Davis (1971) and Diamond (1971) have pointed to some unremedied defects as among the causes of a more recent derailment of the same express (Arrow, 1971), and reference has already been made to the disastrous results of two Hahn enthusiasts' specials.

This combination of fierce rigour in the theory and unheeding slackness in its application seems to parallel closely the examples of technological innovation and fire-testing mentioned earlier; and there are others which readers may call to mind. It cannot be the fault of the people concerned; it cannot be simply (though it may be partly) the fault of the peculiar character of economic theorising. One might postulate a law that the sum of rigour is a constant: thus the greater the rigour of the formal model, the weaker the connection between that model and the reality which it may be used to interpret. The price of precision is not only error, but ignorance: the rigorous theorist or experimenter doesn't know what it is he doesn't know. But since each of us believes he understands the significance of his own model best, the verb 'to abstract' may be conjugated: I abstract, you over-simplify, he (or she?) fudges.

Search and screening

If bounded rationality makes abstraction unavoidable, and if any abstraction creates ignorance, but lower levels of abstraction are expensive, what are the implications for problem solving? Where a great deal of ignorance is inherent in the situation, as in the quest for a new drug or for a corporate strategy, it may be best to use a variety of approaches in series, beginning with the simple and highly abstract, with the object of eliminating most of the possibilities before undertaking a comprehensive investigation of the few that remain. In one way or another, this seems to be what often happens; and it helps to explain why later detailed study seems often merely to confirm an apparent predisposition in favour of a project.

Such a finding, which might otherwise be interpreted as a sign of inefficient decision-making, is highly rational when such detailed studies are so expensive (certainly in their opportunity costs) that it is unwise to undertake them unless the odds against success have been drastically reduced, but where the techniques for improving the odds necessarily leave a margin of ignorance to be reduced by more elaborate studies. Thus prototypes, experimental plants, and test-marketing are by no means wasted if they usually confirm previous predictions. They would be wasted if predictions were always confirmed, but there seems no present danger of that; they would also be wasted if they usually failed to confirm predictions, unless there were no ways by which those predictions could be improved at reasonable cost. 'Reasonable' can be given a precise meaning by using the notion of the value of information, but since that notion depends upon concealing guesswork under the title of subjective probability, the price of precision (though it may be worth paying), is, in this instance also, error and ignorance.

The idea of a series of partial models has been formally developed by Gallagher (1971) into a scheme of sequential screening, and applied to the problems of innovation in the chemical industry. Sequential screening is a kind of negative sequential search: instead of trying the most obvious candidates first, it begins by eliminating the most unlikely. The basic justification is the same – economy of effort in making choices under conditions of partial ignorance; but the characteristics of the ignorance are different in the two cases. Sequential search is appropriate when two conditions are present: first, the contemplated alternatives can be ranked according to the subjective probabilities of success, and second, this ranking is negatively correlated with the likely cost of testing the option. Fulfilment of the second condition is not difficult when, as often, both estimates are heavily influenced by the same factors (in particular, the experience of the decision-makers); but it is a necessary, though usually overlooked, condition for producing a well-defined programme of sequential search. For if the most promising solutions require a great deal of investigation, and the less promising are rather easier to decide on, the assumption behind the notion of sequential search breaks down.

In decision situations where there is little prior confidence in the success of any available choice, and where the costs of demonstrating success are high, but the costs of a partial investigation, which may be adequate to demonstrate failure, are low, the best policy may be a strategy of selection by progressive rejection. To select is to reject, and it is sometimes easier to eliminate the many than to choose the one. This can be seen most obviously in the emergence of new pharmaceuticals and pesticides. Both of these involve the injection of chemical substances into complex biological systems, and, if one is interested in the adoption of the new product, into complex social systems too. The interactions are, to put it mildly, not well understood; thus it is not easy to choose a winner. However, it is easy to throw out some obvious losers, because the system is sufficiently decomposable for us to be confident that failure within a specific artificially-isolated subsystem entails failure in the more complex environment.

The ideal sequence of screens depends on two factors. The first is the relation between the costs and the direct benefits of each screen, the latter being measured by the costs saved through avoiding further investigation of candidates which will eventually fail: thus the success of a first-stage screen in eliminating a candidate which would otherwise be rejected only at the test-marketing stage, having consumed a great deal of time and effort, can outweigh failure to eliminate a large number which will be thrown out cheaply in the next round. The second factor is the extent to which the results of one screening process will help to improve the efficiency of the next – as judged by these two criteria. Shackle (1972, p. 391), in a more general consideration of handling partial ignorance, emphasises this second factor. 'Study of the existing and available evidence is chiefly relevant as the character of this evidence governs the need for additional and complementary evidence.' This consideration is perhaps not always explicit enough in practice.

Theories as screens

The screening process starts inside people's heads (in Eddington's terms, we all have our own fishnet); but in many scientific contexts the first formal screening is by laboratory experiment. Although, in relation to the full complexity of the system being explored, such screens are very inadequate, yet compared with the alternatives they are usually highly efficient; for they deal cheaply with a part of the system which is highly decomposable, at least in a negative sense of not rejecting potential successes. However, laboratory experiment may not always come first. Halothane provides a striking example of the use of theory (Ferguson's treatment of narcosis, together with theories of flammability and stability) to identify fluorine compounds as the most likely source of effective new inhalant anaesthetics, and to eliminate, without test, all but particular groups of those compounds (Bradbury, McCarthy & Suckling, 1972a, p. 106). The effect of this use of theory, according to the research chemist principally involved, was to reduce the search problem from the equivalent of hitting a sixpence with a dart on a football field to achieving the same result on a table-tennis table.

But the value of theory went beyond this: in addition to being a highly efficient eliminator, it also contributed to the design of the experimental screen. For the theory of narcosis predicted that, with certain identifiable exceptions, every compound tested would be a potent narcotic, and thus set the experimenters free to seek other important properties. Moreover, these properties were in part derived from a simple theory of the market requirements for a successful new anaesthetic. Since acceptance by anaesthetists was essential, the new drug must earn their professional assent, and counter the established preference for anaesthesia by injection, which was well founded on the disadvantages of existing inhalant anaesthetics. The experimenters therefore concluded that any new commercially successful inhalant anaesthetic must match the best properties of all such existing anaesthetics, and designed their screen accordingly (Bradbury, McCarthy & Suckling, 1972a, p. 106).

Some kind of theory must always come first; and this example demonstrates clearly the value of a well-defined and appropriate theory, both in avoiding the need for experiment and in contributing to the design of those experiments which are carried out. In the context of sequential screening, economists need not be entirely ashamed of economic theory. If we apply the criteria by which laboratory experiments in such circumstances should be judged, not of producing the answer but of narrowing down the range of possibilities, guiding further elimination, and doing both cheaply, then economic theory does not always do too badly. It is almost always much cheaper than experimentation; and some very simple market theory, for example, will effectively exclude some technological bright ideas before any attention is paid to their technical feasibility, or limit the field of possible diversification. That is justification enough.

Screening error

The sequential screening approach to complex problems attempts to exploit both their decomposability and the power of abstraction (or, in other words, the precision that can be bought by carefully-chosen error), while attempting to allow for the limits of decomposability and the limited sufficiency of the abstractions (or, in other words, the error and ignorance that are the price of precision).

When employed in the analysis of complex problems, both theory and experiment are better at rejection than selection. They cannot be expected to be perfect at either. Thalidomide, referred to in the previous chapter, is probably the best-known current example of a failure to reject; and that experience has led to the redesign of screens for new drugs, in which the rejection of thalidomide by the screen has been used as an essential criterion. It is possible that the new screens will reject some drugs which would be useful; certainly aspirin can produce deformed births in mice. False rejections may, by their nature, never be discovered; but some examples are known. It is reported that a compound now used as a successful insecticide was earlier rejected as an insect repellent; the fact that it killed the laboratory insects was ignored for a long time. On the other hand, perceptive questioning of a laboratory failure led to the discovery of paraquat.

False rejection is likely if the problem is wrongly decomposed. The insistence on inappropriate technical standards has in recent years caused I.C.I. Paints Division to forgo an opportunity to pioneer a new paint. Division scientists discovered that if this paint was applied to wet plaster, and then immediately grasped by one corner, the complete coat of paint could be peeled away from the wall. Such a possibility infringed the scientists' criterion of technical excellence; but it is not very relevant to the everyday practice of do-it-yourself householders, as was confirmed when a competitor introduced a similar paint with great success. Not only has this particular screen now been withdrawn; the Division now places much emphasis on a set of screens carefully designed to reflect customer requirements, as defined by market research.

Occasionally, false rejection may be avoided because the screen fails to work. A notable example concerns the successful new potato variety Pentland Dell. One of the criteria used in the breeding programme which produced this variety, at the Scottish Plant Breeding Station, was immunity to potato blight; but a few years after its commercial introduction, Pentland Dell was found to be susceptible to a new strain of blight. By this time, however, it had been accepted that blight immunity was an unattainable technical target, because of the rate of mutation of the fungus; and it was also discovered that, for many growers, the improved yield obtained from Pentland Dell provided ample compensation for the risk of blight. Similarly one might argue that general equilibrium theory has gained acceptance because it has been adjudged to pass the test, deemed essential, of logical rigour. It has been shown in this and the previous chapter that such rigour can be maintained only – if at all – by eschewing all application; but it has also been shown that the criterion is unnecessary. How many good varieties of potato, and how many useful economic models, have been lost because they were judged by the wrong criteria?

A variety of models

General equilibrium theory may take a valuable place in the armoury of problem solvers. But it cannot claim a unique place, even among the methods of economists. The use of a variety of incomplete models is both an aid to problem-solving and a safe-guard against false solutions. Since information functions can be preferentially ordered only for defined classes of pay-off functions and probability distributions of events, is it not reasonable to assume that no single method will be best for all problems – even all problems of a certain class? Though all models are incomplete, they are incomplete in different ways; and different kinds of incompleteness confer differential advantages and differential weaknesses. That, no doubt, is why 'a host of wise scientists have been saying that science should be regarded as a means for providing a variety of alternative descriptions of a given set of data' (Bradbury and Dutton, 1972, p. 64).

The value of such alternative descriptions is emphasised by Simon (1969, p. 77). 'All mathematics exhibits in its conclusions only what is already implicit in its premises. . .Hence all mathematical derivation can be viewed simply as change in representation, making evident what was previously true but obscure.

'This view can be extended to all of problem solving – solving a problem simply means representing it so as to make the solution transparent.' Except in pure mathematics, it would be more accurate to say that solving a problem involves replacing it by a (supposedly) analogous problem, the solution to which is transparent. All models are 'as if' models, as Friedman has clearly seen. But all such replacements entail a risk that the transparent solution may turn out not to be a solution to the original problem at all. This is the great danger of seeking the 'one best way', or the 'golden key', as a management consultant has called it. The reason for having a variety of models for complex problems is not to increase the chance of finding one that is a good fit, but to provide a group of models with different fits, and which between them provide a good prospect of finding a good solution.

None of this implies the abandonment of specialism. It does imply building on to our specialisms a better understanding of their limitations than university education often provides – for it is the pursuit of rigour in the treatment of the abstract subject that contributes to the neglect of rigour in the treatment of real-world problems. As Shackle (1972, p. 150) argues, it is the essence of general equilibrium theory that the clarity of its insights derives from the austerity and formality of its abstraction – just as does the clarity of a careful laboratory experiment. Both are very useful heuristics – provided neither is mistaken for a description of reality. If we become more aware of our ignorance, we can make more effective use of the sufficiency of our abstractions, and avoid paying such a high price for precision.

4

The rationale of the firm

Knowledge is the business.

P. F. Drucker (1964, p. 104)

The argument of the previous chapter led to the conclusion that the price paid in ignorance for the benefits of abstraction may be reduced by using a range of different abstractions. A study of the firm as a system might then begin simply by recognising that, in Machlup's (1974, p. 273) words, 'to explain and predict the behaviour of particular business firms. . .is not the main purpose of the marginalist theory of the firm and, if it is used for this purpose, it will be rather unreliable and will utterly fail in far too many cases'. The shift of emphasis entailed in developing an economic analysis of organisational behaviour is thus adequate reason for trying another approach.

But to rely on this justification would be very unsatisfactory, for the presence of firms in a market system would be left unexplained. Moreover, there is a very promising alternative: by deriving sufficient conditions for the existence of firms from the body of general equilibrium theory, it is possible, not only to provide them with a sound theoretical base, but also to identify the topics of analytic interest in an economic study of firms. The analysis thus derived will later contribute to an understanding of the rationale and use of economic theory.

The derivation of such conditions is the primary purpose of this chapter. Some of the relevant conditions will be found among the standard criticisms of the efficiency of a pure market system; but the first, and principal, line of argument is a restatement and development of that put forward by Coase (1937).

The search for equilibrium

Given some highly restrictive assumptions, it is now well-established that a general equilibrium system, with perfect competition in all markets, possesses a solution set, which may be both unique and stable. How such a system behaves if no equilibrium exists is not clear. But even if it does exist, some awkward problems remain. The solution set of prices does indeed provide all the information (apart from technical data assumed to be already available) required for decision-making within the economy; and in the simpler models decisions have to be made once only. But in order to provide this information, that solution set must carry two guarantees: first, that these are the best prices available to both buyer and seller, and second, that they apply to any quantity which may be offered or demanded by any transactor. The second guarantee is equivalent to an assurance that all traded goods and services are perfectly liquid; the corollary that any can serve as money justifies the practice of analysing general equilibrium systems in real terms.

Since these guarantees can apply only to the solution set, they are sufficient to identify it; but how are they to be provided? To that crucial question no satisfactory answer has been given. We may neglect, for the moment, the problems of ignorance which forbid the complete listing of the basic data from which the solution set might be computed; even if such a list exists, how is the computation to be done and how are the results to be disseminated to the decision-makers?

The need for some answer to such questions was appreciated by two of the earliest exponents of the general equilibrium method in economics, Walras and Edgeworth; and no one has yet improved on the suggestions which they offered. Walras invoked the aid of an auctioneer, who would call out a set of prices, receive bids and offers for sale and thereby calculate the excess supply or demand at those prices for each commodity or productive service; on the basis of this calculation, he would then try a revised set of prices designed to eliminate excesses of both supply and demand. This process of guided trial and error (*tâtonnement*) was to be thought of as continuing until the elimination was complete, thus demonstrating that the solution set had been discovered.

Now Walras' auctioneer is very obviously a *deus ex machina*, a benign and disembodied character (he neither seeks reward nor consumes any part of the output of the system, and once his job is done he disappears from the story) who is introduced to sort out a tangle which the human actors are quite unable to resolve. There is clearly nothing in the specification of the general equilibrium model which would lead us to expect his appearance. But it rather spoils the point of the argument to demonstrate that the attainment of equilibrium in the absence of any human direction rests on the guarantee of active and beneficent divine intervention.

Perhaps Edgeworth thought so too; at any rate he suggested that this process of trial and error might be managed, more cumbrously but without the auctioneer, by a prolonged series of direct bargains. The market would thus be rather like a provincial stock exchange which operates without jobbers – for there must be no jobber's turn in price-making. But it would differ from such an exchange in one critical respect: no contracts would be binding, no exchanges would take place, no production or consumption plans would be implemented, until everyone was satisfied that he had obtained the best set of deals available. One might expect all this to take rather a long time; but, however long it takes, for that length of time all clocks must be stopped, all processes must be suspended, human metabolism must cease, the running-down of the universe must be arrested. It is not obvious that Edgeworth's proposal altogether escapes the need for divine intervention.

Yet, whatever method may be used to discover the general equilibrium solution, this complete suspension of activity until it is discovered is essential. It is essential for two reasons. First, until the equilibrium prices have been established, no supplier knows what to do. For as Richardson (1960) has clearly demonstrated, the existence of excess demand (or supply) in the market cannot, of itself, establish the need for any particular supplier to alter his planned volume of sales, since it tells him nothing about the size or effect of his competitors' responses. For that, he needs to know the elasticity of market demand and supply, precisely the information which, for the individual, the equilibrium analysis claims to dispense with. Perfect information, in this model, can exist only in equilibrium: out of equilibrium there can be at most one person with adequate knowledge. Therefore the simultaneous equations must be solved simultaneously, not sequentially; and no commitments must be made until equilibrium has been reached.

If they are, we encounter the second difficulty. In the present state of theory, if production, consumption, or trading starts before the solution is known, the initial endowments which are premises of that solution may no longer be parameters of the final outcome. As everyone who was raised on the long run/short run distinctions of partial equilibrium should recognise, there is no reason why a producer who has committed himself to capital equipment on the basis of non-equilibrium prices should thereafter make production and employment decisions identical to those which he would have made had his investment decision been better founded. Short-period analysis deals with the consequences of past error; it can therefore have no place in a theory of perfect adaptation.

The possible effects of false trading on income distribution, and thus on supply and demand functions, worried Hicks (1939, pp. 127–9), who in the end had to content himself with the belief that asymmetric income effects were not very likely, even though Marshall's (1920, pp. 335–6) discussion, to which Hicks refers, explicitly notes the probability of such effects in the labour market. Clower's (1965, p. 113) sardonic comment that 'it is heartening to know that income effects can be ignored if they are sufficiently unimportant to be neglected', though a little hard on Hicks, who was perfectly honest about the possible significance of the problem, is a fair comment on the state of this part of the theory. If false trading (or false production or false consumption) starts, then the general equilibrium solution without false trading may no longer be valid. Indeed, the system may never reach an equilibrium at all. No adjustment process is specified; as far as the formal theory can tell us, anything can happen.

But this is not all. Not only can we not (formally) say what will happen if non-equilibrium prices are on offer; we cannot even be sure what will happen if the true equilibrium prices are available. For they may not be at all obviously right in particular local markets; and then either resources must be consumed in seeking further information (a process which is likely to invalidate the premises on which the set of prices was based), or local markets may diverge from equilibrium, with lagged income effects which are beyond the scope of the type of analysis by which the equilibrium of the system was determined.

Thus, as Richardson (1960, p. 80) has pointed out, 'equilibrium is not secured merely by the existence of a particular set of economic activities in themselves, but by their co-existence with a particular set of beliefs'. That is why the solution set has to be guaranteed. But standard equilibrium theory pays even less attention to beliefs than to information. Only a Walrasian auctioneer can act as guarantor. In Edgeworth's system everyone has to provide his own guarantee; and that can be done only by ascertaining that every transactor in the economy is satisfied. Otherwise, the transactor has no means of distinguishing between equilibrium and non-equilibrium prices, which he is required by the theory to treat quite differently. The system therefore achieves no economies of information.

Such difficulties have not gone entirely unrecognised by general equilibrium theorists, and much work has been, and is being, done on transactions costs and models of temporary equilibria and sequence economies. Hahn's (1973b) research programme is at least in part intended to cope with some of the difficulties. Yet the fundamental difficulties are inherent in the method. The knowledge that a particular set of prices is an equilibrium set must be a public good, and must, therefore, by the very logic of the construction, be in sub-optimal supply; and the attainment of equilibrium must be the result of a process, and therefore incapable of rigorous analysis by a method which operates by defining (and defining inadequately, as Richardson has observed) the conditions in which that equilibrium has already been achieved.

We can only conclude, therefore, that as an attempt to provide a formal, rigorous explanation of how resources are allocated in a market economy, general equilibrium theory is a total failure. Not only does it begin by assuming the answer; it specifies a system essential components of which (perfect competition and perfect knowledge) can only exist once the assumed answer is found, and a system which possesses no means of searching for an answer, or even for identifying it when discovered. The question 'as old as Adam Smith' has been lost in the attempt to formulate it precisely. The formalisation does, however, have one great virtue; it makes clear what is wrong with it.

The assumption that equilibrium prices are both given and guaranteed may be the most critical in economics. Its withdrawal has wide theoretical implications. Clower and Leijonhufvud have shown how this can lead to an intellectually respectable macrotheory, in which different degrees of liquidity and the special features of money must play essential roles. It also ties the notion of income very firmly to expectations, thus providing the basis for a theory of profit, explaining why the accountant's task of asset valuation is inherently impossible, and justifying the distinction between income and cash, which is now well-established in capital budgeting, but has so far been effectively quarantined there. The absence of liquidity undermines perfect competition too; indeed since the ability of every transactor to buy or sell as much as he wishes at the going price implies the absence of any excess demand or supply, it is difficult to see how perfect competition, like perfect knowledge, can logically exist outside equilibrium, and therefore how it can formally be considered as a system for determining anything. It is, however, a different set of consequences that will be considered in this chapter. The non-existence theorem which is the logical foundation for macroeconomics, monetary theory, and imperfect competition, is also the logical basis of the firm.

If optimal decisions throughout an economy simply require the determination of quantities by the application of freely available prices, incorporating the two guarantees just discussed, to well defined preference sets and production possibilities, then indeed everything could be decided in the market. In such circumstances the subsystems of resource allocation commonly known as firms have no function to perform which cannot be done at least as well without them; if their management involves any cost at all they cannot exist. (That a theory of the firm which assumes that firms do not exist may nevertheless, within limits, prove very useful is explained by the argument of the previous chapter.) However, if the very special prices required by the general equilibrium system are not available at all, or can be obtained only through some Walrasian or Edgeworthian process which absorbs resources and thus invalidates the system into which it is brought, then the situation changes. Now there are costs attached to the discovery of appropriate prices (it is not clear what might now be meant by 'equilibrium prices') and to the discovery of trading partners; and even when discovered, prospective partners may need some persuasion (involving some resource costs) that the proposed deal is fair.

Decision costs and size of firm

These costs can in part be avoided by substituting a formal organisation for a series of impersonal specific contracts, as Coase argues. That explains why firms exist. However, continues Coase, the operation of a firm also involves costs, and these costs – costs of organisation, costs resulting from mistakes, and possibly the supply price of some factors of production which need additional inducements to forgo their independence – are likely to increase with the size of the firm. These increasing costs of superseding the market, balanced against the costs of using the market, determine the point of equilibrium at which it is just worthwhile incorporating another transaction within the firm. Thus the size of firms is determined by an extension of the familiar method of defining equilibrium conditions for a system of optimal choices; and not only the reason for the existence of firms, but 'the whole of the "structure of competitive industry" becomes tractable by the ordinary technique of economic analysis' (Coase, 1937, p. 398). It has not been so treated: Richardson's (1960, 1972) attempts to relate structure to information needs have had little impact, and thinking about industrial structure is still dominated and distorted by technical economies of scale.

Though Coase's argument is founded squarely on the premise that, in the market, prices and partners have to be discovered, his justification for that premise is not theoretical, as in the preceding section, but empirical. His only reference to the assumption in equilibrium theory that prices are given is the simple observation: 'But this is clearly not true of the real world' – and even that appears only in a footnote (p. 390). Nor does Williamson (1967), in his review and extension of Coase's argument, raise the question of how, in equilibrium theory itself, the relevant prices are logically to be established. He does, however, develop his empirical criticism over a couples of pages. He does not question the logic of Kaldor's (1934b) argument that deterministic static equilibrium provides no function for management, but quotes with approval E. A. G. Robinson's (1934, p. 250) riposte: 'In Mr

Kaldor's long period we shall not only be dead but in Nirvana, and the economics of Nirvana. . .is surely the most fruitless of sciences.' Now that the economics of Nirvana have become the dominant source of intellectual prestige in the subject, the question of its fruitfulness is a critical issue, and a recurring topic in this book.

Williamson (p. 125) argues that equilibrium theory can be rescued from Nirvana by the device of substituting stochastic for deterministic equilibrium. In stochastic equilibrium, 'the firm is required to adapt to circumstances which are predictable in the sense that although they occur with stochastic regularity, precise advance knowledge of them is unavailable'. This contrast between a series of decisions in response to circumstances which change within predetermined limits and a single decision taken once only is crucial to the argument, since it is the organisation of this adaptive process which provides the function for management.

By whom the firm is thus required to act is not stated; indeed it is not at all clear from the text whether it is every new circumstance or rather some fraction of them to which the firm must respond. In fact, the replacement of certainty by a succession of uncertain future states provides no theoretical grounds for challenging Kaldor's conclusion: for general equilibrium theorists have established the existence of equilibrium solutions in such circumstances, based entirely on a set of present bargains in appropriate contingent claims markets. In some formulations this equilibrium does not even require interpersonal compatibility of expectations. Thus Williamson's quasi-static conditions are not sufficient to justify an ongoing process. His premises, like Coase's, are empirical after all.

But they so easily need not be. Clearly the general equilibrium model under uncertainty calls for even greater faith in divine benevolence than the simple model: and there are some particular theoretical advantages in considering the firm (like money) as a substitute for a group of contingent claims markets. The incentive thus to undertake present commitments is the hope of future reward. Since there can be no guarantee that present market prices are equilibrium prices, there is scope for a private valuation of resources which is different from their market valuation. Differences in valuation are the basis of profit opportunities (as explained in Chapter 9), and therefore encourage the private search for technical or market information which may reveal such an opportunity; they also provide a reason for entering into those imperfectly-specified contracts which Coase sees as the defining characteristics of a firm. Thus profit and the firm are joint consequences of partial ignorance.

Since the firm economises on transactions costs by substituting one general agreement for a host of particular deals, it requires some structured procedure (which may well involve elements of hierarchy, group pressure, and collective bargaining) to arrive at the specific terms of exchange in the situations as they arise. Wherever the degree of ambiguity in the contract is significant, there is clearly room for a discussion of the balance between inducements and contributions which is much wider than the traditional economic analysis of the supply and demand for labour.

The major part of Williamson's article is concerned with analysing how the costs of co-ordination (or control, as he prefers to call it) increase with the size of the firm, and therefore set a limit to that size. His basic reason for these increasing costs is the technological limitation of the human brain, and the consequent restraints of bounded rationality – the factors discussed in Chapter 1. Thus, once decision-capacity is fully employed (which appears to happen at a fairly low level of complexity) any additional information can be obtained only by the sacrifice of some existing information: the opportunity cost increases.

Some of these costs may be avoided by increasing the number of decision-makers, but unless each makes his decisions entirely on his own (in which case there is no firm, in an analytical sense) communication is necessary between them, and communication between brains of limited channel capacity is liable to add distortion to the costs incurred by the sacrifice of other mental activities. This distortion will not usually be random – a point which, in this article, Williamson ignores, though he does note that it is an increasing function of dissonance between the objectives of the decision-makers. For now that we have dropped the assumption that relevant information is available without cost to all who need it, the control of information becomes a possible means of achieving one's objectives. Systematic distortion is most obviously likely in a hierarchical system, where the interpretation of the incompletely-specified contract is nominally at the discretion of the superior.

Every management consultant profits from the fact that information will be made available to outsiders which is not made available within the company itself. Organisations tend to frustrate the very purposes for which they are designed; the creation of a formal communications system inhibits certain kinds of communication; the process of bringing resources together outside the market ensures that they are not fully used. Though means are available to combat these difficulties, these means have their own costs, and are subject to diminishing returns. The relationship between individual objectives and organisational design and control is clearly an important area of study, which will receive a little attention in later chapters.

Thus, within Williamson's model, the greater the size of an organisation, the greater the loss of both detail and accuracy in the information on which its decisions are based. Furthermore, these difficulties affect the transmission of information and instructions down through the hierarchy too, so that the behaviour of the operating units corresponds even less closely to the intentions of the decision-makers and (a point Williamson leaves to be deduced) therefore even less closely to the real needs of the situation. If one adds to Williamson's analysis the element of time, even in the artificial sense which seems appropriate to this quasi-static model, one must expect an increasing lag between the initial reception of information and the action to which it eventually gives rise, and therefore an increasing chance that the action taken will be out-of-date and inappropriate to the existing situation. All in all therefore, there are good reasons, even in quasi-static conditions, for expecting management, in each industry, eventually to become increasingly costly. The argument that, within such a theoretical framework, long-run cost curves must eventually rise seems to be established. The output at which they rise and the rate at which they rise may differ greatly between industries; and there is of course no general reason why this output should be small enough to avoid the analytical problems caused by economies of scale.

The Coase–Williamson analysis can be applied to questions of growth, as well as to questions of size. Williamson's observation (p. 136) that 'increases in experience lead to refinements, short-cuts, and routinisation, all of which permit increasing the span of control for a fixed level of control loss' provides a direct link with the analysis developed by Mrs Penrose (1959): for here is one of the major ways in which the managerial services available to a firm tend to increase over time, and thus lead, in Coase's terms, to a search for new transactions to take over either from the market (by expansion from within) or from other firms (by merger). Extension of the bounds of knowledge within the firm permits extension of the bounds of the firm: the greater the ability to decompose the existing system the easier it becomes to incorporate additional subsystems.

The speed and extent of the increase of managerial services depend on the pattern of experience: the stability of the pattern determines the degree of routinisation that is possible, the frequency of its repetition the time that must elapse before an adequate sample is available on which routines may be based. The efficiency of a firm's procedures may be quite highly dependent on the particular characteristics of its business, and the managerial economies to be gained from expansion may then be available only if the expansion is into activities with similar characteristics. A firm taking on activities for which its existing procedures are not suited may suffer significant diseconomies – as may be readily observed. But it may be only by such trial and error that it can discover the limits of sufficiency to its operating abstractions.

The size of firms, and the groups of activities which it is profitable to incorporate within a single firm, will clearly be affected by the efficiency with which a market operates and by the state of management technology. Organised markets facilitate small-scale operations; the development of the product division structure by Du Pont appears to have been essential to the emergence of successful diversified corporations, and must therefore be rated the most important innovation ever produced by that innovative company. The amount of dissonance is important too; hence the emphasis in many large organisations on a wide variety of devices for reducing it; hence also the fact that much larger organisations appear to work satisfactorily in times of national emergency (such as in Britain between 1940 and 1945) than at other times.

The irrelevance of economies of scale

Since much emphasis is usually placed on the effects of economies of scale, it is important to realise that technical economies alone are not sufficient to account for the existence of firms. In a state of general equilibrium, the balance of processes can be achieved perfectly satisfactorily by the market. There is indeed no lack of examples of vertical disintegration to preserve appropriate scales of operation at each stage of production: the manufacture of milk-bottle tops, dyeing, plating, and advertising, to mention a few. Even a single giant machine or power station could be used by very many independent operators if their respective rights and payments could be precisely determined in advance. But of course, if equilibrium cannot be guaranteed, then the existence of such technical economies provides a powerful reason why the swing from market transactions to the imperfectly-specified contracts of formal organisation may go very far. Technical economies thus do not explain the existence of firms: they do help to explain why some firms are large.

It is worth pausing at this point to summarise the implications of the preceding analysis for the long-disputed question of the size of the firm in general equilibrium systems. In the previous paragraph we have argued that in the equilibrium solution there is no role for indivisibilities – that, as far as technology is concerned, the firm can be as large or as small as one wishes. Nor can one quarrel with Kaldor's (1934b) conclusion that this solution implies no managerial limitations on size, since it implies no management. Thus we are led to support Sraffa's (1926) argument that the firm operates under conditions of constant costs. Given perfect competition, the size of the firm is therefore indeterminate. It is also irrelevant to the existence of equilibrium, since it is impossible in the system as specified for anyone to charge more for a commodity than anyone else is prepared to accept; and however large a firm may be, it can have no cost advantage over its smaller competitors except through some inherent and inalienable initial endowment. Though perfect competition may no longer be quite essential to the proof of a stable and unique equilibrium solution, such a solution does seem to imply perfect competition.

In fact, it is perhaps more accurate, and probably more helpful, to say, not that the size of firm is indeterminate but irrelevant, but that the question is meaningless. In conditions of perfect knowledge, the theory of the firm is very simple: there are no firms. The firm exists because of the costs of handling ignorance.

Thus the economy is decomposed into a set of decision-making systems; and as with the example of watchmaking, the advantages of such decomposition are closely related to the problems generated by change. If a solution set, once discovered, were never disturbed, then there would be no need for any intermediate level of organisation between the individual and the total economy. Since general equilibrium theory attempts no analysis of the adjustment process, it has no need to consider the advantages of intermediate levels. A general equilibrium system is constructed like the watches made by Tempus, and has similar limitations.

The firm and its environment

But, again as in the watchmaking example, there is more than one level of decomposition. Richardson (1972) has drawn attention to the way in which clusters of firms are created by the development of imperfectly-specified contracts between them, and has explained these contracts in terms which are readily assimilable to the analysis just offered. Firms economise in the need for information and in the costs of frequent decisions by forming 'a trading relationship. . . .which is stable enough to make demand expectations more reliable, and thereby to facilitate production planning' (p. 884); instead of attempting to establish contingent claims markets in situations where the necessary complete listing of possibilities cannot be achieved, they organise subassemblies within the economy to encourage the ongoing search for knowledge, and the effective transfer of new technology. These are examples of what is sometimes called uncertainty-avoidance; but it would be theoretically sounder to say that what is being avoided is part of the cost of handling uncertainty through market mechanisms – including the logically infinite costs of creating a system of contingent claims markets when there is no way of knowing when the search for a complete listing has reached its goal.

Richardson argues that the principal reason for the existence of two types of non-market co-ordination, within firms and between them, lies in the different ways in which activities may be related. He sees the firm as primarily a device for the grouping of similar activities, requiring similar capabilities. The problems of communication and control which, in Williamson's view, set the limits to the size of the firm, are certainly likely to be less within a group with similar problems, and therefore likely to be using similar abstractions. Richardson's argument that limits of similarity tend to put a limit on size appears to be based on such considerations: 'the scope for co-ordination by direction within firms is narrowly circumscribed. . .by. . .the fact that complementary activities need not be similar' (p. 890).

The market is, of course, the principal means of co-ordinating complementary activities – most obviously, in our textbooks, the activities of production and consumption, but also, and more important in volume, the production and use of intermediate goods. The use of imperfectly-specified contracts does not abolish the market, but modifies it in a degree which, according to the terms (tacit even more than explicit) of the contract, may vary from the barely noticeable to the dominant. Richardson briefly considers the influences on the degree of modification. He argues that 'impersonal co-ordination through market forces is relied upon where there is reason to expect aggregate demands to be more stable (and hence predictable) than their component elements' (p. 891). In such circumstances, commitment to a particular trading partner increases uncertainty. It is worth noting that from this point of view a competitive market is not a basis for establishing an equilibrium set of contracts in contingent future markets, but a means of providing assurance that present contracts for future performance are unnecessary. At the other extreme come the activities described by Richardson as 'closely complementary', which require detailed matching of specifications. Here decomposition into markets would prevent adequate attention being paid to external effects; thus the imperfectly decomposable system gives rise to imperfectly specified contracts.

Methods of decomposing the economic system to cope with

ignorance may, as Richardson shows, range all the way from the partial equilibrium subassemblies called commodity markets to 'clusters, groups and alliances'. Since his emphasis is on industrial organisation, it is not surprising that Richardson fails to mention that his three broad alternative methods of co-ordination – by direction, co-operation, or the market – may all be found within business enterprises. He is, however, careful to point out that in many situations there appears to be no clear superiority of any one method, or of any particular principles of decomposition within one method: neither the structure of industry nor the structure of organisations is always the logically imperative precipitate of the conditions under which it operates.

Characteristics of decisions within the firm

The esteem in which Coase's article is held is well-deserved. And yet it owes as much to what he did not say as to what he did. He demonstrated that the decision to reject the market in favour of planning (within the firm) could be analysed by the traditional apparatus; he even remarked (how seriously is not clear), 'In a competitive system, there is an "optimum" amount of planning' (p. 389). All this was easy to accept. What would have been much less easy to accept was the obvious but unnoticed implication of the statement that 'the distinguishing mark of the firm is the supersession of the price mechanism' (p. 389). If decisions within a firm are explicitly not made by using the price mechanism, might it not be a legitimate area of economic enquiry to consider how they are made? Yet this disturbing implication was not drawn by Coase, nor by anyone else. So what could have been a foundation-stone has been treated merely as a coping-stone.

Let us then consider the implications. The total costs of decision-making increase with the number of decisions; therefore a major objective in creating an organisation which will replace market transactions is to reduce the number of decisions, thus spreading decision costs over a larger number of actions. There are three ways in which this may be done. The first two are directly analogous to technical economies of scale: a single decision may determine a large number of simultaneous transactions, or it may determine a long series of transactions. Programming costs can be spread over a large volume of activity by means either of high rates or of long runs: the former depends on uniformity of conditions, usually reflected in organisational structure, the latter on predictable stability over time, which encourages the development of routine procedures. Both methods are related to Adam Smith's discussion of the proper scope for joint-stock companies. The more extensively they can be used, the larger can be the efficient size of the firm.

The third way of reducing the average decision cost for each transaction requires a little more consideration. As has been seen, the cost of using the market is much increased if a succession of uncertain future states is postulated; if the firm, in replacing the market, attempts to behave like an artificial market, not many decision costs will be saved. Therefore the firm, in replacing market transactions, is likely to abandon the attempt to achieve a set of synthetic equilibria in contingent claims markets. This reasoning applies not only to the firm's handling of its own resources, but also to its dealings in the market.

This is not all. One obvious way of economising on decision costs when faced with a succession of uncertain states, as has been noted, is the conclusion of incompletely specified contracts. Another is to concentrate attention on the nearer states, increasing the total of effective decision-capacity by increasing the time-span of its utilisation. Thus it is decision costs, not simply the sequence of states, which provide the rationale for the adaptive behaviour postulated by Williamson. There is another reason for such behaviour: a firm facing stochastic circumstances may not know what the characteristics of the frequency distribution is. (Who, indeed, is to guarantee that the distributions are stochastic?) Thus the outcome of early decisions may be used to help make better decisions later. In particular, a situation in which there are known to be conflicting expectations, though it can formally be accommodated in an equilibrium model, may very well lead to some caution about future commitments. Avoidance of decisions may be very sensible; for if probabilities, and even the set of events to which they relate, cannot yet be properly defined, then any present set of contingent decisions may well be premature. Explicit recognition of this point, and of the extent to which present decisions constrain future responses to new situations, is a

notable feature of Richardson's (1960) analysis. The recognition
of ignorance changes the logic of choice.

Thus the firm's behaviour is not equivalent to the operation of
contingent claims markets. Such a conclusion reinforces the argument that firms cannot be formally incorporated into a general
equilibrium system without denying their essential rationale. It
also implies that the existence of firms is incompatible with Pareto
optimality. That inference, however, tells us more about the limitations of standard welfare analysis as a guide to policy than
about the desirability of abolishing or controlling firms.

If the firm is to economise on the decisions it makes, it must
make them by some different method. Furthermore, if some decisions are avoided altogether, and others postponed, then the firm
must establish, by conscious action if it is not to emerge by default,
some kind of mechanism for choosing when to make decisions –
and about what. Decision processes within firms provide the
major theme of the next two chapters.

Market systems and administrative systems

We have seen how an analysis attributing the existence of firms to
the costs of discovering market equilibrium can contribute to an
understanding of their size, their growth, and their internal procedures. Recognition that the informational basis for such an
equilibrium does not exist strongly reinforces this view. But the
cost of using the price mechanism is not the only reason for the
existence of firms. The firm supersedes the market as the method
of directing the resources within its control; and the long debate
over the relative virtues of planning and the price system has
made it clear that there are other reasons for rejecting the market
besides the cost of operating it.

At least three possible reasons for dissatisfaction with the
market are relevant to the existence of firms. Market allocation
depends on supply and demand conditions which reflect only
private costs and benefits; it may be significantly influenced by
elements of monopoly; and the decision-makers in a market
system may be unskilful or guided by motives other than profit
maximisation. (The third reason, being external to their usual
models, receives less attention from welfare theorists than the

other two.) Where such deficiencies exist, they may be met either by comprehensive state planning, or by the emergence of that limited administrative system known as a firm. Analysis of these deficiencies, like the analysis of the costs of using the market, aids the understanding of the size, the growth, and the internal organisation of firms. To illustrate the possibilities, it will be convenient to take the three reasons just listed for the supersession of the market in the reverse order.

Given all the other necessary conditions, the efficient allocation of resources through the market depends on competent decision-making by people with objective functions which are completely and appropriately specified. It is far from obvious that these requirements will be met: decision-makers may well not be profit maximisers, and even if they are, they may find the maximisation of profit beyond their competence. The market, too, may not be a very effective – and certainly not a very speedy – device for selecting out the efficient decision-makers. Marris (1964) has argued that takeover bids and the threat of bids may enforce significant control; and this argument clearly has some force. But observe what the argument is: to say that a firm which fails to make the right responses in the market is liable to be taken over by another is to say that the ultimate sanction of the market is its own supersession by an administrative system.

The failure of the market to ensure rational action – at least rational by the standards of the organisation taking over – may provide an incentive for either vertical or horizontal integration. Inefficiencies among customers or suppliers can have serious consequences for a firm which does not have easy access to alternative sources or outlets. Thus Aberdeen fish-merchants were drawn into trawler-ownership by the reluctance of trawler companies (for good family reasons) to replace their decrepit vessels, and Courtaulds bought up customers in the hope of improving their sales and thus their demand for Courtaulds' fibres.

Horizontal integration, on the other hand, may present an opportunity to bring poorly-organised transactions within the scope of an efficient administrative system. Much of the argument in favour of the G.E.C.–A.E.I. and Leyland–B.M.C. mergers turned on the superior efficiency of the Weinstock and Stokes administrative systems rather than on technical economies of larger size. Lord Kearton has said that the aim of the Industrial Reorganisation Corporation was to group resources under the control of the rather small number of first-class decision-makers in Britain. The success of such mergers depends a good deal on the extent to which routines derived from the experience of one company are appropriate to another. This is a problem fundamental to the study of management, on which we hope to cast some light in later chapters.

The issue of the skill and motivation of decision-makers is of course not resolved simply by the creation of an administrative system. Questions of organisational design and management control have attracted much attention from psychologists, accountants, and organisational theorists – but not from economists, who have tended therefore to credit administrative systems with more efficiency than they deserve. This is another topic for later consideration.

Market imperfections may prevent any of a group of competing firms from realising many of the potential economies of large-scale operations; and it may be very expensive, if not impossible, for any one of them to expand its market sufficiently to displace its competitors. But, as Dewey (1969) has argued, an industry in which such conditions apply is not necessarily doomed, in the absence of state intervention, to remain in the unsatisfactory equilibrium of monopolistic competition. A merger may commend itself to some of the competing firms as a means of achieving lower-cost output; and it may be encouraged by the assumption that experience in one of the merging companies is relevant to the problems of management after the merger – that there may be genuine economies in the use of managerial services.

Finally, the market may ignore significant external effects, so that the grouping of previously independent transactions under a single authority may change the basis of transactions. For example, an industry of small firms may have a common interest in a supply of trained workers, but as long as trained men can easily move elsewhere, no one firm has much incentive to spend money on training: only a company like Rolls-Royce, which was reasonably certain, because of its size, of keeping a fair proportion of those it trained, could be expected to have an expensive training programme. Hence the need for the Industrial Training Act.

Again, it is hardly sensible for one firm among many to stand out against pressure from suppliers, employees, or customers, even though such pressure may damage them all. Hence the need to *organise* countervailing power. In such cases the formation, or extension, of a firm to incorporate parallel transactions may make rational actions which were irrational (though desirable) before.

The internalising of external effects is a common argument in favour of mergers. If this is a major reason for replacing the market by an organisation, then one would expect that the resultant organisation structure should be designed to secure adequate consideration of erstwhile external effects. It is to be observed, however, that mergers which are publicly justified on the grounds of economies from integration do not always lead to that reformation of the organisation structure which appears to be necessary for the realisation of those economies. One important reason for this is that the process of securing consent to integration may involve promises to directors, senior managers and trade unions that are incompatible with such reformation.

Although the internalising of external effects might provide some justification on welfare grounds for the existence of firms in a general equilibrium system in which such effects were important, theorists would no doubt consider it inferior to public action. Of more immediate importance is the fact that there appears to be no incentive for firms to emerge in such circumstances. Once again, however, the situation changes when one makes allowance for the costs of discovering an equilibrium solution. One of the obvious ways of reducing the costs of search is to reduce the area of search. This may well lead to the neglect of interdependencies which would be taken into account in a zero-cost market equilibrium; and if the creation of a firm can permit some reduction in decision costs, the firm may then be able to include some of these otherwise neglected interdependencies in its calculations. An organisation chart is indeed a formal statement of the interdependencies that are believed to be important: its object is not only to reduce the costs of decisions, in ways noted earlier, but also to improve their quality, by prescribing the recognition of certain effects external to particular managers. It also, by implication, specifies what interdependencies should not be taken into account, and what areas of ignorance should be accepted: for the firm, like the individual, can save on decision costs by ignoring some interdependencies which are relevant. The inter-relationship between decision-making and organisational design provides another topic for further examination.

Ignorance and the firm

Starting from a basis of general equilibrium theory, we have argued that the firm offers a possible substitute for the market system when the information required for the working of that system is costly to acquire and use. The argument becomes even stronger when we recognise that some of that information cannot exist. Whether it is a viable substitute depends upon the costs and quality of decision-making within the firm, including its ability to select the more important interdependencies. Its basic methods of operation must be different from those of the market. It must recognise and define those problems with which it proposes to deal, and it must attempt to learn as it goes along, not only what are the relevant data, but what are the rules of the game.

5

Decision processes

We are not primarily interested in business men, business decisions, business routine and business reactions.

F. Machlup (1974, p. 277)

A classification of decisions

Since the justification of the firm is the reduction of the costs of coping with ignorance, any study of organisational decision-making should logically start by considering how that is done. To facilitate this study, it is suggested that decisions may be classified according to three criteria, each of which relates to one aspect of complexity.

The first aspect may be conveniently called the *width of agenda*, a term, adapted from Kenneth Boulding (1966), which refers to the definition of system boundaries employed for the purposes of making the decision. General equilibrium theory strongly suggests that, for decisions to be optimal, agendas typically need to be very wide indeed, since the conditions in which local decision-making will produce overall optima are very restrictive. But as Boulding (1966, p. 167) points out, 'there seems to be a fundamental disposition in mankind to limit agenda, often quite arbitrarily, perhaps because of our fears of information overload'. This tendency to neglect relevant interdependencies Boulding sees as a serious threat to sensible decision-making: 'what looks like rational decisions under limited agendas often turn out to be disastrous'. Orthodox welfare economics leads to a similar conclusion.

The creation of firms may reduce this risk, in two ways. First, the decomposition of the economic system into organised groups for making decisions within coherent subsystems must logically be regarded as one of those 'improvements in information processing' which Boulding welcomes because they 'remove obstacles to that widening of agendas'. Second, the collective experience of the firm can mitigate the obvious problem that 'we cannot know the cost of limiting the agenda unless we widen it' – a cost which, in Boulding's view, we are dangerously inclined to underestimate. Formal organisations, by such devices as organisation charts, job descriptions and the specification of managerial objectives, define the width of agenda deemed appropriate for each member of the organisation. Of course, every such definition is a compromise between the desire to include relevant interdependencies and the desire to simplify administration; and the fact that a firm may be regarded as a device for beneficially widening the agenda for decision does not imply that it does so optimally. How, and why, agendas are defined is a major topic of organisational analysis, to which we hope to contribute in the following three chapters.

The second method of classification is by specifying the *set of control variables*. This is a generalisation of one of Marshall's most useful ideas, the distinction between the short and the long period. As was noted in the previous chapter, this distinction has no meaning in the general equilibrium world of pre-reconciled choice, but it is very relevant to a world in which decision-making absorbs resources. The short period, in the present analysis, is the period during which assumptions and procedures, like capital equipment, remain unchanged; the cost of decision within this framework is therefore small. In the long period, assumptions and procedures, like fixed capital, may be replaced.

The justification for thus extending the distinction is that decision costs are a form of capital investment undertaken in the hope of the future benefits which will flow from good decisions. Just as no firm can afford to replace its plant every time a slightly better design appears, so no firm can afford to change its policy with every slight potential improvement it may discover. A firm must work within a framework of assumptions and procedures if it is to function at all; and the sunk costs of old decisions are no more relevant than the sunk costs of old plant. But its assumptions and procedures will sooner or later become obsolete, just as surely as its plant. When to replace plant is in fact just one of the general class of long-period decisions. Of course, this simple distinction between long and short periods is very crude (Marshall also used a very short and a very long run), and for that reason it is replaced here by the more general concept of the set of control variables.

Here again is a critical area of study, as may be illustrated by a biological analogy. Most new ideas, like most mutations, are harmful; therefore resistance to change, in organism or organisation, has high survival value. But total failure to evolve leads to extinction.

The third aspect of decision-making may be called, following Simon, and by obvious analogy with computable algorithms, the *degree of programming*: the extent to which the procedure for reaching a decision is prescribed. One obvious way in which a firm may, over time, reduce decision costs without impairing the quality of decisions is by organising its experience. Indeed, one might regard an organisation's activities as an experimental design, sampling some population with the hope of generating economical and effective procedures for future decision-making. From this viewpoint, an organisation might be defined as a learning system incorporating a set of standard programmes. Large organisations have an advantage in the collection of data on which to base programmes; but they also tend to have a greater need of programmes, in particular, programmes for the operation of the organisation as a set of quasi-isolated subsystems.

For the larger the number of people involved at some stage in the decision process (including its implementation) the more difficult it becomes to ensure that all the relevant factors are fairly considered, that information and instructions are not distorted as they are passed through intermediaries, and that everyone concerned will modify his behaviour in an appropriate way. In large organisations these capital costs of major decisions are likely to be particularly high, and must therefore be amortised over a greater volume of activity. Long runs are as necessary for expensive decisions as for expensive machinery. Thus, for most of the time, large organisations need to rely on routines, or cheap highly-programmed decisions; they have very limited decomposability, and can thus cope readily only with isolatable change. By contrast it is the low capital cost of new decisions in small organisations that explains their greater flexibility, and thus their special advantage in situations where frequent major decisions are needed.

Any reduction in decision costs implies some departure from the process that would produce an optimal decision in a world where optimal decisions were costless. It implies the acceptance of a margin of error, indeed of a margin of ignorance. Thus one can never be certain, not only whether the decision was correct, but even whether the process by which it was reached employed the appropriate width of agenda, set of control variables, and degree of programming. It seems therefore inevitable that the analysis just outlined should normally be applied to the decision process that is used, rather than to the situation which gives rise to the process. In very many (if not all) situations, some relevant considerations are omitted, some variable factors are treated as fixed, and some routines are used which do not precisely fit. Such distortions are by no means necessarily bad; for, as has been argued, decisions are normally, and rightly, based on a simplification of a reality which is too complex and costly to be handled directly.

Thus, in appraising a decision process, the important question is not whether it fully reflects the situation – to which the answer is almost always no, as it should be – but whether the degree of abstraction (in all three aspects) is so chosen that the consequent advantages to the decision-makers outweigh the loss of sufficiency which it necessarily produces. We all know that it is better to have an approximate answer to the right question than a precise answer to the wrong question; but often it is only by asking a question which is at least partly wrong that any answer at all can be obtained. Bounded rationality requires some limitation of agendas. What can be achieved by the careful study of well-chosen wrong questions is nowhere better demonstrated than by the success of scientists in explaining complex natural phenomena by detailed investigation of artificially contrived simple situations. The problems raised by this procedure have been extensively discussed in Chapter 3.

Even if obtainable, an answer to precisely the right question may be too expensive; firms exist to reduce decision costs, and must therefore abstract, simplify, and distort. Konrad Lorenz's (1971, p. 253) suggestion that human thought processes have been adapted by evolution to produce 'not absolute truth about outer reality, but just the kind of working knowledge which is necessary for the survival of the species' may or may not be true of human beings: it is undoubtedly true of organisations.

Operating and innovative decisions

As an example of its usefulness, this threefold classification may be used to contrast operating and innovative decision-making. Operating decisions usually share three characteristics. First, their effects are normally very localised, so that decisions may legitimately be made within a narrowly-defined system. Second, they typically involve few elements which can be regarded as variable within the time-span over which decisions will be effective. Third, similar decisions need to be taken quite frequently; thus a standard repertoire of solutions emerges, and, since this repertoire is based on a fairly large sample of experience, it is unlikely that any novel solution would be significantly better. Thus day-to-day problems both require and permit low-cost decision-making.

Major innovations present problems of a very different sort. Their effects may spread widely through an interdependent system, and some of the interdependencies may not be easy to spot; the time-span involved (seven years from discovery to full-scale production is fairly typical for a new chemical product) is a potent source of complexity. The number of potentially-controllable variables may therefore be very large. Moreover, innovations of even a roughly similar kind are likely to be fairly rare, especially within the experience of the relevant decision-making unit; thus the sample of observations is small, and probably non-random. Therefore uncertainty, both about the possible benefits from a good decision and about the effectiveness of different methods of reaching it, is likely to be high. It is most unlikely that innovation problems can be fully resolved by any deterministic or even probabilistic technique. Relatively expensive decision-making may be desirable.

Even in the most innovative organisations, there are far more day-to-day operating decisions than any other kind; it is therefore not surprising that these are the decisions for which most organisations are designed. The emphasis on low-cost decision-making has obvious implications. A formal organisation structure, with its specific allocation of responsibilities, is a device for keeping most agendas narrow. Relevance is defined by the prescription of reporting relationships, which also help to specify the procedure for dealing with problems, while localisation of problem-solving within the responsible unit helps to build up the experience from which low-cost solutions will emerge (possibly to be formalised in operating instructions) and ensures that local solutions, involving few control variables, will be tried first. Various schemes of management by exception are used to isolate the elements in the situation which appear to require attention, and to place the responsibility for action on the appropriate individual. The structure of comparative management ratios employed by the Centre for Interfirm Comparison, which purports to trace the causes of poor performance to specific origins, provides a particularly clear example. A management system combining these features makes use of local knowledge and experience, avoids unnecessary complications, and, if correctly specified, provides for the efficient handling of problems which occur frequently and are limited in scope. This, it must be emphasised, means most problems.

But the most important problems are liable to be neither frequent nor limited; and these such a system does not suit. If it is (for good reasons) the prevalent system, problems which need different handling may not get it. They may not even be recognised as different problems, or indeed be recognised at all. Any automatic warning system will be activated only by the signals to which it is programmed to respond; what was not anticipated will not be noticed. People are rather more flexible; but those who are normally fully occupied on well-specified and familiar tasks may fail to perceive something unusual which was not specified. If it is perceived, it may well be wrongly classified, like the Japanese planes approaching Pearl Harbor, on 7 December 1941. Not only do wide-ranging problems often appear in the guise of little local difficulties (the first sign of the collapse of a market may look very like a normal seasonal fluctuation); since, as has been argued above, even day-to-day problems often have to be forcefitted into the decision procedure, a mismatch between a problem and the normal methods of dealing with it is a very imperfect test of the suitability of those methods. Those with little experience of wide-agenda or many-variable problems are not well qualified to judge the appropriate width or number of variables. They may consequently place their emphasis on keeping down decision costs.

Briggs' bathtubs

There are many examples of the dangers of wrongly classifying a problem: a classic instance is to be found in a book which deserves to be much better known, *The Management Problems of Diversification*, by Stanley S. Miller (1963). The Briggs Manufacturing Company supplied fully-trimmed car bodies to two U.S. motor manufacturers, and because of a decline in car sales found its expensive press capacity seriously underemployed. The company's problem appeared simple: all it wanted was a complementary product to act as a filler, thus absorbing some of the overhead charges on the presses: there was no need for the additional product to be particularly profitable in its own right. The solution appeared simple too: the company had just successfully completed a contract from a large mail-order company for steel sinks, and so it was decided to produce steel bathtubs, which seemed to be just bigger and therefore (in terms of utilising their large presses) better sinks. Thus a narrow-agenda, single-variable problem was solved by a process embodying a high degree of programming.

Unfortunately, the real situation turned out to require a very wide agenda indeed, and entry into the bathtub business was found to entail major changes in company policy. Some of the difficulties which rapidly beset Briggs might be anticipated by anyone familiar with modern marketing doctrine, so they may be outlined first. Experience in supplying two customers with orthodox products of their own specification was not very relevant to the task of selling a new type of bathtub (for Briggs were pioneering steel stampings) to a multitude of plumbing contractors. The previous mail-order contract proved the reverse of helpful; for plumbers regarded mail-order companies, who supplied home handymen, as a serious threat to their livelihood. Furthermore, bathtubs alone were very inadequate as a product line; the company's range had to be extended to brassware and vitreous chinaware, each of which required novel design and production skills.

Now of course Briggs had very little marketing expertise; their strength was in technology. But the most instructive part of this case history is its demonstration of the narrowness of their technological base. Skill in the spray-painting of car bodies proved irrelevant to producing a satisfactory fired ceramic coat on bathtubs. Most unexpected of all was their inability actually to press bathtubs. The heavier gauge, deeper draw, and sharper curvature, all presented formidable difficulties. Eventually they were overcome, but not before Briggs had found themselves engaged in a joint research project with a major steel company to develop a new type of steel specifically for this use. What the company never succeeded in doing was producing bathtubs on its existing presses; three additional presses had to be bought. In the end, the venture was successful; but the original problem was never solved.

The Swindon project

As a contrast to this example of problem mis-specification, one may take the history of W. H. Smith & Son's response to the pressure of an expanding volume of business on the capacity of their book and stationery warehouse in Lambeth (Loasby, 1973). Here again is an apparently simple situation, with an apparently simple answer: find a bigger warehouse. The solution programme, derived in this instance from the experience of similar multiples instead of that of the company itself, prescribed a search for a new site outside, but not too far outside, London. But members of Smith's management were not content with this as a complete problem specification. From the beginning, this detailed problem was seen as a massive opportunity to aid the transformation of the company from an old-established family business that was going nowhere in particular (unless to takeover by someone with a keen eye for asset values) to a tightly-run organisation with clear retailing objectives. So the problem was successively redefined.

The company began by specifying the task as the design of an efficient distribution system, and provided the resources, both from its own management and from consultants, to deal with it. The new warehouse was to be not only bigger, but better. In this respect, although a good deal of effort went into warehouse design, and resulted in a handsome building, the main principles were determined by a programme derived from immediate experience. The multi-storey building in Lambeth, with its massive, closely-spaced pillars, was such a well-recognised obstacle to efficiency that the new building must obviously have a single storey (not quite obviously: there was some discussion of a mezzanine floor) with a minimum of internal obstructions. The latter requirement produced a graceful, triple-arched roof, which, however, when a mezzanine floor had later to be added to cope with still-expanding business, prevented the most effective use of the building's volume. Minimum obstruction in two dimensions was not compatible with minimum constraints in three: the company chose an abstraction which proved (too late) to be lacking in sufficiency. It is noteworthy how many decisions are made with the intention of avoiding last time's mistakes, forgetting Hamlet's warning that in casting off those ills we have we are liable to fly to others that we know not of. In this instance the new ills were certainly far less grievous than the old; nevertheless, by using a flat roof, supported by pillars spaced to conform to a convenient stacking module, the new warehouse could have been both cheaper and of larger effective volume.

However, the design of the new warehouse was, rightly, not the first consideration. Both movement and storage of goods had to fit into a new distribution system, and it was this which received most attention. In the process, it soon became apparent that the information generated by the old system was inadequate for the design of the new; and this discovery, together with a near-programmed decision to computerise, drew attention to both the need and the opportunity to generate information for better management decision. It would be quite unfair to suggest that the need for better information, notably about the relative costs of handling different lines, had not been recognised earlier; but the problem of warehouse capacity was seen as the opportunity to do something about it. Finally, the prospect of a distribution system under control, and ready information about costs and current sales volumes of particular lines, provided the basis for a clear and rational marketing policy. Thus the problem – almost a routine problem – of warehouse capacity played a critical part in the transformation of W. H. Smith & Son that has been visible within the last ten years.

The recital of these two case histories is not intended to suggest that organisations should always seek to widen the agenda for their decision-making, and add to the set of control variables. The decision costs involved in so doing may be very high, as they certainly were for W. H. Smith, since the human resources employed are likely to be some of the most valuable in the organisation; and the justification for the existence of a firm is the reduction of decision costs. No firm could afford to treat every question of a line-filler or of warehouse capacity as the occasion for a thorough overhaul of its corporate strategy: Occam's razor is still a useful guide, even if Briggs nearly cut their throats with it. What is clear is that the correct definition of problems is not always easy; thus the question of how problems are defined becomes a key question in the analysis of firms. That question forms the topic of the following chapter; but before starting that enquiry it is convenient to consider, for the first time explicitly, decision-making as a process.

The decision cycle

Modern microeconomics is advertised as the theory of choice. It will be necessary later to give more consideration to the making of choices; but in a world of partial ignorance, there is much more to effective decision-making than the selection of the correct alternative from the choice set. That this is the overwhelming emphasis of formal training in economics and management science is probably attributable to the pseudo-scientific belief in pseudo-rigour discussed in an earlier chapter, which imposes a requirement for tightly-defined problems. But before making a choice it is necessary to assemble the elements of the choice set; and, to use one of the original operational research problems, it is no use choosing the optimal search procedure for detecting submarines if you are looking in the wrong part of the ocean. The full set of relevant alternatives is not usually given; it has to be found, at a cost – and the cost may be such that it is not reasonable to look for the full set. That set may indeed be impossible to define. Choice must therefore logically be preceded by a search for the courses of action between which choice is to be made. But, as the two case histories clearly demonstrate, before one can even begin to seek possible courses of action, it is necessary to recognise the existence of a problem. One could hardly expect Briggs to consider alternative methods of developing a new steel alloy until they realised that no existing alloy would serve for the pressing of bathtubs.

The argument of the preceding paragraph is familiar to students of management; and it is quite usual to find nowadays in discussions of decision-making a division into three phases, characterised, for example, by Simon (1965, p. 54) as 'finding occasions for making a decision; finding possible courses of action; and choosing among courses of action'. These phases may conveniently be labelled *intelligence, search*, and *choice*. However, as a representation of managerial decision processes this classification is seriously incomplete. A choice is not effective without *implementation*, which may be far from simple, and often imperfectly accomplished. It is dangerous to assume, either that what has been decided will be achieved, or that what happens is what was intended. Partly because implementation is so uncertain, but fundamentally because decisions are made in circumstances and by processes which are liable to lead to error, there is then usually some kind of assessment of the success of the decision made. Such assessments may range from the impressionistic to the very formal; all may be included in a wide sense of the accountant's term *control*.

One reason for choosing this accountant's term is that control procedures are intended (if they are thought out) to identify 'occasions for making a decision'; and thus the decision process becomes a decision cycle. This concept of managerial activity as a five-phase cycle, in which the perceived consequences of one decision may provide the occasion for another, was formulated (using a slightly different terminology) fifteen years ago in an unpublished analysis by a former colleague, D. K. Clarke.

Control forms a major part of the intelligence generated inside an undertaking. It discloses deviations of performance from the planned decision. . .Control will thus provide a stimulus to the appreciation of new events or to new and better understanding of old facts and this will ultimately lead to the revising of old decisions and the taking of new ones. In a closed system control starts afresh the cycle of administrative activity.

Simon (1965, p. 56) quite explicitly divides decision processes into the first three phases only.

It may be objected that I have ignored the task of carrying out decisions. I shall merely observe by the way that seeing that decisions are executed is again decision-making activity. A broad policy decision creates a new condition for the organisation's executives that calls for the design and choice of a course of action for executing the policy. Executing policy, then, is indistinguishable from making more detailed policy. For this reason, I shall feel justified in taking my pattern for decision-making as a paradigm for most executive activity.

Simon's argument that one man's decision is another man's intelligence is sound; and this notion was used by Clarke as one of his ways of interlinking cycles. Simon, on the other hand, seems more concerned to distinguish between decisions than to integrate them. What makes his attitude so odd (apart from the fact that he does actually refer to a 'cycle of phases') is the emphasis which he, along with Cyert and March, has repeatedly placed on a disparity between aspiration and achievement as a stimulus to fresh decisions. The cycle from perception to perceived result is implicit in so much of the work of the Carnegie School that it is surprising not to find it formally embodied in the way proposed by Clarke.

The cybernetic associations are also obvious. On the other hand, it is not surprising to find the cycle absent from formal microeconomics. It could be introduced into the world of contingent claims markets, where the declaration of a particular state of the world leads to the selection of the appropriate set of actions. What happens at that point could be formally regarded as the result of fully-programmed decisions, the programmes having been, of course, embodied in the general equilibrium solution. However, although fully-programmed decisions are of interest in the analysis of managerial behaviour, their interest arises from the fact that not all decisions are fully programmed. But a willingness to leave unspecified, or incompletely specified, the method of making a choice in some possible future situation would be fatal to any attempt to demonstrate the existence of a general equilibrium solution in such circumstances. Thus, although it would be possible to incorporate the idea of a decision cycle into general equilibrium analysis, it appears to be a pointless complication.

In a theoretically sound macroeconomics, however, it may have a vital role. It offers an obvious framework for such ideas as this of Shackle (1972, p. 341): 'Action can be suggested by, and respond to, events outside the mind, only if these events are perceived. But action can itself bring into view what was hitherto latent.' Action may not only reveal what was latent; it may also change the data, as for example in those trade cycle models in which action falsifies the expectations on which it was based and thus precipitates fresh self-defeating decisions. That expectations, influenced by events, give rise to a new set of decisions, was at the heart of the sequence analysis developed by Myrdal and Lindahl. But we are not yet ready to deal properly with expectations.

Applications of the decision cycle

The Briggs story would serve as a very straightforward illustration of the use of this analysis. After the original decision to get into the bathtub business, each turn round the cycle was precipitated by failure to solve the overall problem on the previous circuit. Each time the problem to be tackled was defined narrowly, and its solution merely revealed the next obstacle – like trench warfare in 1916. (The analysis of the Briggs situation presented earlier did not list the difficulties in the order in which they were perceived.)

Another instance of a company lurching round and round the decision cycle, cannoning off constraints, is to be found in Pressed Steel's assault on the domestic refrigerator market in the late 1950s. In contrast to the bathtub story, this assault was consciously undertaken as a long-period decision, based on a new, specially-equipped factory near Swansea; and Pressed Steel seem to have had no difficulty with the technology – they had been in commercial refrigeration for some time, and even had some small-scale experience with domestic refrigerators. But in other crucial respects, Pressed Steel, like Briggs, took decisions that were programmed by their expertise in production engineering for large volumes, which had just been successfully embodied in a new car-body works at Swindon. Their highly-automated production flow at Swansea appeared to offer obvious cost advantages over the small-scale assembly then characteristic of the industry. Moreover, they had a Design Centre award for one of their refrigerators.

Unfortunately, the production lines were designed to supply the bulk of the market, even in the boom year of 1959; and there were already a dozen well-established brands, many of them owned by such major companies as G.E.C., Tube Investments, and Thorn. The prevalent small scale of manufacture reflected the contemporary pattern of monopolistic competition, which was not to be broken simply by a Design Centre award and skilful production engineering.

Now there are few better ways of losing money than to run a highly-automated production line far below capacity; and this was the situation in which Pressed Steel inevitably found themselves. Their urgent problem was then to increase sales. Here again past experience provided the programme for decision. Their main business was in car bodies and railway wagons, produced on contract for a handful of customers. They knew how to deal with such customers; but they clearly needed one who in turn could produce the very large volume of sales for which their production had been designed. There was one such customer about at the time, who happened to be looking for something like refrigerators to add to his product line. His name was John Bloom.

So Pressed Steel took the irreversible decision of committing their whole output to Bloom for direct sale – irreversible because by withdrawing their products from the retail trade virtually without notice they abandoned any future possibility of using conventional channels. Not even John Bloom could offer to take all the potential output from Swansea; so part of the factory had to be converted to the manufacture of Bloom's original product, washing machines, which had no place in Pressed Steel's original plans. Soon after this, Bloom's empire collapsed, and Pressed Steel's major diversification with it.

The Briggs and Pressed Steel stories both suggest the need for careful consideration of complex problems, and the danger of using programmes which are narrowly based. High precision may conceal great ignorance about the limits of its applicability; and a successful pattern of decomposition may break down when exposed to a different environment. But solving all the problems before one starts is characteristic of general equilibrium theory; the creation of a firm represents a commitment to an ongoing attack on problems, and a recognition that it is too expensive, if not impossible, to foresee everything from the beginning. One can hardly help, in an innovative situation, making several trips round the decision cycle. But they could be rather more ordered than in these two instances. Too often innovation is thought of as a linear process, or at best a branching network, and the recycling of problems which continually occurs is considered the result of accidents or mistakes. A more effective approach is to structure decision-making cyclically, accepting deliberately an incomplete definition of the problem at the outset, and providing for a series of redefinitions as partial solutions and new difficulties are discovered. The decision cycle provides a convenient framework for the method of tackling complex problems advocated in Chapter 3, and is used in the scheme developed by Gallagher (1971), which is there referred to.

If such a method is used, it will become obvious that the cycle may sometimes be short-circuited. This may happen anyway. The concept of sequential search implies a simple iteration between the phases of search and choice. Such an iteration may be observed in W. H. Smith's quest for a warehouse site. The Estate Manager was first asked by the specially-created Distribution Committee to produce a list of sites which met certain criteria, within a fifty-mile arc from west to north of London; when the Committee considered the very small number which he had found, they were insufficiently impressed by any one of them to make an immediate choice, but widened the area of search, not by modifying the criteria for the site, but by extending the geographical limits; and the site chosen, at Swindon, was discovered in this second round (Loasby, 1973, pp. 6–9).

The Smith case history also demonstrates recycling from search to intelligence: the realisation that the data generated in the old warehouse was inadequate for the design of the new system facilitated (though it did not alone produce) a redefinition of the company's problem to include an information system designed to meet particular supply and marketing requirements.

If one wishes to investigate the administrative process in more detail, then one must recognise, as Clarke points out, that one phase of a complex decision may itself include one or more complete decision cycles at a lower level of complexity. This is most obvious when one of the phases is delegated. An operational research group, asked to formulate proposals between which a choice is to be made, is operating entirely within the search phase (unless they challenge their terms of reference, which is sometimes very worthwhile); and yet work on that remit will include problem definition, the discovery of possible methods of dealing with it, the selection of one or more preferred methods, some kind of trial implementation (by computer simulation, for instance), and appraisal on the basis of that trial, quite possibly leading to modification of the solution, or even to redefinition of the mathematical form of the problem (for example, from stock to flow, or vice versa).

It is not the intention of this book to pursue the disaggregation of problems any further; if the relevance of the concept of a five-phase decision cycle has been established, that is enough. We have seen that both the cost and the quality of decision-making depends on the agenda on which it is taken (the items included, rather than simply some measure of width), the set of control variables consciously manipulated, and the degree and type of programming used. These considerations emphasise the crucial role of the criteria employed in decision processes, and in each phase of each process: the criteria used to sift intelligence, to direct search, to evaluate choice, to guide implementation, and to appraise the results. The determination of these criteria is the subject of the next chapter.

6

Reference standards

> Even ordinary singular statements are always *interpretations of 'the facts' in the light of theories.*
>
> K. R. Popper (1972, p. 423)

The study of information systems, at present so flourishing, is of recent growth. No doubt its burgeoning owes much to the perception by accountants of a threat to their established position from the development of new information technologies. Yet what are called information systems are too often little more than data systems. An isolated fact is of no significance whatever; but even to collect facts into groups requires some kind of interpretative framework. Before we can collect the relevant facts, we need to know what facts are relevant. As the most fundamental concept of information theory reminds us, data becomes information only when related to some prior expectation. Facts acquire meaning only when matched with theory.

But the matching of facts with theory is not the obvious procedure that so many economic theorists and designers of information systems assume it to be. As the examples in the previous chapter demonstrate, it is possible to fit observed facts into more than one pattern, and the choice of pattern may have profound consequences. All information systems rest on the implicit assumption that we know what it is we need to know – and many of them on the further assumption that the needs of the system users can be accurately gauged by those who design and operate it. That would be an arrogant assumption in any circumstances; but as has been argued earlier, the most critical decisions are liable to arise from circumstances that were unexpected. Thus the most critical information requirements may be those that cannot be programmed into a formal system.

Although the need for interpretation of facts is implicit in the notion of a disparity between achievement and aspiration as the trigger of action in their theory of organisational behaviour, Cyert and March (1963, p. 34) offer no more than the simplest, and barely argued, account of the determination of those short-run aspiration levels which play a crucial role. The aim of this chapter is to provide the basis for a more extended analysis of aspiration levels, and also of the criteria used in other phases of the decision cycle. That basis is substantially derived from the ideas put forward by Pounds (1969) in an article which has apparently been noticed by hardly anyone.

The process of problem finding

Pounds' central concept, analogous to that of information theory, is that problems are defined by differences.

> The word 'problem' is associated with the difference between some existing situation and some desired situation. The problem of reducing material cost, for example, indicates a difference between the existing material cost and some desired level of material cost. The problems of hiring qualified engineers and of reducing finished goods inventories similarly define differences to be reduced. . .
> The manager defines differences by comparing what he perceives to the output of a model which predicts the same variables. . .The problem of understanding problem finding therefore is eventually reduced to the problem of understanding the models which managers use to define differences (p. 5).

Like decisions, these problem-generating models, or reference standards, may be classified in various ways; of the four categories suggested here, three are due to Pounds. They are: *historical*, the record or recollection of some past situation believed to be relevant; *external*, the apparent situation somewhere else; and *planning*, the situation that was anticipated or intended. The fourth category, *imaginative*, some notion of what does not exist but might be created, was proposed by C. W. Suckling.

Pounds also used the category of 'other people's models', to define the class of problems which a manager works on because they have been referred to him by someone else. But although this category is obviously relevant to the question: 'How did managers come to be working on this particular set of problems?', it does not explain how the problems were originally identified. It seems helpful for the present to keep the question of problem finding separate from that of problem allocation.

What determines which models are evoked in a particular situation? This is a question which faces behavioural economists and business historians, but not microeconomic theorists; for microeconomic theory is not concerned with the particular, but standardises circumstances by its choice of assumptions. Perfect competition is the simplest, but by no means the only, way of standardising circumstances: it is where circumstances cannot plausibly be standardised – notably in oligopoly theory – that the traditional approach runs into serious trouble. That is why problems of oligopoly offered behavioural theory its first foothold in economics.

It is important to remember that what has to be explained is not merely the standards employed, but also what subjects people have standards about: not only, for example, why a company should have a certain target for research expenditure, but also why research should appear to be a relevant subject for a standard at all; in many companies it does not. The establishment of a certain kind of standard may itself be considered as a consequence of apparent differences between the existing situation and some higher-level standard, prescribing what models ought to exist and what they ought to do.

Historical standards

Historical standards are, obviously, based on experience, and the assumption behind their use is that the past will prove, in some important ways, a guide to the future. This is the argument for extrapolation. Their content depends on at least three factors. The first is the range and weighting of the experience built into the model – the size of the sample, and also its biases. The second is the accuracy with which that experience is perceived – corresponding to the design of a sample questionnaire and the quality of the interviewing and recording techniques. The third is the interpretation of experience – the quality of the analysis applied to the sample results.

The ordered accumulation and interpretation of experience, especially of experience purposefully generated in controlled experiments, has made science a powerful weapon for the recognition and solution of problems. Pounds notes the contrast with the formation of managerial standards.

the models used by the managers [in the company studied] are almost startling in their naivete. In the same company, electrical engineers explicitly used quite complex theoretical models to help them define problems associated with the design of a relatively simple electronic control system...Managers, on the other hand, based their expectations on relatively small samples of their own experience (p. 15).

Briggs, it will be recalled, relied on a single trial.

The value of a historical standard depends not only on the care with which it is constructed, but also on its continued relevance. Historical standards are good guides in repetitious situations; they are poor guides (and may be actively misleading) if essential elements in the new situation differ from those in the old – if, in other words, one is no longer sampling from the same population. Such situations occur in both pure and applied sciences, as well as in business: Newtonian mechanics doesn't quite fit, full-scale plants fail to work, larger box-girder bridges collapse. The fallibility of experience, even the experience embodied in well-corroborated scientific laws, is a central Popperian theme. In management it happens far more often that experience is used to construct models of quite unjustified generality.

Thus historical standards are of limited help in defining unusual problems. So long as history does, in significant ways, repeat itself, experience is a good qualification for a decision-maker; but when it ceases to repeat itself, experience is no qualification; indeed, if the experienced man should fail to recognise this (which is not always easy), then it is a disqualification.

In his study of diversification, Miller (1963) draws particular attention to the limitations of ingrained historical standards, so well exemplified in Pressed Steel's major venture into domestic refrigeration.

Much of what we call management judgement is actually experience in a particular business context. Diversification to a new business context necessarily tends to upset that judgement.
...the specialised task of the contract suppliers tended to create specialised judgement. For example, high-unit volume and insistent

cost pressures resulted in a system of priorities and work procedures that supported a production-dominated organization and emphasised the value of low margin and high turnover. The problem for executives in such a change is that the influence of previously developed subconscious standards of judgement may not be clearly recognised. There was no reason for automotive executives to regard automotive standards as specialised as long as they kept within the automotive industry (pp.126–7).

Historical standards are particularly likely to foster the concentration of effort on narrow-agenda, limited-variable, highly-programmed activities. In so doing they promote efficiency by speeding the firm down its learning curve. But we cannot escape the problems of ignorance. We cannot discover the costs of keeping agendas narrow unless we forgo the benefits by widening them; we can move rapidly down the learning curve only if we sacrifice our understanding of just what it is we are learning. There is no reason to believe that the choice should always be made in favour of breadth; but it should at least be remembered that there is an inescapable choice to be made.

External standards

The limitations, and possible bias, of one's own experience may be mitigated by also using external standards – which are other people's history, usually as perceived by outsiders. The value of such external reference points is the primary justification for the Centre for Interfirm Comparison, and an important reason for employing management consultants or attending external management courses. The use, or neglect, of external standards as problem-generators may be one of the most crucial factors determining the quality of managerial performance.

What is external must depend on the particular pattern of one's own experience. Academic division of labour, like any other kind of division of labour, favours the development of a limited set of clearly-defined standards for the definition of narrow-agenda problems. The encouragement of well-articulated responses to situations is particularly characteristic of those disciplines which call themselves scientific; and economics has gained most notably in precision by the willingness of theorists to sacrifice breadth. The results have surely been worthwhile; but, like the automotive engineers, theorists have in the process sometimes been unable to recognise how specialised they have become. A belief that low margin and high turnover is the universal requirement for business success is no more absurd than a belief that general equilibrium theory is the theory of choice.

It may sometimes be helpful to distinguish between those external standards which relate to organisational performance and those which concern personal behaviour. The influence of the latter, usually under the title of 'reference groups', is a major topic of sociological research, and any manager proposing to introduce members of another profession, discipline, or trade union into an organisation should think carefully about possible problems. Organisations may be powerful reference groups too; and disparities in organisational style often cause some trouble after a merger – even sometimes after a merger between different departments or divisions of a single organisation.

Planning standards

Historical and external standards are both products of experience. Where do planning standards come from? In an organisation with an established planning system, planning standards will be modified with the passage of time like other standards. They will tend to reflect performance, either in the organisation which is the subject of the plan or in some other organisation which is thought of as a valid reference point.

Nowadays planning may be far more sophisticated than a simple extrapolation of the past. The progress of management science is steadily transferring items of cost to the engineered category (predictable from a knowledge of the required outputs, such as material requirements) from the managed category (where the requisite levels, for example, of welfare expenditure, are unknown and therefore subject to managerial discretion). But this trend should not be allowed to disguise the fact that standards for engineered costs are normally derived from historical experience; it is much easier to establish what a particular operation has cost than what it should ideally cost. Nor is this all. McNamara's record at the U.S. Department of Defence suggests that management science is still some way from successfully engineering the costs of achieving either military or research and development objectives; and the planning of demand is not quite as easy as Galbraith likes to suggest. Ignorance has not yet been abolished.

The technical difficulties of producing a plan that is a more useful problem-generator than other available reference standards are bad enough. But planning is not only a technical problem. In an organisation of any size, whether public or private, commercial or philanthropic, it is highly political. Plans are often meant to serve the purposes of individuals or groups, as well as the organisations to which they belong; and for these purposes the plan may be an end in itself, for example, by establishing the status or autonomy of that individual or group, and not be intended as a guide to action.

Making or modifying a plan is the result of a decision process, and must therefore be initiated by the awareness of a problem. But one of the major practical difficulties in drawing up a plan, as suggested in the previous paragraph, is that it may be intended to solve more than one problem. This is characteristically true of preparing budgets for control purposes. A budget is seen as a solution to the problem: how do we know when things are going well or when action is needed? It offers a solution to this problem by making possible the calculation of variances, a form of management by exception. Variance analysis narrows the agenda by its allocation of responsibility, identifies the relevant control variables, and often elicits programmed corrective action; but it should be remembered that the distinction between offset and non-offset variances (which determines the absence or presence of designated problems) may depend on both the method and the level of decomposition. However, the budget is also seen as a solution to the problem: how can we evaluate the performance of subordinates? It offers a solution to this problem by providing a standard against which they may be judged.

But these are different, indeed conflicting, problems. An effective budgetary control system for the first purpose is one that is an efficient problem-generator, in other words, one that reveals, by throwing up variances, a sufficient number of matters for attention. But for the manager whose performance is being evaluated, an effective solution to the second problem is a budgetary control system which generates very few, or even no, problems. As Pounds comments: 'Among other things, plans are organisation-ally defined limits of managerial independence. So long as the manager is able to perform at least as well as his plan requires, he expects, and is normally granted, the right to define his problems as he sees fit' (p. 8). Thus the conflict between objectives itself generates a problem. In the firm studied by Pounds – according to him a successful firm – the solution was unequivocal; every time a proposed budget proceeded a step up the hierarchy it was relaxed, in an open conspiracy to avoid a situation in which any manager might lose his right to manage.

A similar concern to preserve this right is evident in the sales forecasting behaviour studied by Lowe and Shaw (1968). The rewards of the area managers in a retailing company were seen to be related to their relative position in a league table of perform-ance compared with their sales budget, the budget being based on sales forecasts which originated with the managers themselves. There was accordingly a general tendency to underestimate sales, where such estimates were thought likely to be acceptable at Head Office. A few unfortunate sales managers, however, in areas of declining population, felt compelled to mortgage their future by inflated forecasts, rather than incur the immediate displeasure of a senior management which was believed not to appreciate their special difficulties. They sacrificed future security in an attempt to preserve their present independence.

Imaginative standards

Like planning standards, imaginative standards cross the bridge from the past to the future. But the differences are twofold. First, while plans prescribe targets (what should be), imaginative stan-dards suggest hypotheses (what might be). Second, while the process leading to a plan can be analysed, the process leading to an imaginative standard involves a creative leap which can, at best, be rationalised. It may – perhaps it must – draw on past experience and analogy (historical and external standards) for its components: but though it may be possible to create conditions favourable to the emergence of imaginative standards, it does not yet appear to be possible to produce them on demand.

Yet their importance is immense, as Dubos (1961, p. 44) observes.

During many thousands of years, men have used the elements of the real world...to imagine – that is, to create in their minds – other worlds more reasonable, more generous, and more interesting. These acts of imagination have had an enormous influence on history... For...in many cases new processes and tools have found their place in civilization only when they could be used...to bring into being the imaginary worlds first conceived in the abstract by the human mind.

The way in which a new hypothesis generates experimental problems for the scientist is well known; and one of the great merits claimed for Popper's philosophy of science is the encouragement of bold falsifiable speculations by scientists who had previously been constrained to caution by inductivist methodology (Lakatos, 1970, p. 181). But imaginative models can generate fruitful problems for management too. To convert a fact which is accepted into a problem to be solved may often be the key to progress. Uncertainty reduction may be the principal activity of both science and management; but it is uncertainty creation which provides the major opportunities for both.

The recognition of problems

However, it must be recognised that some element of creativity may be involved in the use of any reference standard. The problems which are apparent are not necessarily the problems which are relevant. Skill in the generation and selection of reference standards is an important part of what is usually called perceptive management.

The validity of standards is an issue most frequently raised in connection with external references. Why should the experience of another organisation be thought a relevant criterion of one's own achievements? It is common enough to encounter protests at the use of such a measure, especially when its acceptance would define an unwanted problem. The initial reluctance of Esso's Fawley management to accept the relevance of performance at Standard Oil's Louisiana refinery had to be overcome before they could be persuaded to deal with inefficient working practices

(Flanders, 1966, Chapter 2). Willingness to generalise from a small sample of one's own experience may be complemented by refusal to consider the experience of others. There is overmuch protesting of uniqueness.

On the other hand, there are real dangers in transplanting a standard into a new situation without re-examining the assumptions on which it is based. It should be noted here that the question is essentially the same as that involved in the continued use of a historical standard in changed circumstances. The more specific the standard, the narrower is likely to be its range of usefulness.

This is not a general argument against precision in standards. Not only have precise standards repeatedly proved their worth in science; their effectiveness as problem generators was very clearly demonstrated by the study of investment decisions carried out by Williams and Scott (1965). A number of these decisions produced results which were felt to be unsatisfactory; but, whereas failure to achieve a clearly-defined target stimulated successful remedial action, performance which was below vague expectations proved a weak incentive. There is an obvious lesson here for the management of research projects. In the evaluation of such projects scientists find precision on technical issues both easier and more congenial than precision on commercial prospects. The consequence is liable to be a misallocation of resources: the technical reference standards define clear problems and attract much effort, while generalities about the market are unlikely to be reviewed. Economic theorists face similar temptations.

The emphasis here placed on the reference standards by which facts are judged, too often neglected by the designers of information systems, does not justify a neglect of the data flow, which they rightly stress. Reference standards without relevant facts are as incapable of defining problems as facts without reference standards. Since it is not always possible to produce whatever facts would be convenient, it may sometimes be necessary (and often worthwhile) to modify reference standards to suit those facts which are available. This principle may be used to justify the use of some rather crude measures of success in industry, education, and econometrics; but it must be remembered that by so doing one is gaining information about one's model at the cost of increasing doubts about its relevance. The difficulties discussed in Chapter 3 are very pervasive.

A further difficulty concerns the validity of the information itself. Doubts may arise under either of the two heads familiar to statisticians: sampling error or observational error. It is always possible that an apparently surprising observation is merely an outlier of a distribution centred on the reference standard, or, more insidiously, that an apparently normal observation is an outlier of a distribution centred far away from the standard; and in many situations (especially those in which major decisions may be required) it is just not possible to acquire a sample large enough for statistical confidence before making up one's mind. Macroeconomic management provides some obvious illustrations. Second, the reports may simply be wrong.

What makes this double difficulty so intractable is that often the quality of the information is judged by the reference standard against which it is to be compared. As noticed earlier, this is characteristic of experimental science, where the hypothesis is so regularly used to judge the quality of an experiment that it is quite normal, when a hypothesis is apparently disconfirmed by an experiment, to conclude that it is the experiment, not the hypothesis, which has failed.

In practice, the difficulty in experimental science can often be overcome by using a hypothesis to test single experiments, but a large number of experiments to test the hypothesis; but when we are talking of single critical events, this solution is not available. The ability – or luck – to distinguish between false and true alarms, or false and true security, then becomes critical. If it is ability, then it seems to be related to the ability to widen the agenda in appropriate directions, thereby admitting a greater range of evidence. The advantages of such widening, particularly in critical situations, favour the use of multiple reference standards; thus as a practical matter of decision-taking in an uncertain world, some scheme of objectives, such as Ansoff (1965) has proposed, is likely to be more effective in identifying genuine problems than any single-valued criterion, such as profit.

So far we have discussed the perception of information by the potential decision-maker. But much of the information which he perceives originates with someone else; and this introduces a new group of difficulties. What is information to the originator depends on his own reference standards, and if, as is likely, they are not identical with those of the decision-maker, then irrelevant data may be provided, and relevant data suppressed. Even where relevant data are provided, they may not be offered in a form which evokes the appropriate reference standard. In the language of information theory, the cypher used to decode a message may be different from that used to encode it. This phenomenon can be observed as a frequent cause of unintended problems in negotiating situations.

Distortion of information is not always accidental. There may be strong incentives to distortion, as is well-established in the related problem of eliciting individual preferences for public goods. Within an organisation, managers being evaluated by a budgetary control system who have not been able to fudge the budget enough to avoid the risk of unfavourable variances may be able instead to fudge the figures which the budget is to be used to assess. For example, in a consulting firm, case budgets have to be kept low enough to sell the case; but undesired overruns can often be avoided by such devices as the working of unbooked overtime, the use of secretaries, whose time is charged to overhead, to do work which would otherwise be done by professional staff, or booking time to another case which is running under budget or is just beginning – and which may therefore need to be rescued by similar measures later on. Such expedients do nothing to improve the quality of forecasting; indeed, by concealing instances where a budget is unjustifiably tight, they may simultaneously perpetuate these practices and lead the firm to bid for, and obtain, an increasing amount of unprofitable business.

This particular practice is not obviously acceptable as a second-best solution. However, the avoidance of problems is often a useful skill. Not only may it sometimes be impractical (especially from a subordinate position) to insist on the use of appropriate reference standards; once one admits that consensus within a large organisation is no more attainable – and perhaps no more desirable – than Pareto optimality, then the effective working of the organisation may depend on the suppression of at least some of the latent conflicts, by avoiding either the juxtaposition of conflicting standards or the appraisal of a situation by a standard that would generate conflict. The position of the individual in the organisation is considered more fully in Chapter 8; and some examples of the avoidance of conflict between groups are given in the last part of this. But first it is worth considering briefly the significance of reference standards in the solution of problems, once perceived.

The perception of solutions

The nature of the decision process implies that solutions are no more likely to be uniquely defined than are problems; but their perception can be similarly treated.

Medawar (1967) has emphasised the necessity of some apparent means of solution as a condition for entering the decision cycle of scientific research; indeed, this condition is so crucial that Medawar is prepared to characterise scientific research as 'the art of the soluble'.

Good scientists study the most important problems they think they can solve. It is, after all, their professional business to solve problems, not merely to grapple with them. The spectacle of a scientist locked in combat with the forces of ignorance is not an inspiriting one if, in the outcome, the scientist is routed. That is why some of the most important biological problems have not yet appeared on the agenda of practical research (p. 7).

In management and economics too, the visibility of some means of solution is critical; many unsatisfactory situations remain untackled because no one knows how to set about them. Often the degree of ignorance is so great that it is impossible to be sure that there is indeed any solution to be found. Boulding (1966, p. 163) follows a similar observation by commenting that 'existence theorems might have a profound effect on behaviour, because of their effect on the willingness to search'. This is assuredly true; but Boulding does not notice that the perception of solutions, like the perception of problems, may be false, because the criteria used for recognising either may lack sufficiency. It is at least possible that existence theorems in welfare economics have produced an excessive willingness to search for non-existent policy solutions.

The objective is to find some means to reduce, and if possible eliminate, the difference between the apparent situation and the chosen reference standards. In Pounds' (1969, p. 5) words, 'The process of problem finding is the process of defining differences. Problem solving, on the other hand, is the process of selecting operators which will reduce differences.' It has been emphasised already that the defined difference may not accurately represent (or even represent at all) a relevant problem. But even if it does, the solution may be one that affects the perceived rather than the real situation; for instance, by changing the scope or content of reports. Clearly one of the objects of any effective problem-generating procedure is to ensure, as far as possible, that the solutions proposed to the problems generated are relevant to genuine threats or opportunities, and not merely a means of eliminating apparent differences.

What determines the visibility of solutions? In Pounds' scheme, 'Because problems are defined by differences and operators can be executed to reduce differences, strong associations are formed between problems and operators. The problem of devising a production schedule can ordinarily be "solved" by applying the operator "lay out production schedule". The problem of "increasing sales volume" can sometimes be "solved" by applying the operator "revise advertising budget" ' (p. 5).

Such strong associations are often found; but it is worth enquiring how particular solutions come to be attached to particular problems. An obvious line of investigation is provided by the set of reference standards used to explain the recognition of problems. Thus the difference-operator combination may itself be the product of experience, a historical standard. Different people, of course, have different experiences, and therefore favour different solutions. (Compare, for instance, the various ways of dealing with industrial disputes in different organisations.) Once again, there is a substantial risk that in dealing with infrequent problems, experience may be dangerously misleading.

Alternatively, new solutions may be discovered by analogy with other difference-operator systems. 'Always reduce a problem to one you have already solved' is the mathematician's method; if one cannot make a precise conversion, then look for a problem with a similar kind of structure which has already been solved. Either type of sequential search implies confidence in the standards, historical or external, which are used. Ansoff (1965) and

Bradbury, Gallagher & Suckling (1973) both propose methods of search and evaluation which are designed to challenge unjustified confidence in such standards. Attempts at redefinition are often important, especially when a problem seems intractable in its original form. If, indeed, as Simon (1969, p. 77) argues, 'solving a problem simply means representing it so as to make the solution transparent', then the encouragement of alternative means of representation may be the key to the effective solution of novel and complex problems. Thus, just as part of the value of employing management consultants and of using management courses lies in the greater range of extra-organisational models which they provide for problem finding, so another part of their value lies in the greater range of extra-organisational models which they provide as a basis for suggesting solutions.

At a more academic level, the development of alternative forms of theorising may be more useful than continued refinement of a theory which is already well-developed; and the value of inter-disciplinary work may depend less on general similarities between disciplines than on highly-specific differences. Since it is by defining differences that problems are recognised, and by redefin-ing them that they are often solved, interdisciplinary variety should be accentuated, not concealed: it offers the prospect of discovering at least a path to a solution by a drastic change in the representation of a problem. The case for a range of different models, put forward at the end of Chapter 3, has both a negative and a positive aspect: it offers some protection against the insuffi-ciency of abstractions, and a chance of finding an abstraction which will be more effective.

Though strong associations between problems and solutions often exist, this is by no means an invariable rule. It probably appears a stronger rule than it is, partly because investigations of search behaviour have tended to concentrate on repetitious situa-tions, and partly because complex problems are often force-fitted into simpler categories, and subjected to an inappropriate degree of programming.

Where the association does exist, the solution depends on the way in which the problem is defined: and the ability to define problems in more than one way carries dangers as well as advan-tages. For example, where alternative definitions (each with its

solution attached) are possible, a supervisor who accepts his subordinate's definition of a problem is effectively delegating the
decision, even though he may believe he is delegating no more
than the intelligence function. Moreover, there are solutions in
search of problems, and the prospect of applying an attractive
solution may cause a problem to be distorted to fit; and since
problems normally have to be distorted anyway, this is not always
easy to spot. Fortunately, however, although some choices are
disastrous, there are often a number of satisfactory solutions; it is
notable how often several different management styles or product
policies seem to work well enough, even in the same industry.

From Bridge House to Swindon

To illustrate how the concept of reference standards may be
used to analyse a complex situation, we may consider W. H.
Smith & Son's handling of the labour problems involved in the
transfer of their book and stationery warehouse from Bridge
House, in Lambeth, to Swindon (Loasby, 1973). In the new warehouse, the company secured a reduction of more than half in
shop-floor labour; a substantial reduction in overtime (and,
therefore, sometimes a reduction in take-home pay); and a transformation of working practices. Moreover, all this was achieved
without damaging, indeed, while probably strengthening, the
company's generally good relations with the National Union of
Printing, Bookbinding and Paper Workers, one of the powerful
unions in Fleet Street. Altogether this was a noteworthy accom-
plishment. How was it done?

The first element in the company's success was that the changes
in working practices were embedded in a physical transfer to a
quite different, and much more attractive, building. This had two
helpful consequences. On the one hand, transformation was so
comprehensive that all existing landmarks were swept away, and
the historical standards of Bridge House made obviously irrelevant as a starting point for argument. The complexity of the
reorganisation made it impossible, for example, for either
management or workers to attribute the loss of any particular job
to any particular change. On the other hand, for those workers
who moved, Swindon offered so many advantages in better

homes, shorter journeys to work, better working conditions, and, for many, promotion, that there was a general disposition to count blessings rather than seek causes of complaint. The move evoked an alternative set of standards, relating to working conditions and home circumstances, which defined satisfactions instead of problems, and which dominated other standards. Morale after the move was very high.

The second element was the skilful (if not entirely deliberate) way in which the company managed to decompose their managerial system, and to make a constructive use of conflict within management to sharpen the issues which they had to resolve. The planning of the new warehouse and its operating methods rested on a conscious rejection of much of the company's past experience, and a search for relevant external standards. This was reflected, for example, in the employment of consultants, in a North American tour by the Supply Director of that time, and most clearly, because it reversed a previous decision, in the appointment of a Supply Centre Manager who was very familiar with modern warehousing methods, but refreshingly ignorant of the assumed special features of the book and stationery business or of W. H. Smith & Son.

By thus limiting the agenda and evoking a specific set of reference standards, the company devised an efficient distribution system; but the wider consequences of such bounded rationality might have proved disastrous. For although it could fairly be argued that by 1963 Smith's operating traditions had become an obstacle to beneficial change, yet the traditional pattern of its labour relations remained a great asset. There can be few problem areas in which the neglect of tradition and precedent may be more dangerous than in trade union bargaining; for trade unions are, in general, among the most conservative, and even, in its literal sense, reactionary groups in society. The reorganisation of Smith's distribution system could have produced, quite unwittingly, such obvious violations of the historical standards of the union officials and their members as to precipitate serious trouble; and between the announcement of the move to Swindon and its actual completion the company had to face two years of extreme vulnerability.

The avoidance of such conflict was the professional responsibility of the Staff Director and Staff Manager; but it is not too great a distortion to claim that the Supply Centre Manager, as custodian of external standards of good distribution management, was balanced by the Labour Adviser as the custodian of traditional references in labour relations. By virtue of his formal position as Manager of the News Dispatch Department, the Labour Adviser had necessarily to be well-informed about union attitudes, and his interest went well beyond his formal duty, and to such effect that he had created the position of Labour Adviser for himself. By each concentrating on their own expertise, the Supply Centre Manager and the Labour Adviser presented two sharply-defined sets of reference standards, which indicated clearly where the introduction of modern operating procedures could cause trouble. As a result, Smith's management were never caught unawares by any approach from the union.

The third element was the use, wherever possible, of in-house bargaining. The company enjoyed, as it had sought, the confidence of the Father of its Chapel, a sturdy and honourable man, who, like Smith's management, bargained for agreement, not for victory. Thus he, and his committee members, were very happy to negotiate on the basis, primarily, of reference standards derived from experience within the company, rather than the standards of Fleet Street, which, though external to them, were the historical standards of their Branch Secretary, whose territory it was. Nor had Smith's any desire to evoke Fleet Street standards, either in relation to the substance of agreements or in union–management attitudes. The Branch Secretary himself had no wish to interfere: he was fully occupied administering a huge branch with a tiny staff, and therefore quite happy to accept the Chapel's satisfaction as the criterion of his own. He was necessarily involved in the major negotiations about the move, but much of the detail was left to the Chapel, and the Branch Secretary's attitude was clearly affected by the general confidence between Chapel and management.

In the substance of negotiations, the influence of reference standards is manifest. The union had a policy of no redundancy, and this policy the Branch Secretary insisted must be applied to the Swindon project. But Smith's wished to employ far fewer people at Swindon. This dilemma was resolved, to the satisfaction of both parties, by a three-part agreement. First, any employee who wished should be allowed to move to Swindon. Second, there should be a generous transfer scheme, so that there could be no suggestion that the firm was trying to discourage transfer. Third, there should be generous payments to those who did not move. Some members of Smith's management had doubts about the wisdom of the first part of this agreement, because of inflated ideas about the numbers likely to move; but all supported the other two principles, and by conceding improvements to the already quite favourable terms in response to union pressure, confirmed the Branch Secretary's favourable view of the firm. Thus Smith's secured the reduction in employment, and the Branch Secretary avoided redundancy; for to leave your job because you have turned down a good offer is quite different from being fired. This is not a matter of cynical semantics: the agreement is a credit to all concerned.

The avoidance of any dispute over redundancy was assisted by the company's fortunate inability at that time to provide any firm forecast of employment at Swindon. In their desire to give as much information as possible, the company regretted this; only later did they realise the advantage of obscurity. For if there was no figure for employment at Swindon, no one could calculate the number of jobs to be lost; and as has been remarked earlier, precision in standards is a major influence on their power as problem generators.

The importance of precision in defining problems was confirmed by a later turn round the decision cycle. By then, the Branch Secretary had gradually come to accept the figure of 200 as the likely employment for his members at Swindon; and 200 was what he expected to get. By this time, however, the Swindon management were beginning to think of a much smaller figure; both the numbers required and the relevance of Bridge House experience were dwindling in their estimation. This conflict between Swindon planning standards and the Branch Secretary's expectations produced the nearest approach to crisis in the Swindon story.

It was not very near. After an internal debate which turned partly on the relative importance of operating efficiency at Swindon and of avoiding trouble with the union, and partly on the relative likelihood of each, the problem was resolved when Smith's decided to take up the Branch Secretary's offer, originated earlier, to provide volunteers from the branch. This decision involved some departure from subjective suboptimisation at Swindon, but it replenished the company's fund of goodwill with the Branch Secretary: there could hardly be a more convincing sign that Smith's were not trying to get rid of union members than their willingness to take on additional workers from the same union. Thus the number of volunteers for Swindon was brought into line with the Branch Secretary's expectations. Not surprisingly, the number who eventually moved was rather less; but that was not the firm's fault, and could not be a source of dispute.

It is of course possible to present this whole episode as an example of optimisation subject to constraints. Such an approach would, however, tell us nothing of the process involved; nor would it confront the main issues. For, even in hindsight, neither the constraints nor the objective function can be confidently specified. The pervasiveness of ignorance prevents a unique objective definition. Complex problems must always be simplified and often artificially decomposed; frequent redefinition through successive decision cycles may be needed to build up a satisfactory solution. At each stage, however, problems in their current form may be defined by differences – differences between what is perceived and the reference standards by which it is assessed.

7

Objectives in organisations

Constraints are obligatory, objectives are optional.
C. W. Suckling

The previous two chapters have suggested, and illustrated, methods of analysing decision processes, and proposed a scheme for investigating the origins of the particular criteria which are used in particular circumstances. Neither the details of decision processes nor the characteristics of particular circumstances are of interest to economic theory; in modern microeconomics choice results from the application of a well-defined preference function to a fully-specified set of available alternatives.

Producers' preferences

The standard theory of the firm is, however, particular in one very important respect: the firm's preference function requires nothing but the maximisation of profit. This specification has been criticised on three counts: first, that the objective is not simply profit; second, that the objective function is not maximised; and third, that the concept of a unitary preference function cannot properly be extended from individuals, for whom it was designed, to collectivities such as firms. It is the purpose of this chapter to explore the logic of objectives in organisations, and in particular the bases of these criticisms. As usual, the discussion will be related both to the analysis of actual behaviour and to the requirements of efficient decision-making.

Consumer theory has no need to concern itself with the content of preference functions, but only with their form. The doctrine of revealed preference enables us – entirely hypothetically, for in economic newspeak 'revealed preferences' are not even the subject of enquiry – to infer preferences from the behaviour which they are used to explain. The primary purpose of consumer theory is not to learn about consumers, but to contribute to the construction of economic models; and the interest in these models is in their formal properties, not in the actual quantities of any particular goods or services consumed, or produced. Thus, while it is convenient to exclude the possibility of total satiation of wants, it is of no consequence whether leisure is an inferior or a superior good.

It was once assumed that profit maximisation was the precise equivalent in production of the standard assumption of consumer behaviour. But as Scitovsky (1943) pointed out thirty years ago, this is not so: if profits are to be maximised, then the entrepreneur's willingness to engage in profit-seeking activity must be entirely independent of his income. The consumer, and the worker, may use an increase in income to buy additional leisure; the entrepreneur must not.

This restriction is essential to the existence of the perfectly competitive equilibrium. For whereas a worker, by opting for an additional hour of leisure, obtains it (in a perfect market) by the sacrifice of an amount of income which exactly reflects the value of the lost product and thus leaves everyone else in the economy exactly as well off as they would have been had he chosen to work instead, the entrepreneur is the agent by which these very conditions are secured. Since the entrepreneur is the agent of equilibrium in production, profits are a kind of transactions cost, which poses a well-known threat to optimality – and indeed, as has been argued in an earlier chapter, a threat to deterministic equilibrium analysis.

Competitive pressure will not resolve the difficulty, for the presence of a small number of single-minded profit-seekers could not enforce profit maximisation on their fellows. The profit-seekers would clearly make more profit, but that would no more influence the others than the knowledge that his contemporaries who have chosen to work longer hours are receiving larger incomes would cause a worker to revoke his preference for greater leisure. The higher profits earned by the single-minded would appear as a rent, and would not attract new entrants whose preference functions were more widely based.

Thus profit maximisation implies a special assumption about

the content, and not merely the form, of the entrepreneur's preference function; and the device of postulating zero income-elasticity of demand for leisure on the part of all entrepreneurs is a handy escape from some awkward problems. The need for such a special (even if, as Scitovsky argues, not entirely implausible) restriction can be avoided altogether by recognising that the equilibrium conditions discussed are those in which no decisions of any kind are required, and that there is thus no role for either profit or the entrepreneur.

As far as the analysis of perfect competition is concerned, therefore, the whole argument amounts to very little. But economists do make much use of the assumption of profit maximisation; and it should be generally recognised that it is much less innocuous than the very general standard assumption about the maximising behaviour of the consumer. As a matter of logic, managerial objective functions can claim to be rather more general – the opposite of what is frequently asserted.

Williamson (1963, 1964) has effectively demonstrated that it is possible to produce an objective function, comprising staff, discretionary spending for investments, and management slack absorbed as cost, which has the notable qualities that it includes profit maximisation as a special case, yet outside this special case predicts (using the customary device of comparative equilibrium analysis) different responses to changes in either the rate of profits tax or a lump-sum tax, the latter implying equivalent responses to a change in fixed costs. Thus, for example, while the output of a profit-maximising firm would be unaffected by either change, Williamson's firms would increase output in response to an increase in profits tax (because the cost, in after-tax profits forgone, is reduced) and reduce it in response to a rise in fixed costs (to release funds for utility-increasing costs). The model is thus usable and significant for the traditional comparative-static purposes of predicting the directions of change; to predict magnitudes one would need to know not merely the components of the managerial preference function, but also its detailed specification, just as one would for predicting the magnitude of consumer response to a change in circumstances.

Two other well-known suggestions for specifying managerial objectives in terms other than profit maximisation are those of

Baumol (1959) and Marris (1964). Baumol postulates the maximisation of sales revenue, subject to a profit constraint, Marris a constrained maximisation of the firm's growth rate: each justifies his specification as a surrogate for a range of managerial objectives, such as those summarised in Williamson's triple function. Both models yield some predictions which differ from those of profit maximisation (changes in fixed costs, for example, affect price and output), and both can be used – indeed, Marris' model is designed explicitly to be used – for the non-traditional purpose of analysing the growth of firms.

Costs as commodities

If the proposals of Baumol and Marris have attracted rather more interest than those of Williamson, it is probably in part because they seem to offer a method of tackling a different problem, rather than threatening an established answer to an old problem. Another possible reason is that they rather successfully obscure a critical methodological issue which Williamson's model leaves out in the open – though Williamson himself has not drawn attention to it. Sales revenue or growth rates are very imperfect surrogates for managerial utility: there is no general reason to believe that it is a matter of indifference to the managers whether, for example, price-cutting, increased promotion, or an emphasis on product quality through research is the means chosen for increasing sales, or into what new areas their firm diversifies in its search for growth; indeed it is generally true that a managerial objective function will lead to some sacrifice of sales and growth, as well as profits, as the price of achieving the managers' maximal set. It is clear that Williamson's managers maximise neither sales revenue nor growth rate.

But this is the trouble. Wage theory has long recognised, in its concept of net advantages, that such factors as the convenience of the hours and the physical conditions of work may affect the market rate for the job. But the job itself must be technologically determined. All costs must be engineered, and the choice of production method (including the choice of managerial system) must be based on allocative efficiency. Costs themselves must not be a subject of preference. It is, however, the essence of Williamson's model that unnecessary costs should be a direct source of satisfaction, and that leisure-preference should be exercised, not only in choosing the hours of work, but also in choosing its intensity, and therefore its productivity. From the manager's point of view, allocative efficiency is non-optimal.

That is a disturbing conclusion. It invalidates, for example, as a simple welfare proposition the precept that x-inefficiency should be eliminated. X-inefficiency is the term coined by Leibenstein (1966) to refer to most of what is popularly meant by inefficiency: everything beyond the distortions attributable to market imperfections. Leibenstein's claim that welfare losses due to such slack in the system are far greater than the losses resulting from the misallocation inherent in imperfect markets has been disputed; however it is not the significance but the logic of the argument that is at issue here. The presence of slack must be a result of choice; and one of the principles of economic purity is that one must never second-guess the decision-maker. Therefore if slack exists it must be presumed to be someone's preferred state, and its elimination must involve moving someone out of his preferred state. Nor can one explain all existing slack – though one can explain some – as the product of an optimal balance between the costs and benefits of removing it. There is no more logical justification for excluding slack from the welfare ideal than for excluding leisure. It can only be done by ruling that certain preferences are illegitimate.

These daunting consequences of admitting more complex managerial motivations are powerful reasons for keeping hold of the familiar nurse of profit maximisation. There are also good reasons for doing so on grounds of its sufficiency. No one has yet proposed a managerial objective function which does not entail the use of profit either as a component or as a constraint: any other element may be left out of some formulation or other, but never profit. Why not therefore concentrate on the one common factor? Profit also has the great advantage of being in the same dimensions as the prices of inputs and output; and the requirement that it be maximised allows us to formulate an optimisation problem, which on the basis of much experience, embodied in both historical and external standards, promises to make possible the use of techniques known to be fruitful. No precise results are expected: economists rarely mark any scale on their expository diagrams.

The use of such a model does not imply any belief in a firm's desire or ability to maximise profits. It is an indication – not an infallible indication, as Williamson's analysis demonstrates – of the kind of thing that is likely to happen. It is a very quick and simple (once one has been trained) way of obtaining a first approximation. It is when economists act as if it were the last word, rather than the first, that objection should be taken.

So far, the discussion has remained entirely consistent with general choice theory; that it should call into question the standard equilibrium analysis serves to demonstrate that general choice theory is not an adequate basis for that analysis. Even the assumption of perfect knowledge has hitherto been maintained. It is now time to remove it.

Partial ignorance: decomposition of objectives

One of the consequences of partial ignorance is the decomposition of simple objectives. Thus, even if one wishes to maximise profits, if one is not clear about the relevant demand or cost functions one may be driven to make use of separate, though related, targets for revenue and costs. General choice theory is enough to sanction the idea of a well-integrated set of preferences; it is the inadequacy, in conditions of highly imperfect knowledge, of any such well-integrated set that justifies the use of a loosely-related group of objectives, even if none of them is itself a direct object of preference.

It should be emphasised that Cyert and March's (1963) treatment of objectives is not of this kind. The objectives they propose, for profit, sales volume, market share, stock levels, and volume and stability of production, emerge from a discussion on the stabilisation of a management coalition, to which they contribute in some imperfectly-defined way. We are not yet ready to discuss the need for coalitions. If, however, we turn to Drucker (1955) or to Ansoff (1965), we find reasons for specifying a set of objectives which have nothing to do with the maintenance of coalitions, and everything to do with the inadequacy of knowledge. Both authors are interested in the prosperity of the business, and their sets of objectives are explicitly justified on that basis. Thus, for example, Drucker (1955, p. 60) declares that every business needs targets in every key area, and lists the following eight: 'market standing; innovation; productivity; physical and financial resources; profitability; manager performance and development: worker performance and attitude; public responsibility'.

Drucker's reasons why such a set is necessary emerge from his discussion of the inadequacy of a single profit target.

...the search for the one right objective...is certain to do harm and to misdirect.

To emphasise only profit, for instance, misdirects managers to the point where they may endanger the survival of the business. To obtain profit today they tend to undermine the future. They may push the most easily saleable product lines and slight those that are the market of tomorrow. They tend to short-change research, promotion and the other postponable investments. Above all, they shy away from any capital expenditure that may increase the invested-capital base against which profits are measured; and the result is dangerous obsolescence of equipment. In other words, they are directed into the worst practices of management (p. 59).

Now theorists may object that the behaviour condemned by Drucker is not profit maximisation. But Drucker's point is that in the practical business situation, any definition of profit maximisation must be arbitrary, and dangerously insufficient. It is because one cannot specify with confidence any single criterion for all decisions that multiple objectives are needed. 'Objectives are needed in every area where performance and results directly and vitally affect the survival and prosperity of the buisness' (p. 59). Perhaps we should add to that sentence of Drucker's the phrase 'but in ways that cannot be precisely defined'.

Ansoff is quite explicit that the justification for his system of objectives – indeed, the reason why corporate strategy exists as an area for either theory or practice – is partial ignorance. In general, the longer the time horizon, the greater that ignorance is likely to be, the more doubtful is the accuracy of quantitative measurements, and therefore the more dubious becomes the attempt to maximise anything. 'A way round this obstacle is to abandon efforts to measure long-term profitability directly and to measure, instead, characteristics of the firm which contribute to it' (p. 50).

The implicit assumption in this policy is that we know what contributes to long-term profitability, even if we don't know how it contributes. The earlier discussions on reference standards, and the examples cited, suggest that the factors contributing to long-run profitability are not always easy to identify in a practical way. Take, for instance, Ansoff's best-known concept: synergy. It may be easy to agree that developments which exploit synergy from existing activities are likely to be more profitable than those which do not: but what developments are synergistic? Had they been able to study *Corporate Strategy* beforehand, Briggs might well have argued that their bathtub project enabled them to exploit very powerful technological and production synergies.

Partial ignorance: satisficing standards

The consequences of partial ignorance extend beyond the types of objective that are used; they also affect the way in which they are defined. Objectives are maintained as a disjoint set, not because they are independent, but because we do not know how to specify their interdependencies. Optimisation of the components of an objective function must be suboptimisation, for local optimisation is only optimal in a perfectly competitive equilibrium. In conditions of partial ignorance the establishment of a set of target levels may well be better than the attempt to optimise any sub-objective. The attempt to achieve target levels is what Simon calls satisficing behaviour; and satisficing may be the way to optimise.

However, the question may be approached at another level. One may argue that our ignorance of the future, and the extent to which our bounded rationality forces us to decompose systems in misleading ways and artificially to restrict our agendas, means that we have no means of identifying an overall optimum even if we could find one. The system optima of economics are defined only in relation to conditions which we know cannot exist. Profit maximisation has no unequivocal meaning outside the economists' model. Thus, whenever we use an optimising model – and it is very often convenient to do so – we must rely on some judgement of what is good enough. There is no alternative. If, for example, we choose to make our investment decisions on the basis of an

optimised investment portfolio model, rather than by reference to
some target criteria, we are merely substituting for the question
'how good does the prospective return have to be?' the question
'how good does the specification of the model have to be?'

The use of an optimising model may be the chosen way to
satisfice. Of course the satisficing levels are not uniquely set, as an
optimum may be uniquely defined – but only within the framework imposed by the model used. That may be unfortunate, but
it cannot be helped. If reference standards are avoided inside our
models they must then logically be applied to the quality of the
models themselves. We have already considered the question:
by what criteria should one judge the claims of the supporters of
general equilibrium theory? We have suggested that this is a
question amenable to reasoned debate, but not to be settled by
reference to the optimising content of that theory, or by assertions
about its optimal nature.

Individual rationality

Though the discussion has been in terms of organisational problems, none of the arguments in this chapter so far have turned on
the particular character of an organisation as a structured group
of people. Where the word 'managers' has been used, the singular
could be substituted for the plural without changing the sense.
Partial ignorance and bounded rationality cause each of us to
maintain a poorly-integrated and incomplete list of objectives,
mainly expressed in terms of target levels. We have been talking
about general choice behaviour.

We have not even made use so far of the concept of the salaried
manager. There is no general reason why the owner-manager
should not sacrifice profit for other objectives; nor why he should
be endowed with a fully-specified objective function. Although
the features hitherto discussed are of particular interest when they
occur in organisations run by a number of managers none of
whom has a substantial shareholding, it is important to establish
that they do not logically depend on such an organisational setting. They are consequences of complexity and ignorance.

Boulding (1966, pp. 165–6) reaches similar conclusions by
another route.

Even though ethical theory does not come out with any single formula for relating subordinate goals to ultimate goals, it can state with a high degree of certainty that given the complexity of the human organism, no single value index can ever serve without question as a measure of the ultimate goal. . .

The quantification of value functions into value indices, whether this is money or whether it is more subtle and complicated measures of payoff, introduces elements of ethical danger into the decision-making process, simply because the clarity and apparent objectivity of quantitatively measurable subordinate goals can easily lead to a failure to bear in mind that they are in fact subordinate. The development of accounting is an interesting case in point. . .With the development of accounting, the measurement of profit became much more exact, but as a result also, certain other elements of the total value situation became less prominent and, therefore, neglected, such things for instance as morale, loyalty, legitimacy, and intimacy and complexity of personal relations.

In this passage Boulding is reminding us both that concentration on profitability is liable, as Drucker has emphasised, to undermine true long-run profitability and also that profit is itself a very narrow objective in terms of human potentialities and of human satisfaction. If the economic system cannot enforce a narrow concern with profit, there is no need for the analyst to do so. Indeed, in specifying any single objective, the economic logician is exceeding his brief. As Shackle (1972, p. 135) points out, 'In circumstances sufficiently known, reason may tell what action will lead to what end. But reason will not tell *what end ought to be chosen.*' That rationality can only concern itself with means, not ends, is a principle long established; it implies that the specification of objectives in a logical system must depend on their contribution to some further objective. Only subobjectives can be defended by logic alone; and as Miller and Starr (1967), like Boulding, have argued, rational decision-making in a complex and uncertain environment requires multiple subobjectives. In such an environment it is, paradoxically, the desire to maintain coherence of action in response to a stream of events that dissuades us from reliance on a superficially coherent objective function.

By postulating the existence of a preference ordering defined over an extensive commodity space (or, nowadays, over commodity attributes), but making no attempt to characterise the contents of that space, consumer theory manages to avoid this problem, at the cost of complete agnosticism (not to say amorality) about the contents of the resulting equilibrium. Production theory will not work without something more precise; but the standard choice of profit maximisation cannot be defended on any grounds of logic, and certainly not by claims of consistency with consumer theory, but only by arguments of practical convenience. Those are strong arguments; and it is a great pity that general equilibrium theorists seem so often to confuse the requirements of practical convenience with those of formal rigour.

Objectives, inducements and authority

It has been shown that there is no need to invoke a multiplicity of decision-makers in order to justify abandoning the notion of a unified objective function; complexity and ignorance are quite enough. But their effects in loosening the relationship between objectives will obviously be reinforced if each objective becomes the specific responsibility of one or two individuals. The consequential problems of delegation and control will be considered in the following chapter. But the substitution of a group of managers for a single decision-maker not only compounds the difficulties of integrating any given set of organisational objectives; it extends the set.

That an extension is, in general, logically entailed by such a substitution is most clearly seen by examining the circumstances in which it is least likely: a strict managerial hierarchy, in which formal authority, including the power of appointment and dismissal, is vested in a single individual, whom we may call the managing director. This managing director may be the controlling, or even the sole, shareholder; the question of ownership is irrelevant to the general argument that follows. The traditional economic assumption in this situation is that the appointed managers act simply as agents of the managing director; if their actions differ at all from those of a sole entrepreneur, the cause must lie in difficulties of communication. If knowledge is perfect, then there are not even communication problems, and the size and complexity of a firm have no effect on its behaviour. This was a familiar line of argument in the nineteen-thirties, when

economists were concerned with the theoretical relationships between size and efficiency, and could find no limits to size in circumstances which provided no problems for managers to solve.

The assumption that in a complex organisation only the objectives of the managing director are relevant to organisational
decisions is defended by two arguments. First, the market enforces
profit maximisation on all firms, and therefore excludes all objectives within a firm which are not strictly subordinate to this,
and second, acceptance of the firm's objectives is included in the
labour services which the managing director buys. In countering
these arguments there is no need to invoke market imperfection;
the latter, as much as the former, requires very specific restrictions
on the content of individual preference functions. That such
restrictions are necessary to produce a profit-maximising entrepreneur has been demonstrated already. But in an unconstrained
preference set, the salaried manager, like the entrepreneur, may
obtain satisfaction not only from the proceeds of work, but also
in the process of work. Thus the organisation's objectives enter
into the supply price of labour. Instead of hiring managers to
carry out a predetermined policy, a firm may have to formulate
a policy that will succeed in attracting managers. The argument
applies also to other kinds of labour: it has been suggested,
for example, that a programme of basic research is a necessary
cost of obtaining top-class applied scientists, because they are
unwilling to work for an organisation with no commitment to
pure science.

Once again, conclusions derived from general choice considerations are reinforced by the effects of partial ignorance. The
likelihood that objectives may have to be used as inducements
is increased by the fact that the firm, by its nature, relies on
incompletely-specified contracts. The manager's activities within
the firm are subject to some discretion, on his part as well as by
his employers, and compatibility of objectives is one of the inducements to exercise this discretion in the firm's favour.

This concern with objectives as an instrument of organisational
cohesion has emerged quite strongly in recent writings on organisation. The older, simpler, view regarded organisational cohesion
as a problem of authority. Acceptance of authority was partly a
matter of convention, partly a matter of clear lines of command,

and partly a matter of report, sanctions, and incentives. None of these is sufficient to ensure conformity.

Authority implies a monopoly (within defined limits) of the right to decide; its antithesis is complete independence, like perfect competition. But though perfect competition may be defined in terms of perfectly elastic demand, completely inelastic demand is not acceptable as a definition of perfect monopoly. Nor is there any unique relationship between the share of a market held by a single firm and its ability to control price. There is no simple correlation between monopoly status and monopoly power. That power depends, in the short run, on the alternatives open to customers, and, in the long run, on the possible consequences (such as the emergence of a new competitor, the organisation of countervailing power, or restrictive legislation) of too free an exercise of the power which the monopolist apparently possesses.

Similarly, although complete independence implies complete absence of control, there is no degree of authority which confers absolute power. Even when there is no possibility of escape from a superior's jurisdiction, there are alternatives to full obedience, let alone to full co-operation; and in the long run, too ruthless an exercise of nominal authority may encourage the emergence of a more benevolent rival, the organisation of subordinates' unions, or even revolt.

The existence of some limits to authority has long been recognised; the Czarist system of government in nineteenth-century Russia was once described by a contemporary as 'absolutism moderated by assassination'. Barnard (1938, p. 163) transformed the concept by insisting that authority could not be imposed: 'the decision as to whether an order has authority or not lies with the persons to whom it is addressed, and does not reside in "persons of authority" or those who issue these orders'. The need to secure acceptance has been emphasised by the buoyant demand for managerial services in recent years, and has been a central theme in a number of studies of motivation and behaviour in organisations. Probably the most influential, as it is the most readable, of these studies is McGregor's *The Human Side of Enterprise* (1960), which argues the case for improving managerial effectiveness by a deliberate attempt to use the organisation to satisfy some managerial goals. Underlying this argument, and later variants, is the idea, popularly associated with such psychologists as Maslow (1954) and Herzberg (1968), that among the important human needs and motivations are some, like the need for satisfaction from a job well done, and acknowledged by one's peers or superiors to be well done, which can most easily, and sometimes perhaps can only, be met within an organisation.

To anyone trained as an economist, an obvious limitation of this social psychological approach is that its adherents are so concerned with an organisation's need to provide satisfactions to its members that they pay little attention to its need to satisfy its customers. But since non-Marxist economists have made it a point, not merely of principle, but even of virtue, to treat producers' preferences as illegitimate, even in what purports to be a general theory of choice, they are in no position to be very critical of this new emphasis among analysts of organisational behaviour, which indeed developed as a reaction to the consumer-dominated school of 'scientific management'.

However, a more rounded view is provided by Barnard's (1938) suggestion that customers, employees (of all grades), suppliers, and shareholders should all be regarded as contributors to the success of the enterprise, and that sufficient inducements must be offered to each category to elicit the contributions which only each can provide. Cyert and March (1963, p. 30) have similarly argued that 'ultimately it makes only slightly more sense to say that the goal of a business organization is to maximize profit than to say that its goal is to maximize the salary of Sam Smith, Assistant to the Janitor.' There is no reason why, in a complex and uncertain world in which the interrelationships between objectives are not clear, the objectives of the organisation should be regarded as free from influence by any of these categories.

Conclusion

That firms attempt to maximise profit is a very special, though often convenient, assumption. General choice considerations are sufficient to establish that, even within the analytic world of perfect rationality and perfect knowledge, a complex preference function is as reasonable for a firm as for an individual. This is true even of a one-man business; in a multi-person firm, however hierarchical, the preferences of all its members are, in principle, relevant. Thus complex organisations exhibit the characteristic problems of group preference orderings.

The logical consequences of partial ignorance are first, to introduce subordinate objectives into the preference set, second, to replace the well-defined function with a cluster of loosely-related objectives, and third, to substitute satisficing criteria (even if cast in optimising form) for optimisation. The second consequence imports the problems of group preference even into the individual's situation. Thus the next question to require attention is that of organisational cohesion. Before turning to that question, however, it is worth observing that none of the issues discussed has turned on the structure of ownership. Indeed, as the following chapter will confirm, for the analysis of organisational behaviour the separation of ownership from control has no qualitative consequences whatever.

8

Organisational structure and behaviour

> Things get done because people want them to be done,
> and in the last resort the success of industry depends on
> its members being willing to contribute beyond the limits
> of what might reasonably be expected of them on occa-
> sions when the situation demands it.
>
> C. W. Suckling

Economics and organisation theory

Complex problems must be simplified: agendas must be restricted,
the set of control variables curtailed, and questionable procedures
imposed. The sufficiency of such abstractions cannot be guaranteed, yet they can hardly be designed afresh for every occasion.
Similar abstractions are likely to be used for problems which are
deemed similar; and definitions of similarity are often provided
for us. Each academic discipline imposes its own categories on the
phenomena which it claims to investigate, through a process
which is neither consciously controlled nor well understood by
historians or philosophers of science. Organisation theorists, on
the other hand, seek to discover the principles of abstraction for
organisational problem-solving. So, in a very important sense, do
economists. Both groups are concerned with similar issues: the
allocation of problem areas among decision-makers, in ways that
avoid or mitigate discordant decisions; information requirements
and information channels; and the effects of incentives on behaviour. That these topics are common to both should not be surprising, since formal organisations and a competitive market are
alternative systems of resource allocation.

Economics, it might be said, is the organisation theory of the
economy. Most economists would no doubt dismiss any suggestion
that the present condition of organisation theory bears comparison
with the tightly-argued conclusions of formal economic analysis
and the well-documented correlations of econometrics. Economics,

after all, claims to have solved the problems of designing an economy – in principle. Pareto optimality is a universal criterion, and perfect competition (in the absence of externalities) ensures Pareto optimality. To be sure, the resulting distribution of welfare may be judged far from ideal, but any deficiencies on this score are properly attributable to an unsatisfactory pattern of initial endowments among the members of the economy, and therefore properly corrected by revising this pattern – admittedly a non-trivial operation; as a mechanism for the efficient allocation of the resources provided, perfect competition is unassailable. But the apparent superiority of these grand abstractions is founded on illusion. Both the Pareto criterion and the perfectly competitive design apply to fictional systems; economists have evaded the problems of complexity and ignorance.

One important reason for the apparent inferiority of organisation theory is that it tackles more fundamental issues. The need for such a theory rests on the limitations of human capacities for receiving and processing information; complex problems have to be shared because it is impossible for any one person to handle them adequately. Despite the overwhelming theoretical emphasis on the working of a disaggregated market, it is not at all clear why in economic equilibrium one person should not decide everything, since in equilibrium there is nothing to decide.

Organisational design is an option of difficulties which contemporary economics scorns. It is necessary to decompose a system which is only partly decomposable, and by so doing to define, explicitly or implicitly, the set of externalities deemed to be relevant at every level in the system. The formal hierarchy is a device for internalising the externalities between a specific group of people by bringing these externalities within the remit of a common superior. Given the limited capacity of the human brain (even computer-aided), including its speed of operation, this is also a device for ignoring all other externalities.

For economists, life is much simpler. Factors and commodities (or perhaps, nowadays, product characteristics) occur as quite distinct natural families; and a complete and unambiguous list of these families is provided at the outset, perhaps by our beneficent auctioneer. This listing is treated as a trivial problem of classification. Moreover, this is the only problem of classification.

Since it identifies only two levels of analysis, the individual and the economy, general equilibrium theory has no need to collect families into groups; neither industries nor product categories such as food and clothing have any role in such theory. Nor can there be any question of selecting relevant externalities for internalisation at intermediate levels. All externalities are external to the individual and internal to the economy; it is all or nothing.

This simple classification system has the enormous advantage of eliminating all problems of aggregation, and is just one among many examples of the skill of economic theorists in so defining their models that the really difficult issues never appear on the agenda. But though this greatly facilitates the construction of logically watertight theories, it seriously inhibits their useful application. The problems of aggregation are very awkward, and cannot be evaded in many practical situations. Precisely because general equilibrium theory has been so successful in evading them, it can offer no help whatever in their solution. General equilibrium theory keeps itself unspotted from the world; but it can do so only by living as a hermit.

Thus, in a fundamental sense, the general equilibrium theorist is not concerned with the organisation of the economic system, but only with the working of a system which has been designed by someone else. The creation of products, the creation of skills, the creation of markets, all are excluded from his vision. Of course, products hitherto not produced may begin to be manufactured, skills hitherto unused may be called into service, markets hitherto deserted may become populated; but those products, skills, and markets must all have been included in the grand list, and have been known to be included in the grand list, before operations began. The economic theorist studies the rules of the game; the organisation theorist begins by designing the game. The system of the economist is sterile; no act of creation can be tolerated. No wonder the entrepreneur leads such a dispirited existence in the economics textbooks.

Organisation structure

Four principal criteria for structuring organisations may be observed. The original criterion was functional expertise: similar activities, such as production, marketing, finance, personnel, and so on, should be grouped together. This is the principle of organisation by factor input, assumed in all standard theories of the firm. The first major alternative to emerge was a structure by product: where the interdependencies between, say, the production and marketing of paints are more significant than the common expertise between the production of paints and the production of explosives, then paint rather than production or marketing defines the sphere of joint activities. The product division system represents a reversion to the assumed organisational principle of the market. The third basis of organisation is by process or stage of production, and the fourth by geographical area; each may be considered a special case of the second.

Many organisations use more than one basis; and within the nationalised fuel and power industries in Britain, all four may be simply demonstrated. The allocation of responsibility between the nationalised industries in this sector is clearly by product; within electricity supply the division between generating board and area boards is by stage of process; the area boards themselves are regional organisations, geographically structured; and at district level they employ functional officers. The use of different bases at different levels clearly complicates the channels of communication; but the organisations concerned presumably prefer those difficulties to the alternative difficulties implicit in some other structure.

A tightly defined structure not only determines where an organisation's problems are worked on, but also helps to determine what problems they shall be, how they are defined, and what solutions will be attempted. By defining the responsibility of a person or a group, it prescribes the agenda deemed to be appropriate, specifies the decision variables, and establishes a learning programme. As was observed in Chapter 5, each part of an organisation is a kind of experimental design, sampling certain kinds of experience: its members will usually act as if the sample was properly drawn, although almost certainly no one will have given any attention to that point. Procedures may be laid down; if not they will grow up; and information about the world, and about other parts of the organisation, will be shut out. Such a structure reduces the information content of problems to a level which the decision-making units can handle; it resists the intrusion of ideas. Much of the operating success of an organisation depends on its ability to decide cheaply, and that usually means keeping agendas narrow, variables few, and decision processes highly programmed; so highly programmed, in fact, that choice virtually disappears from many decisions.

Organisations of this kind may be very successful; but the source of their success makes them crisis-prone. Their range of sufficiency is likely to be very small. Different problems, even within the same department, may require agendas which differ not merely in width but also in content, and it is not clear that the set of problems faced by an organisation over a reasonable period of time can be adequately mapped on to any single highly-specified structure. As Ansoff and Brandenburg (1971, pp. 709–711) point out, even the effective management of timely changes in output levels may exceed the scope of the abstractions which are most efficient for stable outputs. Innovations, whether of activity or organisational form, may be fatal to operating abstractions – and operating abstractions may be fatal to innovation, as was shown in Chapter 5.

The questions thus raised cannot even be posed in the language of general equilibrium theory; for such theory not only requires all problems to be properly defined, but requires them all to be specified at the outset. There is no place for the unexpected. But they are precisely the questions which arise naturally from the analysis of the firm presented in Chapter 4. The firm exists because it is impossible to specify all actions, even contingent actions, in advance; it embodies a very different policy of adaptation to emergent events. Incomplete specification is its essential basis: for complete specifications can be handled by the market. Thus one would expect very tight formal structures to be seriously insufficient.

On the other hand, the firm must justify its existence by economising in decision costs; and so, although its decision processes must be imperfectly specified, they must not be left completely unspecified. Some structure is essential. The concept of an 'organic system of management', introduced by Burns and Stalker (1961) on the basis of a survey of firms attempting to innovate, probably represents the minimum of specification. An organic system seeks to facilitate the consideration of relevant interdependencies problem by problem, by offering direct access between any two or more parts of the organisation; the types of abstraction to be used, instead of being decided in advance, are left entirely for definition by the changing needs of the situation.

Since organisation theorists need some kind of structure to make analysis possible, it is not surprising that the 'do-it-yourself' implications of the organic system have been resisted, and that more recent writers on innovative management have tended to advocate a greater degree of conscious design. Lawrence and Lorsch (1967, p. 212), for example, call for 'the intelligent tailoring of organizations to their task and environments', while Ansoff and Brandenburg (1971) offer a cluster of adaptive and innovative forms.

Because they must cope with complexity and ignorance, both practising managers and organisation theorists must tolerate ambiguity. Not all of the apparent duplication, waste, and confusion is avoidable. Though they must endeavour to impose some structure and achieve some definition, yet they must remember that in organisational design, it is pre-eminently true that precision implies error. Indeed it is precisely the precision claimed for general equilibrium theory which invalidates it as a model for organisational design. For economists of a more Marshallian persuasion, however, there is a basis for co-operation. The imperfectly-specified contract which characterises the firm implies an imperfectly-specified structure, the central concern and dilemma of organisation theory. Moreover, the concept provides a link between organisation theory and the economic study of industrial organisation; for Richardson (1972) has drawn our attention to the obvious but neglected fact that the relations between firms may be imperfectly specified too. The attempt to decompose an industry into a well-defined structure of decision-making units may be no more successful than the attempt to decompose the decision-making system of a firm.

Delegation: determinism or discretion

The decomposition of decision-making within a firm is often discussed under the heading of delegation. Delegation may occur for either of two contradictory reasons. Well-defined structures may encourage extensive delegation, in the belief that choices will be exercised within narrow limits, and that even the worst choice can do little harm. If this confidence is shaken, some of the delegated authority is likely to be withdrawn; and if the superior feels the situation changing, then he may withdraw it before he is disturbed by any decision of his subordinates. Delegation of decision-making implies some commitment to the actions of those to whom a decision is delegated; like other forms of commitment, delegation is limited by uncertainty. Thus senior management may exercise unusually detailed control when unusual decisions have to be taken, or when familiar decisions are surrounded by unfamiliar circumstances. Persistent uncertainty, amounting to ignorance, will tend to impede delegation so effectively as to keep organisations small.

That delegation is nothing more than a convenient way of programming decisions is clearly implied by standard economic theory. Decentralisation (to a market system) is approved only if the local decision-makers can be guaranteed to act as would the central decision-maker, or welfare economist. Perfect competition allows decisions to be safely delegated precisely because the decision-makers have no freedom of choice. If, because of imperfections or externalities, decentralised decisions would not conform to the overall plan, no delegation is permitted. Richardson's (1960) demonstration that the information structure of perfect competition is strictly incapable of prescribing choice has been determinedly ignored; but its acceptance would entail the abandonment of delegation in any circumstances. For optimality in economics is judged from the centre; the omniscient economist always knows best. Thus only the illusion of choice can be tolerated; general equilibrium theory is fundamentally authoritarian.

But in a complex and changing environment, large organisations, if they are to prosper, may have to reject determinism in favour of free will. Delegation may be used, not to programme choice, but to encourage initiative. Amid the uncertainties and chances of war, the initiative, or lack of it, shown by subordinate commanders has often proved decisive. Nelson both demonstrated much initiative as a subordinate and fostered it as a commander; and Slim (1956), rating as 'one of my most helpful generals'

(p. 311) the Japanese commander at Kohima who missed a great opportunity by conforming strictly to his orders, praised his own subordinates for their ability 'to act swiftly to take advantage of sudden information or changing circumstances without reference to their superiors' (p. 542). Such actions were, of course, within the overall scheme; but in industrial situations even the overall scheme may not be immutable. In an attempt to inhibit the subtle censorship of current ideas, a Research Director in a large organisation told his scientists that 'the objective of the Research Department is to change the corporate strategy'.

Organisational cohesion

Whether considered as a pattern of delegation or as a structured set of problems, organisational design exhibits this essential feature: if a complex organisation is to cope successfully with uncertainty and change, its decision-making systems must remain incompletely specified. That, as a matter of logic as well as design, its set of objectives must also be incompletely specified was the conclusion of the preceding chapter. If objectives and structure are both imperfectly specified, what can be said about the integration of an organisation's activities?

Let us then examine the logic of organisational cohesion. Even if a manager were to identify completely with a fully-specified organisational preference set, it would not be rational for him to use this set for his decision criterion without some direct incentive to do so. For these organisational preferences would be collective goods, to the achievement of which his own actions – unless he is one of a small number of senior managers – could contribute little. The general principle applies: what must be freely available to members of a large group, if it is to be available at all, will not be individually sought. A common purpose may be a useful fiction for cementing the organisational coalition; but it must be a non-operational goal. Organisational performance depends on joint purposes.

Thus incentives must be linked to subobjectives if they are to prove effective. That in itself is enough to rule out the possibility of a perfect incentive system. But when we take into account the likelihood that managerial preferences will include some of the performance-satisfactions discussed by Maslow (1954) and Herzberg (1968), the difficulties increase. The maintenance of organisational cohesion is the function of a management control system: by measuring a manager's performance in terms of his contribution to overall objectives, and motivating him to improve the performance so monitored, formal methods of control are intended to ensure the effective jointness of managerial and organisational objectives.

But the control system does not simply prescribe the rules; it is part of the game. The type of control system used may become a vital influence on the decision whether to join an organisation, and on the quality of performance as a member. On the one hand, the absence of tight control may make it easier to accept membership of a group among whose members one suspects are some with rather different preferences: tight control may specify a contract in ways which make it unacceptable. That is why party discipline is such a critical issue for the British Labour Party, which is a very diverse coalition. On the other hand, the freedom to exercise discretion within fairly generous limits may be a major component of the manager's preference set. But if this freedom is to be used as an inducement to join the organisation, then the manager is being offered, not merely a chance to join in the formulation of the organisation's objectives, but the right, within limits, to pursue his own objectives when making decisions as an employee. Thus the attempt to align individual and organisational objectives through a formal control system may actually impede managerial performance.

Even if the offer of managerial discretion is not used as an inducement, some discretion is inevitable in the absence of perfect knowledge. This discretion may arise from three causes. First, the degree of ignorance about possible future states, and of the impact of a particular decision on future results, may make it difficult to assess the correctness of the choice made. If, for example, that choice is made according to the precepts of decision theory, then assessment of the decision becomes assessment of the subjective probabilities used; and even after the event, this is not easy. To falsify a probability estimate it is necessary to demonstrate not merely repeated but reproducible deviations from predictions based on that estimate: otherwise it is not possible to say that the assessment was wrong without introducing fresh assumptions. The more infrequent the type of decision – and the most important decisions are among the most infrequent – the greater the difficulty.

Second, it is almost impossible to review a decision made by a specialist – and still more impossible to review a decision made by a group of specialists – without having the decision made afresh by another specialist or group of specialists: and this, besides being expensive in scarce resources, is liable to reduce the quality of specialist available for such decisions. Knowledge workers must have discretion by reason of the very knowledge for which they are employed, and authority, in the sense of having one's word accepted without question, can flow upwards as well as down.

Third, subordinates have a good deal of control over the information which their superiors use, including the information by which they are judged. This applies both to the setting of standards, as Pounds (1969) pointed out, and also to the provision of information to which those standards are to be applied. Neither the target nor the performance recorded in a control system necessarily represents reality; on the contrary, all formal control systems may be expected to generate misinformation.

Thus managers often have a freedom of choice which is not merely nominal. Organisational objectives, in so far as they are explicit and operational, may specify the limits, but they do not determine the choice. The extent of the remaining freedom may be obscured by the use of the word 'judgement', often used as a label to cover our ignorance of what is actually happening. Managerial judgement does not consist solely of estimates of probabilities and approximate calculations, nor even of setting appropriate bounds to the agenda and the number of decision variables. It also includes the selection of the criteria by which a choice should be made; and even when the aim, for example, of increasing market share, is prescribed, the actual tests to be applied to specific proposals are still likely to be subject to substantial discretion.

Firms as coalitions

If the classical organisation theorists' prescription of delegation and control cannot be relied upon to achieve integration, neither can the collaborative methods advocated by members of the human relations school. McGregor (1960), for example, appears to suggest that a set of organisational objectives should emerge as a kind of consensus from the involvement of managers in the process of objective setting, and this notion, together with similar ideas put forward by Drucker (1955, Chapter 11), can be seen, sometimes in a degenerate form, in the practice of management by objectives.

But full consensus is hard to achieve, and hard to maintain. It is not easy to imagine how any complex organisation could endure on that basis. Fortunately, partial ignorance and bounded rationality come to our aid; for it is no easier to recognise the existence – or absence – of a consensus than of an optimum. Full consensus on objectives is not necessary to keep an organisation together; nor is it necessary to effective decision-making. The problem of integration need not be completely resolved. Even the individual need not fully reconcile his internal conflicts, since neither the interdependencies between the components of his preference function nor the interdependencies in the complex situation to which it is to be applied can be fully understood, or properly taken into account even if they were. Schizophrenia is indeed a problem, but moderate inconsistency is not. If this is true of the individual, then surely it must be true in the greater complexity and amid the additional obscurities of decision-making within an organisation.

These beneficial obstacles to possibly destructive rationality form the basis for Cyert and March's (1963) bold attack on the problem of organisational goals. In effect, they extend Coase's notion of the firm as a set of incompletely-specified contracts by viewing it as a coalition on imperfectly-specified terms. They go further by explaining how the coalition may be preserved through the avoidance (conscious or unconscious) of full specification. By thus neatly avoiding all the formidable difficulties associated with group preference functions, they liberate economists from their virtual confinement to the analysis of groups with identical pre-ference pre-orderings, technically dubbed teams. If organisations exist to combine a variety of skills, and if satisfaction arising directly from the participant's specific role is to be included in his preference set, then such very special groups are unlikely to provide a very effective basis for organisational success.

Moreover, to restrict analysis to such groups excludes most of the significant features of organisational behaviour: if all members of a community had identical preferences, the analysis of economic systems would be rather uninteresting. Economic systems, like the American Constitution in the view of Supreme Court Judge Holmes, are made for people of fundamentally differing views. Formal organisations do not readily accommodate fundamental diversity, but the accommodation of substantial diversity is an essential part of their activity. In coalition-building, as in marketing, the essential question is: what are the benefits to whom? Indeed, the formation and maintenance of an organisational coalition is a marketing task, just as establishing distribution channels and winning customers is coalition-building. Thus the factors of partial ignorance and bounded rationality, which are so destructive to traditional analysis of individual choice, are the very factors which make organisational analysis possible.

Cohesion is obviously more likely if all potentially conflicting demands can be satisfied simultaneously; and this may be possible if organisational slack is present. The use of organisational slack is usually regarded by commentators as simply a distribution of excess profits derived from market imperfections, which is not a topic of much interest among economists. But the concept was put forward by Cyert and March (1963, p. 36) as a consequence, not of monopoly, but of partial ignorance. Potentially conflicting claims may all be satisfied, not – or, rather, not necessarily – because there are excess profits to share out, but because the demands of coalition members are moderated by their failure to appreciate the full value of alternative opportunities. To discover alternatives requires search: and the costs of search tend to give the existing organisation a protective margin. This phenomenon would be called exploitation in a perfect information model – but it is a phenomenon of imperfect information. Search must be stimulated by the awareness of a problem; but in some instances it is only by search that the information necessary to stimulate it could be revealed. Thus the coalition is preserved, and protected from those external changes which simply affect the amount of slack available. Slack permits the effective decomposition of the system: thus it stabilises both the form of the coalition and its policies.

However, there is a potentially-dangerous consequence, which Cyert and March do not recognise. The firm is partially insulated from changes in the facts, but much more vulnerable to changes in expectations. If, for whatever reason – and there are many possible reasons – external references set a new level of expectations, or a different and more demanding set of standards are evoked, then an acceptable set of inducements may overnight become unacceptable. In the words of the old song, 'How are you going to keep 'em down on the farm, now that they've seen Paree?'

Another fact which tends to protect the coalition from shocks is the use of non-operational goals. They have a double virtue. First, they provide a set of reference standards which cannot define problems, and second, by occupying some of the limited capacity for ratiocination, they leave less room for standards which might. Political manifestos are rich in non-operational goals, and objectives such as progressive, sound, beneficial, innovatory, co-ordinated, and well-planned, appearing in company documents have very little content. One should not underrate the contribution of non-operational objectives to the success of coalitions. When critical problems must be faced and tackled, meaningful objectives are essential, but in situations where conflict would be damaging but its resolution is not important, a little well-designed obscurity can be very helpful. Such an argument has clearly no place in any model based on the artificial concept of perfect rationality.

The remaining three factors discussed by Cyert and March are all devices for restricting the agenda. The first is sequential attention to goals, which may be used, either between departments, to assure each in turn that it is a centre of interest and assistance, or within a department, to avoid the need to make explicit the exchange rate between departmental subobjectives. This policy may be seen as a direct defiance of the basic principles of operational research; and it may lead to locally-satisfactory decisions which prove disastrous, or to the pathological state of management by drives; but it can also have value in preserving the coalition, as well as facilitating low-cost decision-making and some kind of learning.

A similar advantage, and similar risks, are implicit in the policy of local rationality, which is indeed the equivalent at one point of time of sequential attention to goals. In this respect, the division of an organisation into subunits, usually seen as creating problems of co-ordination, may be seen as a method of avoiding problems, by giving coalition members at least partial custody of their own objectives, and restraining outside interference by keeping incompatibles apart. Particularly where parts of an organisation embodying very different reference standards have no great need to work together, the preservation of organisational distance – which may, or may not, mean physical distance – can avoid many problems at little cost. Once again, however, there is a risk; if, for any reason, such organisational distance is reduced – for example, by a change of policy (such as the introduction of a matrix structure) which entails close co-operation between previously remote parts of an organisation – quite unexpected troubles may result.

The final method discussed by Cyert and March is typified by the use of the company's budget both to stabilise expectations and to concentrate attention on practical matters. Reliance on precedent to the exclusion of disruptive external standards serves a similar purpose. This particular method is important to them because it provides a pragmatic justification for the set of organisational goals which they employ. They use the remaining factors just discussed primarily to explain the stability of the coalition and thus to lend plausibility to their concentration on programmatic response to operating problems. Their object is not to explain how long-run or wide-ranging problems arise, but how they are avoided. In the course of our examination we have tried to suggest how this type of analysis can also be used to explain the emergence of internal dissonance in certain situations. The tendency to emphasise narrow-agenda, limited-variable, highly-programmed decisions, noted in Chapter 5, may have high survival value. But it does leave the organisation open, not only to the risks of major error there noticed, but also to the possibility that a change in the basis of decision-making may undermine the coalition.

This picture of the firm is rather like Keynes' view of long-run expectations; in both cases stability is based on concealing our ignorance by the use of devices which give an illusory appearance of certainty – or at least of well-ordered probability. Within such a formal structure, which relies on the absence of certain kinds of communications, organisational stability, like the stability of the demand for money or for capital investment, is likely to be fairly well insulated from minor shocks, but very vulnerable to major upheavals. Just as awareness of the extent of our ignorance about the future may destroy our willingness to undertake commitments in the commodity markets, so awareness of the extent of the differences between individual objectives within a large organisation, or even serious uncertainty about the extent of those differences, may destroy the willingness of many contributors to continue their contributions.

The stability of a coalition cannot be guaranteed: even a local decision may sometimes offer a chance to modify the implicit terms of an imperfectly-specified contract. Many intra-organisational bargains are no more enforceable than contracts with British trade unions; and since definitions of problems are necessarily imposed on a situation, an opportunity for revision may occur, or be made, at any time. Some of the more intractable problems within an organisation occur when a situation gives rise to very different problem definitions by different parties: when, for example, a simple expedient to solve a local difficulty appears as a threat to established status. In such situations, the hierarchy of objectives may become unclear: status may be important because of the power it gives to influence decisions, but decisions may be important because of their effect on status. In a similar fashion, politicians may wish to win elections in order to determine policy, but may also choose their policy in order to win elections.

However, the analysis of organisational behaviour need not be as confused or as confusing as these comments might suggest. Many problems are handled without regard to their ramifications; many implicit conflicts of objectives are not recognised, or at least not recognised as stimuli to action; even the displacement of objectives which is often cited as an organisational weakness may become an important source of cohesion, as individuals accept the objectives of their jobs as equivalent to their own, even when, on reflection, they could be clearly recognised as different. In dealing with complexity, ignorance can be very helpful.

The decision-maker in the organisation

In arguing that the integration of decisions within an organisation can (indeed, must) be left incomplete, we have necessarily allowed scope for managerial choice. Managerial discretion poses a problem for the behavioural school of economic analysis as well as for the adherents of simpler views based on the optimisation of a well-defined objective function. Contrary to the impression usually given by its advocates, satisficing theory does not, in general, provide unique predictions of organisational behaviour, even for a theorist who presumes to define the search space.

There are four reasons for this. First, although anything more than satisfactory performance may not be required, neither is it necessarily penalised. It may be assumed that managers expect it to be penalised by a rise in the level of future performance deemed satisfactory – a venerable fear; otherwise the preference for other satisfactions must be a personal preference, not deducible from organisational goals. Second, the relevant satisficing goals must be those accepted by the individual; and, as we have seen, these may comprise a different set, as well as goals pitched at different levels, from those attributed to the organisation.

Third, there is no reason why the subset of minimum solutions within the feasible set should contain a single element; satisfactory performance may often be achieved in several ways. Even if we assume that the first satisfactory solution will be that chosen, the answer is not unique unless there is a unique process of sequential search. (Nor indeed is it clear why the first satisfactory solution discovered should be a minimum solution.) What appears to be the obvious solution to someone with a particular pattern of experience may not be at all obvious to another, whose experience has been different. Unique satisficing solutions depend, if not on certainty, at least on well-defined ignorance.

Finally, even if all resources not needed to meet minimum objectives are deliberately directed towards meeting personal goals, the pursuit of these goals may have significant effects on the history of the firm. A research department created solely to satisfy the scientific or status interests of the research director cannot be guaranteed never to produce a commercially valuable idea. Indeed, Cyert and March (1963, p. 279) observe that 'slack provides a source of funds for innovations that would not be approved in the face of scarcity but that have strong subunit support'. This observation, though entirely in accord with their general analysis of organisational behaviour, finds no reflection in their detailed predictive model.

All these difficulties are least obvious in the analysis of short-run decision-making. These are the conditions which may be expected to produce organisational learning and standard solutions. But in the handling of situations which occur infrequently organisational learning will be rudimentary, and there can be few standard solutions.

The pattern of narrow-agenda, closely-specified, programmed decision-making which is the staple of behavioural types of analysis is indeed plausibly represented by such analysis; yet it is also in such circumstances that the more usual optimising types of model are at their best. It is no accident that operational research techniques have proved most successful in formulating decision routines for stable systems. Some of them are strictly confined to such systems: standard methods of optimum stock control, for example, can be highly destabilising in response to substantial changes in demand. But the complications of individual preference and uncertainty are most apparent in studying organisational response to, or searches for, major changes.

Polaris: the preservation of managerial independence

Simon (1969, p. 11) argues that properly-designed systems will be decomposable, and will therefore be governed almost entirely by external factors. But, as we have seen, there is usually no scheme of decomposition which is adequate for a large and complex organisation, or for the solution of a complex problem. Thus 'the behaviour of the system will only partly respond to the task environment; partly, it will respond to the limiting properties of the inner system' (p. 13). Rather than concerning themselves with the design of systems which might be decomposable, economists and organisation theorists might concentrate on the fascinating problems of imperfect decomposition, as has been done by Sapolsky (1972) in a study of the Polaris project.

By the criteria which have been used to assess it, the Polaris programme has been an outstanding success in an area beset by varying degrees of failure. 'The missile was deployed several years ahead of the original. . .schedule. There has been no hint of a cost overrun. As frequent tests indicate, the missile works. The submarine building was completed rapidly. Not surprisingly, the Special Projects Office [which managed the programme] is widely regarded as one of the most effective agencies within government' (p. 11).

The popular assumption has been that this success was achieved by careful planning, and a careful monitoring of progress; and on the basis of this assumption the PERT system (Program Evaluation Review Technique) has been vigorously promoted as a new and remarkably effective method of management control. Plausible advocates of a new technique for dealing with intractable problems always gain a hearing. But a formal control scheme can make only a limited contribution to the effective management of complex and open-ended problems: Sapolsky argues that PERT did indeed make a substantial contribution, but in a very different way from that claimed.

In fact the Polaris programme was neither originated nor effectively controlled by government. The proponents of the project had first to gain acceptance against the scepticism or downright opposition of most of the influential members of the U.S. defence establishment, including most of the top-ranking officers in the Navy, the service which was to operate the Polaris fleet. No doubt in part because of the absence of spontaneous support, the advocates of Polaris were very unwilling to hand over control of the project once it had been accepted as a major programme.

The proponents then had two distinct and only partly complementary subobjectives. First, they wanted to attract a broad base of support for the Polaris both inside and outside the Navy. Second, they wanted to prevent the rest of the Navy and the rest of the government from interfering in the management of the Polaris program. To gain the first subobjective, a unique demand for the F[leet] B[allistic] M[issile] system had to be established; to gain the second, confidence in the unique management abilities of the Special Projects Office had to be established. Both were achieved (pp. 42–3).

The skill in coalition-building by which the original advocates of a submarine-based missile system succeeded in gaining for their own objective a decisive place in the governmental preference set will not be discussed here; but it is a standing warning against the assumption that somehow governments act as impartial and wise interpreters of social preference, or even the more modest proposition that subunit objectives derive from higher-level policy.

The advocates of the Polaris system did indeed believe that their proposals were in the interests of the United States, but their success in mobilising a successful coalition in support of those proposals did not make them willing to concede any decisive share in the management of the programme to other members of the coalition. 'The basic objective of the Polaris proponents was to gain the organizational autonomy required to deploy a force of FBM submarines in the shortest possible time...Given their basic objective, they sought to obtain the resources and authority to control independently the design, construction, and maintenance of the FBM force' (p. 41). In other words, they wished to safeguard their managerial independence. For this purpose, the fellow-members of the coalition became rivals: 'the obstacles to success were the many agencies of government' (p. 42). Governments are not in general known for their ability to entrust projects of this magnitude to groups of people without subjecting them to a continual flow of enquiry and suggestion, if not direction. Having created a unique demand for submarine-based missiles, clearly distinct from all other methods of strategic bombardment, the Polaris group now had to create an image of unique managerial competence.

This independence was achieved and preserved by two principal methods. First, much care was taken not to offend potential critics, and indeed to provide many of them with funds for projects in which they were interested but which (whatever the recipients of the funds may have thought) were most unlikely to limit the freedom of action of the Polaris managers: thus many of those who might have wished to exercise control, or who might have called for the exercise of control by others, were impressed by the performance of the management as it affected them. Second, there was a deliberate (and no doubt sincere) attempt to discover and apply new methods of control within the Special Projects Office. Prominent among these was the PERT system.

However, Sapolsky makes it clear that neither PERT nor any other novelty produced a tight control over the development of the Polaris weapon system. What the methods did achieve was a very large degree of freedom from interference for the project managers. They had to spend rather little of their time explaining and defending detailed decisions, and considering outside suggestions. The value of PERT was not that it provided a means of managing the project, but that, by substantially insulating them from outside pressures, it left the managers free to get on with the job of management.

Rather than ensuring that cost and time schedules were met, PERT gave the management much more freedom to set schedules which could be met. The Polaris management effectively wrote its own project specifications and set its own targets; and it did so to provide continuing freedom of action. The successful marketing of the Polaris idea and of the management skills of the Special Projects Office established a wide area of management discretion. 'Its ability to meet self-generated estimates. . . stems from its own unique advantage – overwhelming and dependable political support. The Special Projects Office and the Polaris contractors provided honest accurate estimates because they could afford to provide honest accurate estimates' (p. 182).

Sapolsky points to the one clear example of an optimistic estimate in the Polaris story to clinch his case: this occurred at precisely the point at which the Polaris proponents were trying to break away (quite justifiably, in retrospect) from a joint Army–Navy programme. At that time support was still being built up, and cheapness was one of the relevant considerations. Later, the demand for Polaris appears to have become price-inelastic over the relevant range; certainly all appropriation requests were granted in full by Congress. Such generous funding facilitated the strategy of supporting projects by potential critics to keep them busy and content.

Polaris: management of the project

The Polaris project not only demonstrates how managers may secure their independence; it also, encouragingly, shows how that independence may contribute to the achievement of overall objectives. Polaris was lucky, as perhaps any large and complex innovation must be lucky if it is to be an outstanding success: when one is exploring the unknown, one cannot guarantee to find what one is seeking no matter how well-organised the search. But the project was well managed. However, it was managed on principles very different from those introduced during the McNamara regime, and which were supposed to be in part based on the Polaris example.

The political element has already been emphasised. The operation of the American Defence Department under McNamara was apparently based on the assumption, eagerly taken up in Britain, that many national issues could be removed from partisan debate and resolved by the clinical application of managerial techniques. The great vogue for cost–benefit analysis was a product of this assumption. But any belief that major issues of national security (or of airport location) can be handled by a pure rational process, which will produce results acceptable to all reasonable men, is a chimera: differences of objective, our limited ability to process information, and the inevitable absence of some of the information – about the future, and about future discoveries – all ensure this result.

The relationship between project management and the contractors was also totally at variance with the McNamara principles of effective management. The Special Projects Office did not use a prime contractor. This was in part because the first scheme accepted was for an additional element in an existing Army development programme, and the Army's prime contractor was not thought suitable to handle the very different project which eventually emerged. It also had the great merit, as far as the managers were concerned, of leaving them in control. But, as Sapolsky makes clear, these people were not technically competent to manage the development. Yet they ran it, and ran it successfully. They ran it because at every critical decision point they possessed more than one source of technical expertise, and also no doubt because of their technical limitations – they could not impose their own technical solutions.

They relied on a system of imperfectly-specified contracts; the specifications were incomplete not only in detail but also with respect to boundaries. This had two effects: first, it provided design alternatives, in a situation where no one could be sure that any particular idea would be the best, or would even work; and second, it encouraged the provision of such alternatives, by holding out the prospect of a larger share of the programme for the progenitors of successful ideas, even outside what might be thought their remit, and the prospect of loss of business to the lethargic or unimaginative. Thus the project managers relied on the processes of competition to achieve what they were not capable of achieving by the use of formal organisational control.

Sapolsky is very critical of the idea that innovatory projects can be treated in a highly programmed way.

Reducing the number of subunits that can generate technical alternatives can reduce the immediate costs of development by reducing the pressures for independent projects, but as it does nothing to reduce the uncertainties of development, it cannot improve the efficiency of the weapons acquisition process. Actually, such a reduction could increase the cumulative costs of development by forcing all allocation decisions to be made with less information than one might otherwise have (p. 204).

The attempt to produce major innovations involves a search process. The imposition of a single formal search structure on this process may prevent the most attractive options from ever appearing in the choice set. Insistence on the original target of a persistent selective weedkiller would have prevented I.C.I. from developing paraquat, which is non-selective and is inactivated by contact with the soil (Bradbury, McCarthy & Suckling, 1972b). One way of encouraging a wider search is to increase the number of search parties working from different bases with different schemes of search. Of course it is wasteful to look in the wrong place; but it is even more wasteful so to restrict the area of search that one fails to look in the right place.

The greater the degree of ignorance, the greater the dangers in using an organisational structure, or a theoretical model, which is based on assumptions, explicit or implicit, of certainty, or at best of uncertainty defined as a complete listing of all the possibilities. A formal organisation structure implies such a complete listing; most formal structures imply a very brief listing. But in most situations of uncertainty, and above all when innovations are being sought, the available lists are far from complete. Thus, as Sapolsky says, 'a disciplined hierarchy seems capable of suppressing precisely the information needed to cope with such uncertainty' (p. 204). Precision leads to error, and formal rigour to a loss of sufficiency. Some imperfection in the specifications is necessary, not only for organisational cohesion, but also for the successful handling of problems.

9

Expectations and employment

Choice is always amongst thoughts, for it is always too
late to choose amongst facts.

G. L. S. Shackle (1972, p. 280)

Expectations and equilibrium

Whenever decision-making is decentralised, within either a market or an administrative system, the compatibility between decentralised decisions and system objectives is inevitably at issue.
As we have seen, economists are much concerned with this question, and are likely to approve of local rationality only if it is
guided by the relevant opportunity costs. The principle of
opportunity cost requires each project to be judged by standards
which are external to it: optimal business decisions require the
use of private opportunity cost, welfare optima the use of social
opportunity cost. Thus the study of market systems, from this
point of view, is a study of the criteria which they provide for
– and, indeed, enforce upon – the decision-maker.

This study, of course, reveals the unique virtues of a system of
perfect markets. Perfect competition in the market for his product ensures that each producer's price is determined by the
market price, and that his marginal revenue is therefore an
exact measure of the value of the corresponding increment of
consumption. Perfect competition in the factor markets ensures
that his factor costs are likewise externally determined, and are
an exact measure of the incremental benefit accruing to the
suppliers of productive services. Perfect competition in all other
markets is also required to guarantee that factor prices also
measure the marginal value product of those factors in their best
alternative use: it is because of its pervasive effects on cost levels
that an element of monopoly anywhere calls into question allocative efficiency throughout the economic system. Finally, perfect competition ensures that only by endeavouring to maximise

profits can the producer attain that level of normal profit which is a condition of remaining in business in the long run. It thereby interlocks the structure of the theory by converting profit maximisation from a criterion imposed on the model by the theorist's methodological necessity to an endogenous constraint of the system; within the theory it ensures that profit, like all other input prices, is a measure of opportunity costs, and enforces strict adherence to the external standards which determine the prices of all outputs and all inputs.

How are these cost and value levels set? In a continuing perfectly competitive equilibrium, again the answer is easy. The firm's costs and prices have been determined by competition, so that its historical standards are an image of the relevant external standards; and since the firm is in equilibrium, the past is a perfect guide to the future. Thus historical, external, and planning standards coincide. If they do not coincide, the theorist is in trouble; and if the firm is not in equilibrium then, in general, they will not. Such ambiguity of standards is simply not acceptable in standard theory; which explains Mrs Robinson's (1953–1954, p. 85) quip that one cannot get into equilibrium; one must always have been there. In this, as in many other respects, the concentration on equilibrium situations provides an invaluable method of problem avoidance for the theorist.

No mention has yet been made of imaginative standards in this discussion of standards in equilibrium. The reason for their omission is simply that in equilibrium there is no need for imagination. Indeed, it can be dangerous, because any notion that things might be different could wreck the equilibrium. In no equilibrium model, however elaborate, can there be permitted any development which is not obvious to those skilled in the relevant art – nothing that, by the criteria presently used, would merit the grant of a patent. All possible outcomes must be specified at the outset.

The market provides the mechanism by which external standards are imposed on a firm's planning standards. But, as is well known, markets do not deal in unpriced effects. Divergencies between private and social costs may cause the unified set of standards to mis-specify the conditions for a welfare optimum; or some socially relevant costs or values may not be represented at all. The signals may be wrong, or they may not exist; the private agenda may be provided with the wrong set of accounts, or the agenda may be too narrow. Consistency between standards is no guarantee that they are at the appropriate level, or even that they are the appropriate set.

Expectations and the theory of choice

In fact, the world offers no guarantees of this sort. They occur only in a world of perfect knowledge, which is certain to be in some obvious respects quite different from the world which we inhabit, and in which the study of economics has developed. Economics exists to deal with problems of choice, with decisions between alternatives that are available and imperfect substitutes for one another; but in the economics of perfect knowledge there is a unique solution; what is more, since the model is in equilibrium anyway, the solution has already been found. The world of perfect knowledge is a world in which all the excitement is already over.

Real choice implies that knowledge is not perfect; for, as Shackle (1972, p. 246) has pointed out, one can choose only among future possibilities, but can know for certain only what is past. 'The paradox of rationality is that it must concern itself with choosing amongst things fully known; but in the world of time, only that is fully known which is already beyond the reach of choice, having already become actual and thus knowable.' The logical implications of this argument have been resolutely avoided by economists, and for good reason, because they are potentially destructive of existing theory, most particularly of axiomatic theory, which prides itself on the strictness of its logic. If choice depends on expectations, then a theory of choice must include a theory of expectations; and as Boulding (1966, p. 161) has remarked, that is no trivial enquiry. 'In the initial state, we have to have some kind of image of possible future states, and it is a very interesting and quite difficult question as to how we acquire this image.' Imaginative models are not easy to handle. Arrow (1972, p. 21) has pointed in one obvious direction by affirming that 'the influence of experience on beliefs is of the utmost importance for a rational theory of behaviour under uncertainty'. That assertion was offered as a criticism of Shackle (the grounds for which are far from clear), but it occurs in a collection of theoretical essays in which his co-authors make no attempt whatever to incorporate such influences in their formal analysis.

In thus ignoring Arrow, they demonstrate that they are wiser than he; for if one admits the influence of experience on beliefs, then one must admit, first, that people with different experiences are likely to have different beliefs, second, that beliefs may be, to varying degrees, erroneous, and, third, that beliefs, and therefore actions, may change with time – sometimes very abruptly. Thus, action no longer depends on the objective facts of a situation (if it is indeed any longer possible to say what are the 'objective facts'), and, as Leijonhufvud (1968) above all has reminded us, experience may lead us away from equilibrium by laying false trails. These consequences are so destructive for the body of general equilibrium theory (which is presumably what Arrow, like other general equilibrium theorists, equates with 'rational theory') that it would be much nearer the truth to say that the total exclusion of both experience and belief is of the utmost importance for a rational theory of behaviour under uncertainty. One can now see the inestimable value of perfect competition in enforcing a common pattern of experience and thus standardising beliefs. The exclusion of genuine uncertainty helps too, and general equilibrium theorists have become very expert at excluding it even in the act of ostensibly dealing with it.

Economists are further inhibited from handling expectations by their assumption that mental processes are not a fit subject for them to study. One has only to think of the enormous intellectual effort expended in producing a theory of revealed preference which was entirely innocent of any reason for preferences (and therefore, necessarily, of any reason for believing preferences to be stable), or among the empiricists, the resolute rejection by Friedman and Machlup of any evidence that can be deemed to have passed through any mind – other than the antiseptic mind of the analyst – to be reminded how profound is this aversion to anything which might interfere with the smooth machinery of logic or statistical method. Thus, if there are to be expectations, then they must be mechanically determined.

Two simple methods are employed. One is to assume the problem away by postulating that people or firms guess correctly; this is a trick favoured by economists claiming to test hypotheses about the behaviour of firms, even though it is well known, for example, that the adoption of target discount rates of 15% after tax has not generally produced equivalent returns for the adopters. The second is to treat expectations as a simple function of recent events, as most notoriously emphasised in some investment models. Here the assumption is either that no thought is taken for the future, or that the future is expected to be identical with the immediate past. When such simple models are used as a component of trade cycle theory, such expectations are used to explain their own falsification; and yet people are supposed to continue forming them in this demonstrably erroneous way.

The two methods imply contrary patterns of behaviour. There is either an assumption of complete rationality, or an injection of ad hoc irrationality into an otherwise rational system, in which investors are supposed to be equipped with all other relevant information, and expert in using it. In neither case is there any learning; the influence of experience on beliefs is carefully excluded.

In this respect as in so many others, Marshall (1920) contrived to avoid the dangers which his successors have encountered. His theory of value is an expectational theory; it is also a theory illustrated by reference to consumption goods frequently purchased, such as tea and fish. The purchaser of such commodities does not have to look very far ahead in estimating his wants, and by the frequency of his purchases can build up a sample of experience sufficiently large to justify the assumption that expectations are correct. Moreover, the established patterns of trading relationships in particular markets – a feature of Marshall's analysis which has much disturbed the purists – provide good reasons why expectations should converge. Marshallian preferences are rationally stable, for Marshallian expectations are based on trial and error, in circumstances where there are many trials and where errors are of small consequence and easily corrected. Thus Marshallian values are based on the application of reason to beliefs derived from ample experience. This is very different from the modern theory of rational choice.

What happens to the Marshallian scheme when we come to consider investment decisions? Here the decision-maker has access to few trials and therefore runs a greater risk of error. Expectations based on small samples may be seriously at fault; and they may be subject to drastic revision – not necessarily in the direction of reality – on the receipt of fresh information. Indeed, the examples of Briggs and Pressed Steel suggest that, since confidence may be the direct result of ignorance, it is sometimes the expectation most confidently held which is most liable to be overturned. Moreover, an investment decision represents a much longer commitment, so that the relevant expectations must extend over a much longer period. The information requirements are, therefore, greatly increased in just those situations in which information is least likely to be reliable. Thus, there is not only a greater risk of error, but a greater risk of greater error. Finally, the consequences of error, both for the individual and the economic system, are much more serious. A packet of unpalatable tea is a minor inconvenience; a new giant steelworks based on an outmoded technology is a major disaster.

Keynes on expectations and ignorance

It is precisely this degree of ignorance in circumstances where the consequences of error may be far-reaching, which Keynes took as the basis for his theory of employment. This judgement on a question of much current controversy is based both on the almost totally neglected article of 1937 in which he replied to his critics, and on evidence from the *General Theory*. Much of the remainder of this chapter is devoted to an exposition and commentary on the argument of the article.

For the exposition we cannot do better than turn to Keynes (1937) himself.

more recent writers like their predecessors were still dealing with a system in which the amount of the factors employed was given and the other relevant facts were known more or less for certain. This does not mean that they were dealing with a system in which change was ruled out, or even one in which the disappointment of expectation was ruled out. But at any given time facts and expectations were assumed to be given in a definite and calculable form;...The calculus of probability, though mention of it was kept in the background, was supposed to be capable of reducing uncertainty to the same calculable status as that of certainty itself.

Actually, however, we have, as a rule, only the vaguest idea of any but the most direct consequences of our acts. Sometimes we are not much concerned with their remoter consequences...But sometimes we are intensely concerned with them, more so, occasionally, than with the immediate consequences. Now of all human activities which are affected by this remoter preoccupation, it happens that one of the most important is economic in character, namely, Wealth. The whole object of the accumulation of Wealth is to produce results, or potential results, at a comparatively distant, and sometimes at an *indefinitely* distant, date. Thus the fact that our knowledge of the future is fluctuating, vague, and uncertain, renders Wealth a peculiarly unsuitable subject for the methods of the classical economic theory. This theory might work very well in a world in which economic goods were necessarily consumed within a short interval of their being produced (pp. 212–13).

In the light of this argument, we may conclude that the theory of exchange is a potentially dangerous first approximation to the analysis of economic systems; it encourages a concentration of attention on those goods and services which are currently available, and, even when extended to the exchange of future goods, evades the question of what expectations are necessary in order to justify their creation or preservation, without drawing attention to the potential significance of the exclusion. The theory has, indeed, very reasonable sufficiency for analysing the exchange values of goods which yield their services over a short period; and this success tempts the theorist, as Briggs were tempted, to believe that a minor modification will serve to retain sufficiency in circumstances which appear to be only slightly different. Why not, for example, distinguish goods by their date as well as their physical characteristics? The compelling reason, as Shackle has striven to emphasise, is that the introduction of future time (and no decisions can affect past time, until we become time-travellers) inevitably introduces ignorance, and thus destroys the rational basis on which the theory rests. Time and determinacy are incompatible.

Keynes makes quite clear that it is not a modification of accepted economic rationality but its destruction by ignorance which he is writing about.

the expectation of life is only slightly uncertain. Even the weather is only moderately uncertain. The sense in which I am using the term is that in which the prospect of a European war is uncertain, or the price of copper and the rate of interest twenty years hence, or the obsolescence of a new invention, or the position of private wealth-owners in the social system in 1970. About these matters there is no scientific basis on which to form any calculable probability whatever. We simply do not know (1937, pp. 213–14).

Economic logic, as it has been developed since Keynes' time, has become increasingly specific in its input requirements. Keynes draws our attention to the fact that, for the class of decisions requiring present outlay in the hope of returns far distant in time, the required inputs are simply not available. That emperor has no chance of acquiring any clothes. But without these inputs, the formal models do not just work rather imperfectly; they simply cannot work at all.

Exactly the same problem arises, for exactly the same reason, in the making of managerial decisions. But the response of managers, like the response of economic theorists, is not to abandon choice to chance. That would be to deny the need for either managers or economists. Keynes suggests that in order to generate the inputs required for their quasi-rational calculations, those faced with an otherwise debilitating ignorance tend to rely principally on three techniques:

(1) We assume that the present is a much more serviceable guide to the future than a candid examination of past experience would show it to have been hitherto. . .
(2) We assume that the *existing* state of opinion as expressed in prices and the character of existing output is based on a *correct* summing up of future prospects. . .
(3) Knowing that our own individual judgement is worthless, we endeavour to fall back on the judgement of the rest of the world which is perhaps better informed. That is, we endeavour to conform with the behaviour of the majority or the average (1937, p. 214).

It is not surprising that expectations so founded should be subject to violent changes. It is thus manifest in this article that Keynes' concept of the marginal efficiency of capital was far from a technical reflection of the objective marginal productivity of capital, but instead a subjective, psychological, almost conventional phenomenon. He says as much in the *General*

Theory. 'There are not two separate factors affecting the rate of investment, namely the schedule of the marginal efficiency of capital and the state of confidence. The state of confidence is relevant because it is one of the major factors determining the former' (1936, p. 149). But the message was lost, as Hart (1948, p. 418) feared it would be.

It is entirely consistent with Keynes' view that, as Williams and Scott (1965), for example, discovered, the estimates justifying an investment may be the consequence rather than the cause of at least a provisional decision to invest. It might be objected that this approach makes it difficult to specify the investment function to be used in a so-called Keynesian model. But this is precisely the point: the function cannot be specified, except arbitrarily by the analyst. Keynes is denying the validity of the classical apparatus, and, by advance implication, of the supposedly Keynesian apparatus, as a representation of the macroeconomic world.

Consequences of ignorance: profit and speculation

It is convenient at this point to leave Keynes' own argument for a moment to consider some of the implications of ignorance discussed by Shackle. Future values, and therefore present values of resources with potential future uses, are not objectively determined. 'Valuation is expectation and expectation is imagination' (1972, p. 8): it rests upon some conjecture of what the object or system will be able to do in the future; and clearly the further in the future one is able to look, the greater the scope for imagination. But imaginative models, as has been argued, are not all that clearly tied to individual, let alone general, experience. Imaginative valuations may differ; and it is, in Shackle's view (1972, pp. 409–10), such differences in valuation that give rise to profit. Profit depends on imperfection of knowledge; it results from the successful exercise of imagination in seeing a value higher than the conventional valuation in some asset or opportunity. Such success may be the result of luck or judgement: it is not always easy to tell which after the event, and in any case, there may be little advantage from a policy point of view in attempting to distinguish between the two. Monopoly profit is a different matter, though on the level of abstraction characteristic of formal theory, it is hard to discover any foundations for monopoly other than institutional restrictions.

The prospect of profit acts as a stimulus to the creation of imaginative models, and therefore to many kinds of innovation. But there is a snag. Even after a substantial lapse of time, the valuation of a durable asset may still depend primarily on conventional wisdom about its future uses; thus over this period profits depend on changes in this conventional valuation. Therefore speculation on other people's expectations and behaviour tends to replace speculation on the underlying data. All asset markets are speculative; and the longer-dated the asset, the more likely is this speculation to become a speculation on the results of other people's speculations.

Keynes' occasional purple passages in the *General Theory* are an essential part of his argument, not colourful decorations, as they have normally been regarded. One such passage follows his observation that the more efficient organisation of stock exchanges accentuates this tendency to replace unstable expectations about future events with even more unstable expectations about future expectations of future expectations.

When the capital development of a country becomes a by-product of the activities of a casino, the job is likely to be ill-done. The measure of success attained by Wall Street, regarded as an institution of which the proper social purpose is to direct new investment into the most profitable channels in terms of future yield, cannot be claimed as one of the outstanding triumphs of *laissez-faire* capitalism – which is not surprising, if I am right in thinking that the best brains of Wall Street have been in fact directed towards a different object. . .

It is usually agreed that casinos should, in the public interest, be inaccessible and expensive. And perhaps the same is true of Stock Exchanges (1936, p. 159).

Uncertainty as stimulus or as threat

One of the attractions of speculating on changes in expectations, rather than on further-distant future events, is that it reduces the duration, and frequently the amount, of ignorance that has to be borne. For although moderate ignorance may be a stimulus, ignorance which is too great to handle may paralyse decision. No news may be, in its effects, the worst news of all. The need for a reasonably secure structure as a basis for exploration and creativity has been discussed in an earlier chapter, and the theme will be taken up again in Chapter 11. Such an argument could provide a conceptual basis for distinguishing between desirable (structured, and therefore creative) and undesirable (unpredictable and therefore creation-inhibiting) competition, such as Richardson (1960) has attempted. Certainly where there is too much ignorance for comfort, there are strong incentives to seek ways of reducing or evading it.

Some stability of expectations is necessary to the effective operation of a firm or an economic system; and because policy recommendations are so coloured by equilibrium models in which expectations are no problem, economists are sometimes inclined to exaggerate the merits of free competition. Sometimes at least, the object of agreements between firms is to make possible, not a quiet life, but a life of manageable challenge. The desire for a negotiated environment may be a desire (which economists, from their predilections, ought to commend) for an ordered framework within which rationality may appear worthwhile. Innovations, for example, often need protection in their early stages. Such desires may be seen as part of the rationale of the negotiated environments known as firms, or the inter-firm relationships analysed by Richardson (1972).

The need for some kind of framework, even if partly conventional or even fictitious, also supplies an argument in favour of moderate price stability, including stability of exchange rates. Again the theorist's concern for the virtues of his equilibrium model predisposes him to advocate the free movement of prices in response to changing circumstances – quite illogically, since the theory is formally concerned with stable prices in a stable situation, and can certainly give no formal guidance whatever on the desirable responses to unforeseen change. Where arguments have been advanced in favour of greater stability, they have been based on the costs of administration and of search involved. That argument surely has weight, but there is another argument against extreme flexibility: that, as Keynes argues, it may simply become impossible to find a plausible basis for any price expectation and thus for any rational-seeming decision; and as a consequence (as he did not argue) some highly desirable decisions will not be made.

That partial ignorance affects, not just the detail, but the kind of decision is emphasised in Ansoff's (1965) discussion of corporate strategy. Just as lack of confidence in our expectations drives us to hold cash in order to avoid commitment to any course of action that may prove mistaken, so the firm's policy may be seriously modified by its concern for 'unforeseeable events which may have relatively low probability of occurrence, but whose impact on profitability...would be major' (p. 54). In these circumstances the firm avoids commitment, and seeks flexibility. One form of flexibility is obtained by increasing holdings of cash; others include a deliberate refusal to concentrate on apparently profitable opportunities, or to make large investments in capital equipment with a limited range of use. Ansoff notes that flexibility may conflict with other objectives of the firm: it is no part of his concern to consider its effects upon the economy. However, it is clear that such an account of business behaviour (though consciously put forward as advice, not as description or rationalisation) could be effectively used to fill in some of the details of Keynes' vision.

Willingness to take a chance is essential, but some circumstances may be so disturbed that all bets are off. The threatened destruction of all bases of expectation is one of the major dangers of high rates of inflation. Moreover, the frequent changes (to say nothing of the failures) of policy between and within British governments have made the predication of any decision on a particular government attitude or incentive increasingly dubious, and thus increased the difficulty of securing the desired response to any governmental activity.

Money as uncertainty-equivalent

The consequences of uncertain expectations are effectively concealed by the theorist's use of certainty equivalents. The equivalence may be as false as the certainty. Keynes' own treatment of expectations in the *General Theory* has been criticised on this score by Hart (1948, pp. 421–2).

Perhaps the most crucial shortcoming of Keynes' theory of expectations is his attempt to boil down a system of contingent anticipations into what has been called a 'certainty equivalent'...The certainty equivalent is a will-o'-the-wisp. Generally speaking, the business policy appropriate for a complex of uncertain anticipations is different in kind from that appropriate to any possible set of certain expectations. Trying to frame monetary theory in terms of certainty equivalents means leaving out the specific reactions to uncertainty – which happen to be of fundamental importance for monetary theory.

In fact, since money as a means of exchange is rendered superfluous by the certainty-producing devices of *tâtonnement* or recontracting, and as a store of value by a complete system of present contracts in all conceivable contingent claims markets, it should become clear that money is actually an uncertainty-equivalent. Money, like the firm, is a means of handling the consequences of the excessive cost or the sheer impossibility of abolishing ignorance. This line of argument has been advanced both by Leijonhufvud (1968, p. 307) who asserts that 'the social contrivance of money is superfluous in perfect information models', and by Shackle (1972, p. 160), who declares that 'money is the means by which choice can be deferred until a later and better-informed time'.

Like the firm, money is a device which makes possible incompletely-specified contracts: indeed, as general purchasing power, instead of a set of agreements to purchase (perhaps contingent on precisely-specified circumstances), cash is itself an incompletely-specified contract. People hold cash, just as firms employ people, or enter into working arrangements with other firms, because they are not ready to undertake the set of capital commitments that are essential even to any theoretical investigation of the existence of a general equilibrium. Money and the firm both imply a rejection of the concept of general equilibrium in favour of the continuing management of emerging events.

But there is an important difference between a contract of employment and a promise to pay the bearer on demand. The former is an agreement by which the employee surrenders some control over his future activities in return for an increased security of expectation of income; the firm, on the other hand, by incurring some kind of obligation (which may be rather slight or firmly binding, according to the terms, both legal and understood, of the agreement) and continued payment, acquires increased security of future access to a flow of productive services which can be employed, within limits, at its discretion in the light of future events. The employee gains in security of expectations; the firm gains in flexibility of response. It is clear that such agreements, based on mutual advantage, are quite likely to promote the stability of an economic system. The holder of cash, however, in return for giving up his right to the present possession of goods, retains unlimited discretion over the future use of those resources: he is absolved from giving any indication whatever of the timing or content of his future demands; and there is no automatic provision for meeting his future requirements. The problem is not one of communications, for there is nothing to communicate.

Of course, the ability to hold money is strictly constrained by the amount of money available; and the demand for money is adjusted to the stock of money partly through changes in the price level, but, in Keynes' model, mainly by the rate of interest, in other words by the price of this freedom to postpone decision. What that price has to be is determined by the strength of our aversion to commitment; and as Keynes observes, 'our desire to hold Money as a store of wealth is a barometer of the degree of our distrust of our own calculations and conventions concerning the future' (1937, p. 216). At any one time, there can be postulated a demand curve for this freedom, or a liquidity preference schedule; but for Keynes the most important thing was not that such a function could be deemed to exist, but that it was fundamentally unstable.

Keynes' theory of employment

The level of investment, in Keynes' scheme, is determined jointly by the rate of interest which thus reflects shifts of confidence, and an estimate of the desirability of investment which rests on equally flimsy foundations.

It is not surprising that the volume of investment, thus determined, should fluctuate widely from time to time. For it depends on two sets

of judgements about the future, neither of which rests on an adequate or secure foundation – on the propensity to hoard and on opinions of the future yield of capital-assets. Nor is there any reason to
suppose that the fluctuations in one of these factors will tend to offset
the fluctuations in the other...For the same circumstances which
lead to pessimistic views about future yields are apt to increase the
propensity to hoard (1937, p. 218).

The desire to hoard is a desire to avoid commitment. The
willingness to invest is a willingness to incur specific commitments. It requires some rather special (though certainly not inconceivable) kinds of change in confidence to secure an increased
willingness to make commitments on the part of one group of
people just when another group is trying to go liquid.

If one can summarise in one sentence the theory of employment set forth by Keynes in his article of 1937, it is this: unemployment in a market economy is the result of ignorance too great
to be borne. The fully-specified macroeconomic models miss
the point – which is precisely that no model of this situation can
be fully specified. Of course, what is crystal-clear in the article
was fearfully obscure in the *General Theory*. The struggle to
escape was only very partially successful; and the Keynesians
have long since stopped trying. Keynes' solitary follower among
leading economists has commented sadly: 'A book which concludes, by difficult and entangled steps, that stable curves and
functions are *allergic* to the real human economic Scheme of
Things, proceeded to state this idea in terms of stable curves or
functions. No wonder the critics have worn the Keynesian
garment inside-out' (Shackle, 1973, pp. 517–18). Whether the
theory just discussed is what Keynes really meant may never be
properly determined, for can we be sure ourselves what we really
mean by our attempt to tackle a complex issue? But it is entirely
consistent with a recurrent theme in the *General Theory*, and
the natural – perhaps the only – way of incorporating Chapter
12, 'The State of Long-Term Expectations', into the analytical
structure of the book.

In his preface, dated only two months before publication,
Keynes remarks that 'this book...has evolved into what is primarily a study of the forces which determine changes in the scale
of output and employment as a whole'; and that this requires a

'method of analysing the economic behaviour of the present under the influence of changing ideas about the future' (p. vii). Both money (p. 293) and the marginal efficiency of capital (p. 145) are of critical importance precisely because they link the future to the present. But despite his initial suggestion, by way of a footnote (p. 24), that a 'bundle of vague and more various possibilities' could be adequately represented by a certainty-equivalent, and the use of a term – marginal efficiency – which strongly suggests some objective and constant productivity relationship, he insists again and again that much the most important fact about marginal efficiency is its instability. 'Long-term expectations...are liable to sudden revision' (p. 51); the marginal efficiency of capital is 'subject to...somewhat violent fluctuations' (p. 144); it is 'fickle and highly unstable' (p. 204), 'liable to change without much warning, and sometimes substantially' (p. 249), being 'determined...by the uncontrollable and disobedient psychology of the business world' (p. 317). None of these quotations are taken from Chapter 12, which is devoted entirely to the proposition that the marginal efficiency of capital cannot helpfully be specified as a dependent variable in any equation system.

Keynes' 'Notes on the Trade Cycle' carry the same message. There is no room for any formal mechanical model with fixed coefficients. Changing capital stocks are relevant to changes in expectation, but, basically, the boom is caused by exaggerated hopes, and the slump by exaggerated fears (pp. 321–2).

This emphasis on the critical importance of confidence is a remarkably clear echo of Marshall's explanation of boom and slump in the last chapter of his *Principles*. For Marshall, too, was well aware that the future is unknown, and that ignorance of the future limits both the application of economic theory and the efficient deployment of resources. Marshall's theory of value was very carefully designed to stay within those limits, for he knew the dangers that lay beyond; it was left to Keynes to insist that the whole of the elegant structure of economic analysis rested on a quagmire. No wonder the Keynesians will not listen.

Information or ignorance

The theory outlined in this chapter is not only very different from modern Keynesianism; it is substantially different, too, from Leijonhufvud's reading of Keynes. A decision-maker may be faced with partial ignorance for two general reasons. One is a failure of communication. This may result from the cost of communication (where Leijonhufvud's emphasis is placed), on technical obstacles to communication within complex systems (Williamson's principal source of managerial diseconomies) or deliberate distortion (because control of information may be a means of securing one's own objectives). Only those totally unaware of these factors can place absolute confidence in the data which they possess, however well buttressed with statistical techniques. They will not be quite sure if they can believe what they have been told; and they may be even less sure what to believe about what they have not been told. The second reason is Shackle's reason: the future is unknown. To those having to make a decision on the basis of grossly inadequate evidence, or wondering whether to postpone commitment altogether, it doesn't really matter whether the future is unknowable or merely unknown. But it does make a difference to the analytical approach. One can do something in theory, and sometimes even in practice, to improve information systems; one cannot discover the unknowable.

Let us apply this distinction to the following argument by Mrs Robinson and Eatwell (1973, p. 92):

In a planned economy. . .there are. . .no problems of effective demand, i.e. of ensuring that all that can be produced is sold, for productive resources are directed to meet requirements that have been decided on by the planners. . .The capitalist has to take decisions today about operations which will yield a benefit to him in the future. . .He dwells in a world of uncertainty. . .There is no reason to expect the overall result of their individual decisions to conform to any rational scheme.

One may wonder about the desirability or efficiency of abolishing the need to communicate preferences from people to planners by substituting for them instructions from planners to people;

but even if it were true that a planned economy solved all the communication problems, how can that eliminate ignorance? Mrs Robinson is apparently as aware as Shackle that ignorance of the future was at the heart of Keynes' theory, but she seems to believe that only the iniquities of private enterprise (like original sin) prevent us from enjoying perfect prevision.

The planning process creates an emphasis on communication, on precision, and on consistency. Leijonhufvud's interpretation of Keynes attributes unemployment to the inconsistency which results from a failure of the system to transmit the required set of equilibrium prices. It is a technical problem: a defect in system design. Consistency is certainly a major concern of theorists; it is also a major concern of planners. This can be dangerous, because it presents both theorists and planners with an intellectually challenging and potentially soluble problem which diverts their attention from the more fundamental, and basically insoluble, difficulty. Pareto optimality can be as delusive as the Washington highway planners' vision of 1980.

It is the impossibility of foreknowledge that is at the root of Shackle's argument – and, in our view, of Keynes'. The problems with which they are concerned do not result simply from the absence of the auctioneer. There is no virtue in being consistent if the forecasts are wrong. Few are disposed to find much merit in the massive over-ordering of generating equipment by the C.E.G.B. which was the price of consistency with the 1965 National Plan. This episode is an excellent illustration of Richardson's (1960, p. 87) warning that 'close complementarity between several investments is equivalent to a conductor of error'. Indeed, if one were mildly cynical, one might argue that, since forecasts are always wrong, a consistent, comprehensive plan is bound to be wrong in all respects, whereas an inconsistent plan does at least offer a chance of getting something right. In fact, the forecasts of interdependencies will be wrong as well, so even an apparently consistent plan may turn out to be partly correct. It is the divergency of expectations that is the virtue of competition.

The practical point of great importance is that problems of communication and consistency (and the consequential emphasis on false precision) can so easily become a means of escape from

ignorance. The resulting confidence, having no sure foundation, is vulnerable to many kinds of shock. Recent British
history shows enough examples of false moves based on blissful
ignorance for us not to encourage such false certainty. Perhaps
the only people fit to plan are those who do not believe in planning.

A general theory?

The accepted macroeconomic apparatus, misleadingly labelled
Keynesian, is a challenge to the fundamental notion of economics as a study of situations of scarcity. Certainly in its analysis
of unemployment, it is not concerned with choice situations. But
Shackle's interpretation of Keynes' model is concerned directly
and explicitly with the problems of choice under uncertainty, and
with the ways in which the economic system responds to and
regulates such choices. Its investigation of the causes and consequences of ignorance makes it very different from traditional
theory, and gives it a very good claim to be called more general.
Keynes (1937, p. 222) stresses that, 'The orthodox theory assumes
that we have a knowledge of the future of a kind quite different
from that which we actually possess.' In its dependence on even
more specific and unlikely knowledge, general equilibrium theory
becomes, as Shackle (1972, p. 334) observes, a particularly special
case. 'Micro-economic theory, the theory of value, whether in its
particular equilibrium or its general equilibrium guise, is the
theory of ensured success. Macro-economic theory regards success
as merely one possible, and temporary, outcome of a human pre-
dicament whose quality is manifested and visible in the real course
of history.' Though it is very convenient, and indeed indispensable, for both decision-makers and economic theorists to make
use of analytical techniques which purport to comprehend all
possible alternatives and all possible outcomes, and to fill in gaps
in their estimates of likelihood by the masquerade of that peculiar
kind of knowledge which goes under the name of probability
theory, yet it is wise to remember the insufficiency of these abstractions – in particular, the ways in which the criteria which they
employ inhibit even the recognition of certain kinds of problem.
There is nothing more dangerous than rationality under an

agenda that has been restricted for the explicit purpose of permitting its use. Can anyone really doubt that this was Keynes' (1937, p. 215) view of classical theory when he wrote this sentence? 'I accuse the classical economic theory of being itself one of these pretty, polite techniques which tries to deal with the present by abstracting from the fact that we know very little about the future.' The economic study of information is very different from the study of ignorance.

10

Imperfections of competition

The purpose of a business is to create a customer.
P. F. Drucker (1964, p. 85)

In a perfect market, the analysis of producers' behaviour is very simple; whatever their objectives may be, they have no discretion (though, as argued earlier, this conclusion depends on the distribution of objectives among producers). The full flower of the analysis of perfect markets is found in general equilibrium models; indeed they have difficulty in accommodating any other market structure. Though imperfections of competition may be of interest to industrial economists, they mar the beauties of formal theory. However, it may be worth enquiring once more whether the work of Chamberlin and Mrs Robinson have anything to tell us apart from a warning not to interrupt the majestic progress of that theory. As so often, this enquiry must begin with Marshall.

Marshall and long-run supply

Marshall (1920) did not discuss in detail the formation of consumer expectations, or the problems which might arise if these expectations were ill-founded or insecurely held – although, as we have seen, he was well aware of the significance of these issues. He paid far more attention to the intricacies of cost and supply. One possible reason for his neglect of long-term expectations is the absence of any classification of demand relationships in terms of time-span – in striking, but little-remarked, contrast to the multi-period analysis of costs. The extent to which changes in consumer demand depend on complementary changes in the consumer's capital stock (and therefore on the time allowed for adjustments to this stock) is much greater now than when Marshall wrote; but Marshall might have noted a direct implication of his own analysis. For, if the producer's output response is

determined by the time period, then both the volume and composition of his demand for inputs must be similarly affected; and,
even if we were prepared to treat factor prices quite separately,
we should not forget that the greater part of trade is in intermediate goods. Thus the use of the same demand curve for each
time period of analysis has the effect of excluding intermediate
goods from the general theory of value.

This incomplete analysis of demand was one part of the
Marshallian tradition which his successors in Cambridge took
over without apparent question. His elaborate analysis of supply,
however, they radically modified without realising it, and despite
the clearest warnings. This curious combination of accepting the
relatively undeveloped and changing the well-developed part of
his theory pointed the way to what would now be generally regarded as one of the most notorious blind alleys in twentieth-
century economics.

An essential feature of Marshall's treatment of supply was that
his analysis of long-period costs was not of the same kind as the
analysis of short-period costs. In Marshall's short period, effects
depend on the costs of individual firms; but, as Frisch (1950,
p. 510) has pointed out, his long-period effects 'manifest themselves *by changing the life-cycles of the various firms*'. It is in
order to circumvent the consequent difficulty that 'we cannot
then regard the conditions of supply by an individual producer
as typical of those which govern the general supply in a market'
(p. 459) that Marshall makes use of the concept of the representative firm, a kind of economist's equivalent to the man on top of
the Clapham omnibus. Thus the representative firm of the long
period is a different conception from the firm of the short period.
The attempt to tidy up the theory of supply by combining the two
inevitably ran into trouble.

For it brought into prominence the problem of handling economies of scale in a model which postulated perfect competition.
Economies of scale appeared to be rather important in the world
to which the theory was meant to apply, and indeed Marshall
himself regarded them as valuable instruments of economic progress. But if a firm's costs fall as its output increases, then how is
the firm's equilibrium size to be determined? Short-period costs
can be guaranteed to rise eventually by the assumption that the

quantities of some factors are not readily adjustable: changing factor proportions must produce something like the text book cost curve. But the long period, by definition, is a time of perfect adjustment. Thus as long as economies of scale continue, what can possibly halt the expansion of the individual firm except a falling price for its product?

Marshall had a short answer to that one: old age. In the very long run, Marshall's firms are all dead. Economies of scale may, like advances in medicine, give them a longer life and a more vigorous prime; but it cannot keep them alive for ever. The cleverest economist in the world will not live long enough to drive all the rest of us out of the profession. Whether Marshall's view of business was right is not at present in question: the point is that the dilemma of increasing returns was not, logically, a Marshallian dilemma. Marshallian long-period equilibrium was an equilibrium of the industry: Marshall explicitly denied the existence of a long-run equilibrium of the firm.

He did more. By postulating that firms need time to grow, he rejected, in his own analysis, any concept of the long-run cost curve as representing a set of alternative combinations of price and output that were simultaneously available for choice, as are the price and output combinations of equilibrium theory. Falling long-run costs marked out an expansion path (not necessarily reversible) which an industry could follow through time as far as the growth of the market would permit, and an expansion path which a young and vigorous firm could follow until its vigour waned. A better-managed firm could go further than its rivals; but even the greatest could do no better than Ozymandias, King of Kings. Long-run supply belongs to Marshall's theory of growth.

Imperfect vs *monopolistic competition*

There was plenty of scope for argument whether, or for what purposes, Marshall's theory was adequate for the nineteen twenties; but that was not what happened. Instead, economists attempted to improve on Marshall without appreciating what he was trying to do, and in the process created for themselves a logical dilemma which belonged to a dead world. Few economists have been as rigorous as Marshall in rejecting misleading rigour; and those who criticise him for failure to build a tightly-defined system succeed only in demonstrating their own lack of understanding.

It was here that Mrs Robinson (1933), as she later explained, took her wrong turning. Instead of 'abandoning static analysis and trying to come to terms with Marshall's theory of development' (1951, pp. vii–viii), she saw a splendid opportunity of exploiting this logical contradiction to destroy the whole apparatus of neoclassical theory, with its comfortable implications about the beneficent working of the market. Whereas Pigou had demonstrated that extensive intervention might be necessary to correct for externalities and to remedy an undesirable distribution of income, she sought to show that even within competitive markets, competition could not possibly work as it had been claimed to. The apparatus of equilibrium analysis in her *Economics of Imperfect Competition* was intended, as she complained in her introduction to its second edition (1969), as a reductio ad absurdum of classical analysis, rather as Keynes, in another context, tried to convince his readers of the absurdity of basing analysis on the notion of well-founded and stable investment functions. Both were totally unsuccessful. Formal analysis has no sense of the ridiculous. It requires stable functions and it will have them.

If we are to sympathise with Mrs Robinson, what are we to say of E. H. Chamberlin, whose professional career was carried away and swamped by the consequences of this misguided attempt to help Marshall out of non-existent difficulties? Chamberlin (1933) was actually trying to develop Marshallian analysis on its weaker side, that of demand, not by applying multi-period analysis but by examining the consequences of diverse preferences. He was not concerned with the theoretical implications of continuing economies of scale, and indeed in the debate on scale and the size of firms took the side of those who argued that there were effective cost limits to firm size. But despite the valiant efforts of Dennis Roberston, whose metaphorical style could hardly be expected to counter a demand for strict and delusory logic, the wrong problem had been so firmly defined by the formalists of the nineteen-twenties that no other problem in partial equilibrium price theory could be recognised. Therefore Chamberlin must be saying the same thing as Mrs Robinson, and his protests went unheeded. How far the failure of his fellow economists to listen to him was responsible for the lack of development of his ideas after 1933 may never be known; but it is one of the greatest dangers of economic formalism that it leads to arrogance – usually unconscious arrogance: an assumption that formal models better express the vision of a great mind than its own writings.

The confusion between Chamberlin and Mrs Robinson was accentuated by their use of very similar apparatus, and their similar definitions of equilibrium. It was compounded by Chamberlin's emphasis in exposition on the tangency solution, which was so elegant and so striking that the most determined efforts would have been necessary to convince readers of its intended status as a special case. If profits are to be no more than normal, then in equilibrium average revenue must be tangential to average cost; thus either falling demand or falling costs implies the other, and either is sufficient to exclude the possibility of a technical optimum. But the equivalence of formal models does not imply equivalence of overall theory: the same turnpike may be used for many different journeys. Chamberlin and Mrs Robinson started from different origins, and reached different destinations. But nobody noticed.

Mrs Robinson started with the stylised fact and theoretical presumption of falling costs. Therefore a falling demand curve was a methodological necessity, and she wasted no time accounting for it. Chamberlin explained falling demand curves as a result of diverse preferences and differentiated products. For him it was falling costs that were a methodological necessity – but only, be it noted, for the tangency solution: if there are super-normal profits, falling demand can co-exist with rising costs, or even with a technical optimum. Thus he wasted no time, in his first edition, accounting for the shape of his cost curves.

But methodological necessities may acquire a life of their own; and having given no reason for her falling demand curves, Mrs Robinson slipped very easily into the congenial assumption that they are irrational. The formal theory of imperfect competition gives absolutely no warrant for the emphasis on competitive waste so characteristic of Mrs Robinson's work; and the excess capacity and unexhausted economies of scale which were presented as such striking and undesirable consequences of imperfect competition were already explicit in the assumption of falling costs which precipitated the theory. Chamberlin, in contrast, laid no emphasis on the frustration of scale economies: that a market might be too small to permit the lowest possible scale of production was a thoroughly Marshallian view. Indeed, had not Adam Smith declared that division of labour – the great source of increased productivity – was limited by the size of the market?

That the market limitation could be the result, not only of low overall demand for a product, but of the differentiation of consumer's tastes, was an important development of Marshallian economics. For Marshall, careful as ever, had noticed that, as well as often needing a long time to come to fruition, economies of scale might be impeded by difficulties of marketing.

But many commodities with regard to which the tendency to increasing returns acts strongly are, more or less, specialities; some of them aim at creating a new want, or at meeting an old want in a new way. Some of them are adapted to special tastes, and can never have a very large market; and some have merits that are not easily tested, and must win their way to general favour slowly. In all such cases the sales of each business are limited, more or less according to circumstances, to the particular market which it has slowly and expensively acquired; and though the production itself might be economically increased very fast, the sale could not (p. 287).

Chamberlin's attempt to work out the implications of that paragraph produced no new reason for dissatisfaction with the working of the economic system. Limited markets and differences of taste are facts of life, and no more to be blamed on a particular method of organising production than the fact of human mortality is to be blamed on the system of medical provision. In both instances, the system may fail to make the best of the situation; but the fundamental causes are not to be eradicated even by perfect system design.

Thus the startling discovery of imperfect competition theory, that the absence of monopoly profits was no guarantee of optimality, had no meaning in Chamberlin's theory. The kind of industrial restructuring advocated in Meade's youthful *Economic Analysis and Policy* (1937) (a notable expression of the self-confidence generated in young economists by the apparent power of the new theories of the thirties to remake the world) appears in the light of Chamberlin's model as a serious threat to consumer welfare through its artificial suppression of variety. But the welfare implications of Chamberlin's analysis, that the conditions of perfect competition could be attained only by the frustration of consumers' wants, and that no Pareto optima therefore existed, were not welcome news to anyone. They were perhaps least welcome to the theorists diligently constructing a 'clean' new welfare economics, for which Pareto optimality was indispensable. (Marshall's reference to 'the creation of new wants' would have done for them too.) Thus there was no interest in defending Chamberlin's view (and very little even in understanding it) while the activists continued to assume that monopolistic competition was about remediable imperfections.

Consumer rationality

The basic formal defect of imperfect competition theory is that, given Mrs Robinson's definition of the products of competing firms as identical in all respects other than consumers' attitudes towards them, its demand curves are not deducible from consumers' preferences. If we are prepared to accept consumers' preferences as a foundation either for axiomatic theory or for welfare economics, then we must not presume to second-guess the consumer in situations described as imperfectly competitive. Chamberlin's method is the rational one.

This is not a particularly serious criticism of Mrs Robinson. She has never been one to accept consumers' preferences as the basis of theory, and indeed she was trying to knock down a theory, not build a new orthodoxy. Apart from externalities in consumption, which lead her to the conclusion, directly opposed to that of Marshall, that the total disappearance of a product from the market may actually increase satisfaction, she believes that consumers' preferences are a pasture for firms. She believes (1973, p. 173) that Chamberlin ought to have thought so too.

Firms. . .are continually striving to create monopoly by differentiating their products and manipulating demand for them by advertisement and salesmanship of all kinds. . .Professor Chamberlin himself did not develop the idea of artificial product differentiation far, but devoted his subsequent work to arguing that it was in no way incompatible with the doctrine that the free play of market forces produces beneficial effects for consumers and producers alike.

Consumer manipulation is also a standard theme in Galbraith's writings: since they are formed by the technostructure, consumers' preferences are irrational, and therefore no basis for a properly-run society. Fortunately, this irrationality is not complete; there remain enough pockets of rationality to ensure a good sale for the writings of J. K. Galbraith.

Of course, no sociologist would be prepared to admit that any person's wants were entirely his own creation: they are a product in some large part of the social, economic, and cultural environment – as, indeed, Marshall (1920, pp. 86–91) emphasised. This fact requires great caution in the application to public policy of arguments which take consumer preferences as axiomatic. But the critics of axiomatic preferences are themselves not inclined to be too cautious. Politicians, and academics too, are in the business of preference changing – attitude change is a major educational objective – and the distinction between virtuous and vicious preferences is not an easy one to make. None of those who claim the right to make our choices for us seem very worthy of support.

What is clear is that a presumption of consumer irrationality, though it may seem a natural consequence of approaching the problem of equilibrium with falling costs from the supply side, is a threat to the whole structure of microeconomics. As Andrews (1964) has pointed out, if it is to be a general theory, imperfect competition must apply to the markets for intermediate goods (and why not factor services as well?); but if it does, the purchasers of these goods cannot be maximising their profits, and it is precisely these people whose profit maximisation provides the key to the whole system. If everyone is being bamboozled by everyone else, what is the point of analysis? Yet no one has ever claimed that the theory of imperfect competition is a theory of final markets only, or produced any reason why the necessary ad hoc irrationality should be confined to this class of markets.

Since it is firmly based on consumer preferences, and leads to no automatic prescriptions for intervention to improve welfare, Chamberlin's analysis is not open to these objections. Markets for intermediate goods may well be monopolistic too, and here also the requirements of variety may prevent the exploitation of economies of scale, though, since diversity may often be produced from standard components, one might expect more standardisation and greater volume in intermediate production. The desirability of sacrificing some variety for some scale economies is open to debate, but there is no presumption that such sacrifices should always be made. In contrast to imperfect competition theory, there is a presumption that the loss of variety would indeed be a sacrifice.

Consumer preference and the firm's demand curve

However, that is not the end of the story. The transition from differentiated consumer preferences to the downward-sloping demand curve facing the individual firm is not as simple as Chamberlin believed. The theory of perfect competition also requires downward-sloping demand curves for distinguishable products, but not for the output of individual producers. Chamberlin assumes competition between firms, and something which he calls free entry. The latter assumption raises the question, posed by Andrews (1964): free entry into what? Chamberlin's answer, by anticipation, appears to be that competitors may enter any product group, but not the particular speciality of any existing producer. New entrants may offer close substitutes, and thereby push the demand curves for existing producers to the left; they may even cause the elasticity of such curves to increase; but they cannot produce perfect substitutes. Their offerings must indeed fall sufficiently short of perfect substitutes to permit a significant slope to the demand curves of the competing firms; otherwise there is no point in having any theory other than that of perfect competition. What can keep substitution sufficiently imperfect?

In the postulated conditions of long-run equilibrium with perfect knowledge, nothing can. The same costs are available to all, the same technology is available to all, the same instruments of consumer attraction are available to all. Thus a firm may, in long-run equilibrium, enjoy a market for its differentiated product only on condition that it is offered at a price no greater than any rival would need for a duplicate product package in order to earn normal profits. That is the price which is equal to average cost for the level of output required. If we are prepared to allow for life-cycles of firms, then the price depends on the average costs of the representative firm. Price and output are determined by market demand and supply, both of which reflect the force of long-run potential competition. There is no price discretion; there is no falling demand curve for the individual producer.

Andrews' own argument is developed further, into a model (1949) in which the prospect of long-run reactions dominates short-run actions: thus price is determined by industry supply and demand, while the individual firm's market share depends on goodwill. Price, in effect, is always determined by long-run factors. It is a characteristic of Andrews' theory, misunderstood by his critics, that the prices of products and the outputs of individual firms are not determined simultaneously. Nor were they in Marshall's theory.

One may choose to follow Marshall rather than Andrews in having a separate short-run price theory, in which adjustment time-lags, similar to those which permit quasi-rents until the capital stock can be increased, may also permit monopolistically competitive profits until a successful marketing mix can be duplicated. This expedient may be particularly atttractive in a comparative equilibrium analysis of innovation, where patents may create a limited institutional monopoly, and the degree and durability of comparative advantage helps to explain the choice of pricing policy for a new product.

The assumptions of consumer rationality and perfect knowledge which are held to underlie all major economic theory (except for convenient ad hoc exclusions) also undermine Dewey's (1969) attempt to reconstruct imperfect competition theory. Dewey argues that, in the absence of government restraint, imperfect competition must always end in monopoly. Tangency solutions are unstable, because they offer cost reductions to anyone prepared to acquire additional plants and rationalise production so as to operate a smaller number at their technical optimum; the rationaliser then exploits his cost advantage to engross the market by limit pricing.

This argument may be attacked from many quarters. First, monopoly profits are a collective good to the individual firms, and may therefore not be achieved; but since the normal rules of analysis do not allow one to enquire whether a defined equilibrium can actually be reached, this objection may be overruled. Second, the concentration of output proposed seems to deny that the different firms were in fact producing different products. Having taken for granted that all the costs involved in marketing a product can be subsumed into production costs, Dewey talks of a standard plant, which implies a standard product. Dewey's consumers seem to be very curious people: irrational, yet conscious of their irrationality. They refuse to switch to another seller even though he offers them a similar (apparently duplicate) commodity at a lower price, but are quite happy to switch to this same alternative product at the same price reduction when both are sold by the same corporation. Dewey does not explain why these unexhausted economies should actually be attainable except by producing at a loss.

The model is also wide open to Andrews' criticism. No reason whatever is offered for supposing that new entrants should make do, as Dewey declares they must, with the unused portion of the demand curve, or why they should not themselves establish a multi-plant firm with exactly the same costs and productive potential as the existing monopolist. Dewey's model, by his own account, belongs to the world in which bygones are bygones, and in which there is no advantage in an established position. If Dewey's firms are making above-normal profits, the industry is not in long-run equilibrium. Economies of scale (if indeed they can logically exist, as was queried in an earlier chapter) are open to all, and are no protection against competition. No firm can charge more than would be enough to satisfy another firm in an equivalent position – because, on the assumptions of the theory, such other firms have free entry to that equivalent position.

Dewey's analysis has a good deal of practical plausibility; but the attempt to use the standard equilibrium formulation has destroyed its logic. This has been the fate of all the theories of competitive imperfections. Thus there would appear to be nothing for it but to retreat from this twisting cul-de-sac: imperfect competition depends on irrationality, monopolistic competition is internally self-contradictory. Hicks (1939) was surely right to shun the whole imbroglio, and to work on the beautiful edifice of general equilibrium analysis. He was right, not only for the reason he gave, that the consequences of accepting such ideas were destructive of economic theory, but also because economic theory exposed them as irrational or fallacious. There may be equilibrium solutions for models of imperfect competition; there can be no imperfections of competition in conditions of general equilibrium. The questions over which economists argued in the nineteen-twenties are illegitimate.

Competitive uncertainty

And yet the world is not perfectly competitive. If our formal models lead us to the conclusion that it must be, then we must look to our axioms. That is the great virtue of logical rigour: if the conclusions are wrong it indicates clearly where to look for the reasons. If we look for an axiom to challenge, none is more obvious – at least given the arguments in previous chapters – than that of costless information. It is well known that the inclusion of information costs changes the equilibrium conditions, because some resources must then be employed to discover the optimal pattern of choice, and are thus not available for allocation according to that pattern. Moreover, as was noted in Chapter 4, the knowledge of equilibrium prices – and the knowledge that they are equilibrium prices – is a public good, and therefore likely to be in suboptimal supply. If perfect knowledge is not imposed on our models from outside, the remaining assumptions will not generate it, but will on the contrary lead to imperfect information. Competitive equilibrium requires pre-reconciled choice; and there is no reason to expect any mechanism capable of this pre-reconciliation. Thus competition implies ignorance, as non-economists have always believed: competition is not a state of equilibrium but a process of search.

If markets are not organised for them, then the competitors must produce their own organisation. At one level, this implies the construction of collaborative-competitive groups known as firms; at another, the formation of competitive-collaborative groups known as industries. The boundaries of an industry are notoriously difficult to define; so, surprisingly often, are the boundaries of a firm. We have considered in previous chapters the firm's internal problems of search and choice; let us now consider the problems it faces in the market.

The relevant issues have been explained by Romney Robinson (1971, pp. 33–4) in his critical review of Chamberlin's work.

In the *unorganised* market, each supplying firm, whether manufacturer, wholesaler, or retailer, must hunt up its own customers – or the buyer must hunt up his own seller. These are the markets in which almost all supplying firms find themselves engaged; and common experience tells us that they do not face anything resembling a perfectly elastic demand curve....They are the markets in which products are differentiated.

Robinson follows up this characterisation of the typical industry by asserting that 'the monopolistic competition theory was theory constructed to fit the conditions of unorganised markets'. Certainly Chamberlin's view of the firm employing the three variables of price, product and selling cost conforms much more easily with the idea of a firm searching for customers whose preferences, whose whereabouts, even whose existence, are suspected, rather than known, than do the traditional sorts of model, in which product differentiation appears as a trick, and all selling expenditures are by definition wasteful, if not actually pernicious.

The distinction between production and selling costs is strictly valid only in a world of perfect information. In this alternative view, selling costs are search costs: therefore much must be wasted, as much research is wasted, as much of the time economists devote to building theories is wasted – when judged by the standards of perfect knowledge. Product differentiation is an attempt to discover, as well as to modify, consumer preferences; and this is a two-way process, because consumers often need to discover what the relevant part of their own preference function is.

It would be a mistake to consider these activities simply as a set of transaction technologies applied to the discovery of hidden data. The process is one of invention as well as discovery. The commodity space may be defined for analytical convenience, or to provide a framework for budgeting, but as Richardson (1960, p. 105) reminds us, the list of commodities is always open to addition. 'Imagination, rather than information in any ordinary sense, is what entrepreneurs require in order to discover new ways of combining resources so as to meet consumers' desires.' Imaginative standards, which as we have seen are so dangerous to the preservation of a formal equilibrium, are essential to this competitive process; imagination sees an enhanced value in a new combination of resources, and thus creates a profit opportunity. This creative view of business was forcefully upheld by Schumpeter (1943), and has been eloquently argued by Levitt (1962, 1969) and Drucker (1955, 1964). There are many aspects to competition; but any analysis may be dangerously misleading which forgets the aspect of innovation.

However, this kind of competition lacks the characteristic independence attributed in the model to each monopolistic competitor. As Robinson observes, 'if monopoly means anything, it means the possession of some genuine independence of price policy. And it simply is not true that all firms, or most firms, enjoy such independence' (p. 52). The independence of Chamberlin's firms within their large group depends critically on the diffusion of the effects of their actions among the fellow-members of the group; and, as Kaldor (1935) quickly demonstrated, there is no reason to assume such an effect. Indeed, there are reasons for the opposite assumption: in conditions of limited visibility, one is most conscious of what is nearby; and in conditions of partial ignorance, one is most conscious of those competitors whose activities, for any reason, are most noticeable. One's external references are normally few in number.

The argument applies to customers as well as to competitors: some potential customers are more likely to be attracted than others, and some are more likely to be lost than others. Although this observation may seem to warrant a downward-sloping demand curve, it cannot do so unless each firm's customers have a wide range of different alternatives in mind, whereas each group is likely to consider a relatively small number of suppliers. In general, as Robinson points out, 'The firm's situation is one of oligopolistic interdependence. All monopolistic competition situations are potentially or actually oligopolistic' (pp. 44–5). The path of monopoly, so confidently pointed by Sraffa in 1926, is a false trail.

If, as Robinson and Andrews both argue, actual markets are typically oligopolistic, what happens to the analysis? The apparatus of ceteris paribus demand curves collapses, and the standard method of defining equilibrium conditions fails to work. The reason for the general failure to produce models of oligopolistic equilibrium is precisely the inadequacy of the information which the analyst feels it proper to use. No oligopoly model can be solved on the basis of the assumptions used for equilibrium theory – which makes it just as well that the assumptions used for equilibrium theory cannot give rise to oligopolistic conditions. Oligopoly is the product of partial ignorance, and partial ignorance denies the possibility of a standard type of analytical solution. We are back in the world of ill-founded, unstable expectations.

The only general solution worth considering is that of Andrews, which most economists seem to have been determined to ignore, because it does not fit in with the accepted analytical method. Andrews assumes that learning is effective; but one may be bolder, and consider oligopoly explicitly as a problem of learning in an uncertain environment. It was because this was an obviously reasonable formulation, as well as because no satisfactory solution had been achieved by traditional methods, that oligopoly provided an opening into economics for theories based on explicitly behavioural assumptions.

Such a view of oligopoly is not far removed from the superficially very different analysis offered by Richardson (1960). By looking at the economic system from the point of view of the decision-maker within it, rather than that of its analytical manipulator, he reaches conclusions directly opposed to those of current orthodoxy. The conventional view, of course, is that in perfect competition the price and output of every unit within the economy is precisely determined, whereas under oligopoly they are indeterminate; Richardson demonstrates that, in the absence of the auctioneer, formal perfect competition provides no plausible basis for expectations, whereas oligopoly does at least define the apparently relevant set of competitors, and may well promote the exchange of information which gives firms the confidence to make commitments. It is perfect competition which is indeterminate. The imperfections are what makes the system work.

Though Richardson keeps as close as he can to traditional methods of analysis, he does not attempt to explain behaviour in terms of the formal apparatus of supply and demand curves. One might nevertheless consider, in a loosely-formulated theory, using a falling demand curve to reflect the costs of search. These costs must be borne by someone. They may be borne by the consumer, and indeed if he is sufficiently dissatisfied with the offerings which he sees to be currently available, he may be prepared to put a good deal of effort into his search. Offering to bear some of the costs of search is a way of attracting business, not only for professional intermediaries such as insurance brokers and estate agents, but also for manufacturers. Cheap offers and free trials are attempts to persuade potential customers to experiment by paying part of their costs. As this example shows, price reductions are not the only device for encouraging search: there are many ways of attempting to create a customer, and none of them is, in principle, illegitimate once we cease to assume that the customer already exists.

We should not, of course, assume that such a demand curve, cautious approval for which might be found in the passage from Marshall quoted earlier, is of the same kind as that used in traditional theory. It most resembles the kinked demand curve, which must be drawn from a position of equilibrium, and cannot be used to determine it. How many customers one may gain at what cost depends on how many – and at what cost – one has now. The curve should be thought of rather as indicating an expansion path; it should not be assumed to be reversible, nor as pointing towards equilibrium. It is a device for helping to explain change, rather like a modern learning curve, or Marshall's long-run supply curve.

However, unlike that Marshallian curve, the individual firm's falling demand curve belongs in the short run, if it is to be used in conjunction with any sort of equilibrium model at all. Moreover, the search process may produce income effects, which may modify the original path. At this point one may recall that the absence of secure information is responsible for another set of problems, those considered by Keynes. The connection is perceived by Robinson (1971, p. 58), though not clearly.

A Keynesian underemployment equilibrium presupposes *some* failure within the operating price mechanism – within the system of consumer prices, input prices, or interest rates. But Keynesian economics has not yet been extended from the macro-economic to the micro-economic sphere, to emphasise just *where* within the pricing structure this failure originates. Almost certainly, it has something to do with the fact that most markets are unorganised markets.

Mrs Robinson's (1969, p. vi) instinct, that market imperfections had something to do with unemployment, was sound enough, and the criticism (Loasby, 1971, p. 875) that short-run macroeconomic phenomena could not be explained by micro-economic models of long-run equilibrium, though valid in the context of the accepted set of models, reflected a quite unjustified assumption that the current divisions of economic theory were natural. Keynes explained unemployment by the lack of knowledge which paralyses commitment: at the micro-level this lack of knowledge dissuades firms from the risks of production. Work would be available somewhere at some wage, but where and at what wage is unknown; customers are available somewhere and at some price, but they are unknown too. Ignorance is great, business confidence is low, and therefore commitments are not made. It is safer to adjust quantities than prices. Thus the unemployed man withholds his labour, since he sees some of his fellows still employed at his old wage; the firm withholds its output, since it sees some of it bought at the old prices. Both are afraid to let go, because they do not know where that process will end. They cling to their historical reference standards, and fear the consequences of spoiling the market. Thus they offer quantity signals to a market which requires price signals, and the result is excess capacity and unemployment. There is no path to equilibrium. Indeed, in this fog of ignorance, there is no equilibrium.

A case for competition

Axiomatic theory demonstrates that very special and implausible conditions are necessary to produce an equilibrium that would be regarded as a welfare optimum. It is easy to use this analysis to demonstrate the inefficiency of the market. Thus there might seem to be an especial interest in the demonstration by Lange (1936–7) that a socialist economy could simulate the results of perfect competition; for it might be thought to show, not only that the state can solve the allocation problem, but that only the state can solve it. But the critical question is, not what should the pattern of resource allocation look like, but how is it to be achieved; and the perfectly competitive model, which has defined the terms of the argument, provides no recipe for achieving anything. Actual competition is a process, not a state; and perfect competition can exist only as the description of a state.

The pattern of resource allocation by the state is not determined by the characteristics of any ideal allocation. Those who demonstrate that the market provides inadequate incentives to the supply of collective goods do not always consider what might be the incentive to organise a collective supply; government provision is no simple logical consequence of the failure of private provision. Nor are government officials, or even politicians, free of self-interest: why should they be? The analysis of organisational behaviour applies to them too. The implications need to be worked out with care before government action can be advocated with theoretical confidence. Drucker's (1969, p. 203) view of government may be regarded as too pessimistic: 'the greatest factor in the disenchantment with government is that government has not performed. The record during the last thirty or forty years has been dismal. Government has proved itself capable of doing only two things with great effectiveness. It can wage war. And it can inflate the currency' (p. 268). Its effectiveness in the latter respect has improved even further since that testimony was given. Even if Drucker is exaggerating, it can hardly be denied that government has a spectacular record of failure. Drucker's principal explanation is that government is 'by design a protective institution', and that 'every beneficiary of a government programme immediately becomes a "constituent"' (p. 211). It is notable that Edmund Dell (1973), struggling to find ways of improving the unhappy record of British government's involvement with industry, an involvement which he regards as inevitable and desirable, also emphasises the protective functions of government; he even attributes much of the support for atomic energy and aerospace to the desire to find employment for the large number of scientists and engineers who had been engaged in the war effort. If so, that would surely rank as the most expensive protection racket in history, but for similar American and Russian schemes of outdoor relief.

It is unfortunately too easy to slip from the argument that

government intervention is needed because the market necessarily provides inadequate incentives for some activities which are socially desirable, to the argument that the absence of adequate market incentives is sufficient to demonstrate the case for government support. Thus, if there is a presumption that the market will emphasise private affluence, there is a corresponding presumption that governments will emphasise public profligacy. The choice is between highly imperfect systems.

Part of the case therefore for the preservation of a substantial market system is that governments are hardly pure guardians of the public interest. Since a week is a long time in politics, governments are far too prone to take narrow-agenda, limited-variable, highly-programmed decisions in situations which call for the opposite. Thus, for example, Labour governments created the conditions for financially-inspired takeovers by their dividend restraint in the late nineteen-forties, and functionless property millionaires by their controls on office building in the nineteen-sixties; rent controls and security of tenure for occupants of furnished apartments are the most recent in a long series of measures to ensure that the homeless remain homeless. The results summarised by Sapolsky (1972, p. 1) are, at least in part, inevitable products of the system.

Government continually fails us. Laws which are passed with great expectation often cause larger problems than they were intended to solve. Programs which are announced with great ceremony and apparent commitment often are not implemented. Public agencies which are established to provide innovative and efficient approaches to major policy issues often act with an all too familiar rigidity and ineptitude.

Yet the fundamental logical argument for the market is the argument from competition. It is, however, not the argument that is usually advanced. It is not as a means of achieving the uniformity of behaviour of the perfectly competitive models that competition is valuable. The virtue of competition lies not in constraining all similar agents to the same action, but in encouraging them to behave differently. Pareto optimality focusses our attention on the requirement of consistency; but a competitive system should not be too coherent. In a world where we are inevitably ignorant about some of the past and present, let alone the future, the co-ordination of activities is less important than the perception of new problems and opportunities, and adaptation to them. Competitive success depends on guessing better than one's rivals. Whether the guess rests mainly on skill or mainly on luck is of secondary importance (except perhaps to the purveyors of skills). What matters is that there should be the inducement to try, to be different, and not to conform. The argument for competition rests on the belief that people are likely to be wrong. The argument for political competition rests on the same belief.

According to Sapolsky, the success of the Polaris development was due in significant measure to the encouragement of rival views among contractors. It is necessarily an expensive way of completing a project; but the method of exclusive responsibility for each element has often proved a method only slightly – if at all – cheaper of achieving only failure. Many of the wastes of competition are unavoidable consequences of ignorance. This argument does not imply anything very specific about the number of competitors, in either politics or industry. The desirable number of competitors in the political contest in Britain is at present a matter of some concern; and the value of competition within one of the major British parties has long been an issue. The case for the feudal baronies which characterise I.C.I. must rest largely on their function as alternative generators and recipients of new ideas, joined by a series of semi-permeable membranes, so that such ideas may have some chance to develop, and also some chance of transplantation. In the end, the case against an authoritarian system of resource allocation rests on the same principles as the case against an authoritarian structure in any discipline: part of the case, almost entirely neglected in this book, is that no person, or body of persons, is fit to be trusted with such power; the part of the case that is central to this book is that no one person, or group of persons, can say for sure what new knowledge tomorrow will bring. Competition is a proper response to ignorance.

11

Progress and paradigms

> Formal operations relying on *one* framework of interpre-
> tation cannot demonstrate a proposition to persons who
> rely on *another* framework. Its advocates may not even
> succeed in getting a hearing from these, since they must
> first teach them a new language, and no one can learn a
> new language unless he first trusts that it means some-
> thing.
>
> M. Polanyi (1958, p. 151)

All analysis is selective. The agenda to be used, the set of control
variables, and the solution programme do not derive naturally
and inevitably from the situation to be analysed; they are imposed
upon it. As Popper (1970, p. 52) insists, '*we approach everything
in the light of a preconceived theory*'. Because of our very limited
ability to handle complexity, any representation of a situation
must be incomplete and inaccurate; abstraction entails error and
ignorance. There can be no guarantee that the chosen scheme of
analysis is unquestionably superior to all alternatives, even when
judged by a specific set of criteria – which themselves cannot be
guaranteed to be the most appropriate set. But though, in this
sense, abstraction is arbitrary, it is not usually random. The ways
in which, and the extent to which, the recognition and handling
of problems is conditioned by the structure of a formal organisation were considered in Chapter 8. In this chapter we shall discuss
the abstractions employed by scientific communities.

Paradigms and research programmes

Any group, if it is to be worth calling a group, must operate on
shared assumptions. But the shared assumptions of a scientific
group cannot be simply equated with established truth. Kuhn
(1962, 1970a) has drawn dramatic attention to the significance
and character of these assumptions, which he labelled paradigms;

and more recently Lakatos (1970) has introduced a similar, but more detailed, concept of scientific research programmes. Both concepts embody an agreed group of unquestioned propositions (called by Lakatos the 'hard core'), and a set of procedures (Lakatos' 'positive heuristic') for generating and testing, through the practice of Kuhn's 'normal science', a series of refutable hypotheses, which form a 'protective belt' around the hard core. Refutation of the hard core itself is out of order, as long as the paradigm or research programme persists.

Paradigms provide scientists with their terms of reference. Once such terms of reference are generally accepted, research becomes, in Kuhn's (1962, p. 5) words 'a strenuous and devoted effort to force nature into the conceptual boxes supplied by professional education'. All boxes are empty when constructed: it is the task of the practitioner to fill them. A paradigm must therefore be both comprehensive and open-ended; it does not solve problems, but holds out the prospect of successful solutions to those who formulate and test with skill and care particular hypotheses consistent with the paradigm. For the natural scientist, at least, therefore, it offers 'a criterion for choosing problems that, while the paradigm is taken for granted, can be assumed to have solutions' (Kuhn, 1962, p. 37).

That such criteria are indispensable for the natural scientist is emphasised by P. B. Medawar (1967, pp. 86–7), explaining

why scientists seem so often to shirk the study of really fundamental or challenging problems. . .No scientist is admired for failing in the attempt to solve problems that lie beyond his competence. The most he can hope for is the kindly contempt earned by the Utopian politician. If politics is the art of the possible, research is surely the art of the soluble. Both are immensely practical-minded affairs.

But paradigms are not only essential intellectual tools. As Shackle (1967, pp. 288–9) so clearly appreciates, they also meet vital emotional needs.

The chief service rendered by a theory is the setting of minds at rest. So long as we have a satisfying conceptual structure, a model or a taxonomy which provides for the filing of all facts in a scheme of order, we are absolved from the tiresome labour of thought, and the uneasy consciousness of mystery and a threatening unknown. . . Theories by their nature and purpose, their role of administering to a 'good state of mind', are things to be held and cherished. Theories are altered or discarded only when they fail us.

Shackle is actually so impressed with the comforting role of paradigms that he underplays the intellectual stimulus which they provide. Far from avoiding the labour of thought, they may call for, and inspire, both intense and protracted effort if they are to generate viable hypotheses. But they do allow that thought to be confidently deployed within an agreed structure. Any such structure necessarily precludes limitless possible discoveries; but the rewards for such a sacrifice may be very great. As Kuhn (1970b, p. 247) observes, 'Because they can ordinarily take current theory for granted, exploiting rather than criticizing it, the practitioners of mature sciences are freed to explore nature to an esoteric depth and detail otherwise unimaginable.'

Paradigms permit a concentration on short-run questions; what Kuhn calls normal science is short-run science. In academic work as in business, long-run questions, even if no more intellectually taxing, are much less comfortable, because they tend to open up an unpalatable – and sometimes potentially infinite – range of options. They may require the managing director to consider what business he should be in, or the academic the proper scope of his subject. An acceptable paradigm affords protection from such disturbing speculations.

Some structure must be imposed on complexity and ignorance before any investigation, let alone any decision, is possible. But the mere imposition of a structure is not enough. We must have sufficient confidence to work within it, with no more than an occasional glance over our shoulder to see what is being ignored. We noted in an earlier chapter Clower's (1965) ironic comment on Hicks' (1939) discussion of the potentially disturbing theoretical implications of false trading: 'it is heartening to know that income effects can be ignored if they are sufficiently unimportant to be neglected'. But in any piece of analysis, as in any decision, many factors must be ignored which might be significant; and however careful our selection has been, we still need reassurance that what we have ignored is indeed sufficiently unimportant to be neglected. Paradigms, by restricting the agenda for enquiry, provide the reassurance that we all seek. Logic and evidence can work only within a framework of belief. Confidence in our chosen structure is a prerequisite of commitment to a scientific programme, as it is to an investment decision. Without such commitment, as Keynes realised, there can be no investment; without such commitment, there can be no science.

Paradigms can therefore properly be judged only by their fruitfulness, not by their truth. They are always abstractions, and there is always some criterion by which they are inadequate. Furthermore, if they are to be effective they must be imprecise. Since the set of problems faced by a group of scientists, like the set faced by a formal organisation, cannot be predicted in any detail, some ambiguity in the terms of reference may be necessary for effective response to a specific situation. Ambiguity may also, again as in formal organisations, be necessary to hold the scientific community together; the implicit contract of the research programme may need to be imperfectly specified.

Lakatos (1970, p. 135) provides for imperfection in two parts of a research programme. The positive heuristic 'consists of a partially articulated set of suggestions or hints on how to change, develop the "refutable variants" of the research programme, how to modify, sophisticate, the "refutable" protective belt'; and any particular item in the protective belt is clearly dispensable. But what of the hard core? It is notable that for none of the research programmes which he cites does Lakatos define at all precisely the content of the hard core; nor does Kuhn specify the essential content of any paradigm. This should not be surprising; just because the hard core is taken for granted, it is unlikely to attract critical attention. Often, as in formal organisations, there is no authoritative text to which all can refer; and what texts there are will be open to interpretation. It is even possible that elements of the research programme may be transferred, in either direction, between hard core and protective belt.

That the scientist should have room to manoeuvre – and to manoeuvre within boundaries that are not clearly marked – does not deny the existence of a recognisable structure; it simply makes possible a structure which is acceptable and useful. One implication is, however, obvious. Logically-based disputations about the relative merits of paradigms are of limited value; no paradigm intended to be useful can be defended solely by arguments which relate to its formal elegance or rigour.

But neither can it be defended beyond all question by an appeal to evidence. This is not only because, in a contest between paradigms, the admissibility of at least some of the evidence depends on the acceptance of the paradigm which it is required to support. The difficulty also derives from the function of paradigms as guides to research: from this standpoint the acceptability of a paradigm rests on its promise of future results – in other words, on the problems which have not yet been solved by its use. Because a paradigm defines a set – often a very large set – of possible hypotheses, but makes no claims for the validity of any particular members of that set (some of which, indeed, will be mutually exclusive alternatives), it follows that paradigms, unlike the hypotheses to which they give rise, cannot be validated by formal experimental or statistical methods.

Failure to recognise this distinction has led to much unnecessary argument among economists. The disputes over profit maximisation provide a notorious example. For profit maximisation is not a hypothesis but a paradigm; and whereas a specific hypothesis embodying some version of profit maximisation can, in principle, be tested, the paradigm of profit maximisation cannot. Only in long-period static equilibrium with perfect knowledge is its formulation unique; and no such experimental conditions can be found. Its status as a paradigm is the explanation of its persistence. Lipsey's (1971) attempt to emphasise the testing of economic predictions suffers from a similar confusion: the theory expounded in his textbook is necessarily a paradigm, to which his proposed tests, being designed for hypotheses, cannot properly be applied.

The obverse of a paradigm's continued fertility is the continued existence of unsolved problems. A paradigm which left no issues unresolved would be useless as a guide to further work. Thus, in Newman's (1864) words, when judging a paradigm 'a thousand difficulties do not make one doubt'; on the contrary they offer a thousand opportunities for the deployment of professional skill. In science, as in business, problems may be opportunities in disguise. They may offer new chances to demonstrate the power of our paradigms, if only we have the wit to see how. Provided that they are being steadily resolved, the existence of difficulties is a symptom, not of a paradigm's weakness, but of its continuing strength.

This remains true even when some major difficulties prove recalcitrant. For example, attempts to explain the path of the moon by the application of Newtonian theory failed consistently for sixty years; yet there were no serious proposals for the rejection of Newtonian theory. What was in question was not the paradigm, but the professional skill of the scientists who had failed to derive an appropriate hypothesis from it; and, in the event, confidence in Newtonian theory was justified. More recently, 25 years of skilful and patient work by D. C. Miller, in which many thousand repetitions of the Michelson–Morley experiment produced results clearly inconsistent with Einstein's theory of relativity, evoked nothing but expressions of regret that such a fine experimental physicist should waste his professional career generating data in which no one was interested (Polanyi, 1958, pp. 12–13). For, as Polanyi (1958, p. 138) observes, 'it is the normal practice of scientists to ignore evidence which appears incompatible with the accepted system of scientific knowledge, in the hope that it will eventually prove false or irrelevant'.

Paradigm change

It is, therefore, not surprising that a paradigm, once established, should prove difficult to overthrow. Since its continued usefulness depends on the double condition of unresolved problems and good prospects of their eventual solution by the application of the paradigm, there can be no unequivocal standard by which it can be judged to have failed. Furthermore, since a paradigm, like a management control system, provides the basis for selecting both problems and the relevant variables to be investigated, it may condition its users against even the perception of some of the more fundamental threats. An experiment reported by Bruner and Postman (1949) in which subjects readily identified as normal wrongly-coloured playing cards inserted into an otherwise normal pack provides some formal confirmation of the common experience in all manner of contexts that observations are 'fitted to one of the conceptual categories prepared by prior experience' (Kuhn, 1962, p. 63). A paradigm produces intellectual tunnel vision.

Of course, paradigms are not impervious to attack. If the most strenuous efforts fail to generate hypotheses which successfully predict new facts (or, in Lakatos' terminology, induce 'progressive problemshifts'), but instead can offer nothing more than specific expedients for particular difficulties, then the research programme degenerates, and the paradigm enters a crisis. But apparently degenerating research programmes may be redeemed; there is no unmistakable sign of failure.

It is possible that decisions to abandon paradigms may be too long delayed; for the sequential search programme of science is likely to lead to the troubles of Briggs more often than to the preemptive review of Smith's. Moreover, the commercial criterion is often lacking. Scientists can afford rather more split bathtubs before looking for a new alloy, and will suffer far more in prestige if someone else succeeds in pressing a tub from existing material after they have turned to a new.

Thus something quite exceptional in the way of difficulties must become apparent before an established paradigm can be seriously challenged. As Shackle (1967, p. 288) says, 'Theoretical advance can spring only from theoretical crisis.' To discard an established paradigm is to discard the accepted methods of recognising and solving problems; and, if there are no accepted methods, there is no body of science. A scientific community without paradigms is impossible. Thus some of the current lamentations on the state of economics propose remedies which are, in effect, invitations to abandon economics as a discipline. If a field of study (or the idea of a corporate strategy) is not to collapse, then no paradigm, however dubious, can be abandoned until a replacement is available.

But an acceptable replacement may not be easy to find. As long as an existing paradigm produces results, even with difficulty, the creation of alternatives is a distraction of energies from the immediate challenge; and indeed, the greater the difficulty of working with the existing paradigm, the greater may be the concentration of effort on overcoming it – just as the very weaknesses of a company's policy may absorb the resources necessary to redesign that policy. For these reasons, a new candidate paradigm is likely to appear first in an ill-developed, and possibly misleading form, in shabby contrast to the familiar well-articulated paradigm, the product of a long process of refinement at many hands.

And it will necessarily have very few results to show, in a contest where results are critical.

Moreover, the results are very likely to be, in some respects, irremediably inferior. For the new paradigm is unlikely to be a perfect substitute for the old: it will probably seek to decompose the field of study in a new way, and to employ a different set of abstractions. The controllable variables of one paradigm become exogenous in another; agendas may be redefined; incompatible programmes prescribed. Such differences may well be the means by which the new paradigm claims to resolve the crisis which has called it into being. But the price of success – and there may be no more than an enthusiast's promise of success – is likely to be the abandonment of established solutions to familiar problems: for example, Lavoisier, in offering a solution to the difficulties which were baffling phlogiston chemists, could provide no explanation whatever for the similarities between metals, which phlogiston theory had readily accounted for (Kuhn, 1962, p. 148). Ignorance and complexity compel us often to adopt a different rather than a wider vision: thus 'wider still and wider shall thy bounds be set' is rarely a helpful slogan for paradigm-makers.

The competition between paradigms therefore turns not simply on their relative merits in explaining certain important phenomena, but on judgements about which are the important phenomena to explain. For these judgements there are no generally-acceptable criteria; indeed they cannot be made without excursions into those regions of mystery and doubt from which paradigms, once accepted, serve to protect us. They require a suspension of the incremental method of piecemeal science, and probably the abandonment of some ground already thought to be won. A change of paradigm redefines the set of relevant problems, and the criteria for selecting problems and evaluating solutions: it changes to some degree – occasionally to a large degree – the accepted definition of the scope of a subject. The choice between paradigms is a choice between alternative ways of coping with complexity and ignorance – of deciding what questions shall not be attempted. With its combination of the threatened obsolescence of some established methodology, and the posing of awkward, sometimes fundamental, questions about the nature of a subject, a time of paradigm change is a time of upheaval that for many may be more disturbing than exhilarating. Intellectual retooling is uncomfortable, as well as expensive.

The foregoing argument should not be held to imply that paradigm-choice is irrational, or that scientific progress is impossible. Though for economics the case may be more doubtful, one can normally say, with Kuhn as with Popper and Lakatos, that each paradigm is better than its predecessor for the practice of normal science (Kuhn, 1970b, p. 264). The difficulties of choice arise partly from the imperfect definition of the competing paradigms, and from shortcomings in the evidence, both previously discussed; but they also arise from the use of an imperfectly-specified criterion function. 'Given a group all the members of which are committed to choosing between alternative theories and also to considering such values as accuracy, simplicity, scope, and so on while making their choice, the concrete decisions of individual members in individual cases will nevertheless vary' (Kuhn, 1970b, p. 241).

As Boulding (1966) and Drucker (1955) have emphasised in different contexts, any single criterion is almost certain to be dangerously insufficient; thus a decomposition of objectives into a loosely-integrated set may be both a proper response to ignorance and an essential means of maintaining the joint purposes of the working group. An agreed set of objectives is compatible with disagreement on any specific issue; but it is compatible only with certain kinds of disagreement. As Musgrave (1974, p. 22) has pointed out, even repeated differences in the application of a set of criteria do not justify the argument, espoused by Feyerabend (1970), that the set serves no purpose. Structureless science is a contradiction in terms. On the other hand, as Kuhn (1970b, p. 262) argues, 'variability of judgement may. . .be essential to scientific advance', for it provides a means by which the scientific community can hedge its bets, just as variability of judgement within a competitive economy spreads a society's risks. Strict uniformity of decision is highly dangerous in an uncertain world.

Though originally expounded in the context of natural science (and, indeed, predominantly of physics), the concepts of research programmes and paradigms offer a sufficiently roomy framework for analysing the development of economic theory. The previous chapter contained a critique of the theories of imperfect and monopolistic competition; this chapter attempts to understand and explain them.

The Marshallian paradigm

The Marshallian synthesis on the theory of value was constructed with almost incredible care and subtlety; indeed some of the sharpest minds of the twenties and thirties simply failed to appreciate what Marshall had done, and construed his caution as hesitancy and his subtlety as confusion. But Marshall was facing methodological difficulties which could not be solved, only lived with. Shackle (1967, p. 44) partially explains the situation.

Marshall's self-imposed endeavour was an intensely difficult one. He sought to describe a mechanism of evolution of the firm and industry; to derive the principles of this mechanism from the detailed and wide observation of a segment of British economic and social history. . .and to make his account of this observable productive evolution the vehicle of laws which should be in some degree general and permanent.

Shackle places the emphasis on the problem of explaining a great variety of specific facts by a single body of theory – the achievement of a high level of abstraction without significant loss of sufficiency. But the way Marshall (1890, 1920) tackled the problem evoked a difficulty of a special sort. The key lies in Shackle's phrase 'a mechanism of evolution', which expresses perfectly the inner tension of Marshall's analytical method. This inner tension is perceptible from time to time throughout the *Principles*, and is briefly discussed in the Preface to the Eighth Edition. 'The Mecca of the economist lies in economic biology rather than in economic dynamics. But biological conceptions are more complex than those of mechanics; a volume on Foundations must therefore give a relatively large place to mechanical analogies; and frequent use is made of the term "equilibrium", which suggests something of statical analogy' (p. xiv).

The mechanical analogies gained greatly in force and precision by Marshall's use of the differential calculus, to which he was drawn in part, as he explains in his Preface to the First Edition, because it was such a perfect example of that Principle of Continuity which, in that Preface (as in the motto on the title-page), was set forth as a distinctive theme of the book. But in the last resort, as is made clear in the last Preface he wrote, the differential calculus, or any other device of mechanics, was expendable. 'Fragmentary statical hypotheses are used as temporary auxiliaries to dynamical – or rather biological – conceptions: but the central idea of economics, even when its Foundations alone are under discussion, must be that of living force and movement' (p. xv).

We have seen in the previous chapter how Marshall evaded the statical conclusions from the assumption of increasing returns; and his chapter on equilibrium with reference to increasing returns ends with a warning, unusually blunt for him, that others should do the same.

> The Statical theory of equilibrium is only an introduction to economic studies; and it is barely even an introduction to the study of the progress and development of industries which show a tendency to increasing return. Its limitations are so constantly overlooked, especially by those who approach it from an abstract point of view, that there is a danger in throwing it into definite form at all (p. 461).

But the young do not always take kindly to the warnings of the old. Sometimes, like Peter, they are skilful or lucky, and catch the wolf by its tail; sometimes it is a tiger. A bold venture may end in triumph or disaster. In this instance, it produced a series of short-run personal triumphs; but it has ended in disaster for the subject.

As soon as the workings of a competitive market were approached from a purely abstract point of view, Marshall's paradigm of competition was in crisis. Those who objected, quite rightly, that it was no longer Marshall's paradigm were ignored; after all, it was what his paradigm should have been if only he had not fudged the simple logic of a rigorous model. So the concept of static equilibrium, which Marshall had deliberately confined to the protective belt, became the hardest element in the hard core.

The theoretical argument was forcefully summarised by Sraffa in his famous article of 1926, in which he demonstrated that increasing and decreasing returns were both strictly incompatible with other assumptions of the standard formal analysis, that the size of the firm was therefore left indeterminate by this analysis, and that there was thus no adequate justification for casting that analysis in terms of perfect competition. The logic of Sraffa's (1926) criticism and of his proposed solution are worth examining. The key sentences run as follows.

If diminishing returns arising from a 'constant factor' are taken into consideration, it becomes necessary to extend the field of investigation so as to examine the conditions of simultaneous equilibrium in numerous industries: a well-known conception, whose complexity, however, prevents it from bearing fruit, at least in the present state of our knowledge...If we pass to external economies, we find ourselves confronted by the same obstacle, and there is also the impossibility of confining within statical conditions the circumstances from which they originate.

It is necessary, therefore, to abandon the path of free competition and turn in the opposite direction, namely towards monopoly. Here we find a well-defined theory in which variations of cost connected with changes in the dimensions of the individual undertaking play an important part (pp. 541–2).

These sentences are perhaps so familiar that it will be easier to analyse the argument if they are paraphrased. The strict formal requirements of static partial equilibrium analysis do not permit the conditions which are logically necessary for the existence of perfect competition. Therefore something must go. The cost conditions which make perfect competition possible may indeed be compatible with dynamic general equilibrium; but general equilibrium is a much less usable paradigm than partial equilibrium, and dynamic analysis is still more hopeless. On the other hand, the theory of monopoly offers a readily-available alternative to perfect competition, while still retaining all the usual conditions of static partial equilibrium.

Thus the argument turns, not on the existence of perfect competition as a recognisable state of affairs, but on, first, the internal consistency, and second, the relative usefulness, of competing paradigms. It is important to take these two criteria, of internal consistency and relative usefulness, separately; and it is convenient to begin with the latter.

Imperfect competition or general equilibrium?

Let us accept for the moment Kaldor's (1934b, p. 72) conclusion that 'long-period static equilibrium and perfect competition are incompatible assumptions'. Marshall's theory included monopoly; the new theory had no room for perfect competition, as Mrs Robinson forcefully made clear. When we see some situations approximating to perfect competition, but none, in developed economies, approximating to long-period static equilibrium, what are we to think of a choice of paradigm in which perfect competition becomes an inadmissible market form? Surely the answer is that the choice was soundly based on good scientific practice, which exemplifies at this point the economic doctrine of opportunity cost. Usefulness, rather than immediate realism, is the proper ground for choosing between paradigms. The cost of giving up static partial equilibrium analysis, in terms of existing theory to be discarded, appeared far higher than the cost of giving up perfect competition, and the gains, in terms of alternative theory lying ready for exploitation, were far less.

That this is the relevant basis for choice is confirmed by the reasoning of the most distinguished economist who made the opposite choice, in favour of general equilibrium theory – J. R. Hicks. He stood Sraffa's conclusion on its head: if perfect competition was incompatible with partial equilibrium, general equilibrium was incompatible with anything other than perfect competition. The essentials of Hicks' (1939, pp. 83–5) argument, too, are worth quoting in his own words.

It has to be recognised that a general abandonment of the assumption of perfect competition, a universal adoption of the assumption of monopoly, must have very destructive consequences for economic theory. Under monopoly the stability conditions become indeterminate; and the basis on which economic laws can be constructed is therefore shorn away...
It is, I believe, only possible to save anything from this wreck – and it must be remembered that the threatened wreckage is that of the greater part of general equilibrium theory – if we can assume that the markets confronting most of the firms with which we shall be dealing do not differ very greatly from perfectly competitive markets ...At least, this get-away seems well worth trying. We must be aware, however, that we are taking a dangerous step, and probably limiting to a serious extent the problems with which our subsequent analysis will be fitted to deal. Personally, however, I doubt if most of the problems we shall have to exclude for this reason are capable of much useful analysis by the methods of economic theory (pp. 83–5).

No more than Sraffa, Kaldor, and the others who argued the opposite case, does Hicks appeal to facts. Indeed, he admits that the facts may well be against him. Neither party follows Beveridge's prescription, endorsed by Lipsey (1971), to seek empirical verification. And on this issue they are right, and Beveridge and Lipsey are wrong. For the argument is not about hypotheses – concerning which Beveridge and Lipsey are, of course, correct – but about the kinds of hypotheses and the kinds of data that might be presented for verification; and here the empiricist's prescription is not only inappropriate but often impossible.

The readiness with which Hicks is prepared to accept the exclusion of important problems from consideration as the price of using the paradigm of perfect competition should also be noted. The availability of a paradigm is more relevant than the importance of a problem. Economists are perhaps in general readier than natural scientists to tackle ignorance with inadequate weapons; but this readiness springs from inferior armament rather than superior virtue. And it is, after all, only relative; it would be difficult to maintain that the distribution of economic effort reflects at all closely the importance of economic issues; much less difficult to relate it to the availability of usable paradigms. Nor is this necessarily wrong; for it has been argued by Kuhn (1962, p. 164) that a discipline will make faster progress if its practitioners are insulated from pressures to 'choose problems because they urgently need solution and without regard for the tools available to solve them'.

The illusory crisis and its consequences

So far we have argued that, given the existence of a crisis in value theory, the solution of abandoning perfect competition, though apparently odd, was justifiable. But we still have to ask, was there a real theoretical crisis? The answer must surely be no. The theoretical crisis arose out of a misconception about the nature of the subject, and therefore of the way it should develop. Any usable model must be a mis-specification of the phenomena to which it refers; to refine the abstractions in such a model is often to refine away its sufficiency.

Thus Kaldor's (1934a, p. 122) objective of 'a more rigorous

formulation of the conditions under which it is possible to make generalisations about the factors determining economic equilibrium' must be no more than a subsidiary – and potentially dangerous – concern, since it is obvious that the conditions will never be met. What matters is how extensively they can be violated without seriously impugning the result to which they lead. A strict regard for internal consistency in economic theory is as likely to be a vice as a virtue. Though Sraffa's article appeared to point the way to a more realistic economics, in fact it did nothing of the sort; it was an appeal for formal consistency, which has been such a notable (and not always helpful) feature of the subject ever since. Marshall knew well enough that long-period static equilibrium and perfect competition are incompatible assumptions, and was careful not to commit himself to either.

One immediate consequence of this neglect of Marshall's warnings was the wreckage of Chamberlin's (1933) attempt to expand value theory by a more detailed consideration of market conditions; the urgency and difficulty of the struggle to rescue the theory from the internal contradictions of abstract reasoning made impossible the perception of Chamberlin's work as anything other than a leading contribution to that struggle. The difficulties with which Chamberlin was trying to cope were difficulties on the demand side; but no one recognised that these difficulties existed. 'Theoretical advance can spring only from theoretical crisis'; because everyone was obsessed by a different crisis, Chamberlin's theoretical advance was not – perhaps could not be – understood.

Are we then, as D. H. Robertson (1950, p. 8) suggested, no more than half in jest, 'to regard all that has happened since [Marshall] in this field as a vast crime wave' (p. 8)? Not entirely; for two reasons. The less important reason is that the changing structure of industry did pose problems of fact which appeared to reinforce the problems of theory; any commentary on the arguments of the time which ignores the contemporary concern with these problems must appear unfair to some of the protagonists of change, even though one may doubt the completeness of their success in explaining the new structure by the new theory. The more important reason is that, as is likely to happen when a paradigm changes, the new theory redefined the scope of this branch of economics. As Shackle (1967, p. 65) observes, 'not only the answers, but the questions, were new. The whole notion of what value theory sought to do and the ways its aim should be accomplished had been changed...Primacy had passed from the autonomously self-subsisting technical commodity to the firm considered as a profit-maximising policy maker.'

By setting out to show that 'the analysis of the output and price of a single commodity can be conducted by a technique based upon the study of individual decisions' (p. 15), Mrs Robinson (1933) for the first time appeared to bring decision-making by the competitive firm within the ambit of both theory and empirical research. Though this was far from her intention, she thus not only made possible the development of managerial economics, but determined its characteristic virtues and defects.

The defence of the revolution

That the definition of such an important new field failed to precipitate a flood of investigations was probably largely due to the feeling that research was unnecessary since facts could apparently be deduced from purely geometrical arguments. Logic appeared to make evidence superfluous. Lakatos (1970, p. 137), much more than Kuhn, emphasises the unimportance of evidence in theoretical science: 'the methodology of scientific research programmes accounts for the *relative autonomy of theoretical science*...Which problems scientists working in powerful research programmes rationally choose, is determined by the positive heuristic of the programme rather than by psychologically worrying (or technologically urgent) anomalies.' Similarly, the refinement of the new economic theories took precedence over their testing. Nevertheless, the report, by Hall and Hitch (1939), of the first serious investigation which appeared to show that businesses did not behave in the way predicted, inevitably caused some consternation; the paradigm has been in a kind of crisis ever since.

Many typical features of a paradigm crisis have been visible. There has been no general agreement on the terms of reference for the debate, or indeed on the precise scope of the paradigm under attack. Nor has the attack been well co-ordinated: P. W. S. Andrews (1949, 1964), the only economist to develop both a full-scale critique and an alternative paradigm, published the two halves of his argument fifteen years apart, and in the wrong sequence for maximum effect. On the opposing side, many of the successful revolutionaries, quite properly, turned conservative to protect the newly-established paradigm; and their defence owed little to empirical evidence about firms' pricing behaviour.

Such disregard for empirical evidence, it was argued earlier, is generally appropriate in a conflict of paradigms; and it is particularly appropriate in this instance. For Mrs Robinson's theory was based not, as she claimed, on 'the study of individual decisions', but on the conditions of individual equilibrium, just as perfect competition had been. Both perfect and imperfect competition are empty of predictions about the ways in which firms actually fix prices; studies of pricing behaviour are therefore irrelevant to standard price theory. Perfect and imperfect competition (rather than monopolistic competition, which Latsis (1972) chooses) may indeed be treated as variants of a single research programme; but it is not Marshall's programme.

Andrews saw more clearly than most that the dispute turned on questions not of business behaviour but of the structure of economic models; whether the model should assume atomistic competition or oligopoly, and whether it should be formulated in terms of equilibrium. Part of Andrews' critique offers a remarkable parallel to Sraffa's earlier argument; whereas Sraffa had shown that a strict interpretation of the conditions of long-period static partial equilibrium virtually excluded increasing costs for the individual firm, Andrews (1964), pp. 73–80) now argued that these conditions also excluded falling demand curves for the individual firm. Thus we reach the final condemnation of long-period static partial equilibrium: it is incompatible first, with perfect competition, second, with real-world phenomena, and finally, even with itself.

This rejection of equilibrium theory did not worry Andrews, who had previously developed an alternative; but, as he acknowledged, it worried other people. For it is the concept of equilibrium which is at the heart of the crisis; and the abandonment of equilibrium is a much more fundamental change than that implied by the creation of the theory of the firm, which was developed, in accordance with Sraffa's advice, precisely in order to preserve the static equilibrium method of analysis. Some micro-economists need a theory of the firm; and for some purposes the marginalist equilibrium theory is the best theory we have.

How, then, is the paradigm defended? Andrews' critique, though in its own terms irrefutable, is unacceptable; it has therefore apparently been ignored. Richardson's (1960) work, which is even more subversive, is never mentioned in public. As we have seen, economists have a remarkable capacity for ignoring the un-comfortable. Expositions and explanations of business behaviour which conflict with equilibrium theory, however, have met with vigorous onslaughts, in which the terms of the argument, as is usual in controversies over paradigms, have been defined in a way that comes near to ensuring success. When evidence conflicts with the model, it is the evidence which is found wanting.

Equilibrium theory is justified by assuming its validity. Ration-ality is equated with profit maximisation, which in static equi-librium implies mathematically the equality of marginal cost and marginal revenue; therefore any business observed violating the theory is behaving irrationally, and any alternative theory must assume irrationality, which, as we all know, makes theorising impossible – unless, of course, it be the consumer irrationality which is the not-quite-explicit basis of imperfect competition. Even Cohen and Cyert (1965), who might be expected to be particularly sensitive to this issue, discuss decision-making by marginal analysis as if this were synonymous with rationality. Andrews' own theory has inevitably come in for particularly harsh treatment; but the standard accusation that he is rejecting profit maximisation, rather than equilibrium (which persists even in Silberston's (1970) recent survey) is quite plainly wrong.

However, the defence of imperfect competition against em-pirical criticism has become a subsidiary issue. A defence which exalts formal rigour at the expense of evidence is necessarily vul-nerable to claims of even greater rigour, with even less regard for evidence; and while the defenders have been engaged on this front their base has been overrun. Hicks has triumphed over Sraffa, and the theory of value has undergone a counter-revolution. Monopolistic equilibrium may do well enough for partial analysis; but the logical virtue of value theory requires much more than this. Having accepted the static equilibrium method, and its particular logical requirements, Sraffa's only defence against general equilibrium theory was its fruitlessness 'in the present state of knowledge'. This defence has now collapsed as a result of the devoted work of some of the brightest intellects ever applied to economics, and Hicks' counter-claim that 'under monopoly the stability conditions become indeterminate' has been decisive in rejecting the paradigm of imperfect competition.

Of course, the concept of economic laws as necessarily based on the existence, uniqueness, and stability of equilibrium solutions to artificial equation sets, the concept held by Hicks and other general equilibrium theorists, is very peculiar; but Sraffa not merely accepted these rules of the game, but actually used them as the basis of his argument. Mrs Robinson did not; and it is now her turn to be misunderstood. She wanted to play a different game, and attempted to show that the accepted rules allowed one only to play games that were quite pointless; unfortunately for her, many economists continue to find them fascinating.

Organisational behaviour

Nevertheless, some progress has been made. The exercise of construing business behaviour in terms of accepted theory has revealed much more clearly than before the level of abstraction involved in that theory, so that some economists appear to have given up any pretence that value theory has any concern with business behaviour (Machlup, 1974). This partial withdrawal of pretensions to describe the processes of decision-making by the use of equilibrium theories of the firm has facilitated the emergence of a very different paradigm for that purpose.

The logical justification for a separate paradigm of organisational decision-making was clearly set out for no one to see in Coase's (1937) article discussed in Chapter 4. By arguing that decision-making within a firm was different from decision-making in the market, Coase excluded the detailed study of the former from the application of the marginalist equilibrium paradigm. But it is not surprising that this implication should be ignored, and attention concentrated instead on the skill with which he used the existing paradigm to remove an awkward anomaly in the theory of the firm – the failure, until that time, to account for the existence of firms at all in a specialised exchange economy. The appeal of paradigms is reinforced by success: even their success in explaining their own limitations draws attention, not to those limitations, but to their explanatory power.

Thus it is not surprising that much of the early development of the new paradigm of business behaviour discussed in this book owed little to economists, nor that its impact has been very slight. The failure to recognise economics explicitly as a systems study and the dominance of market paradigms conditioned economists to think of the firm as a basic element rather than as an economic system worthy of analysis in its own right. Managerial and behavioural theories have gained entry almost entirely as models of oligopoly behaviour, because the determination of price and output in an oligopoly was the obvious area of weakness. But even here they have to compete with alternative models, and, much more important, with the tendency to read oligopoly out of the corpus of economic theory. If imperfect competition is debarred by the requirement that economic laws must define equilibrium conditions, then what chance is there for oligopoly – which, anyway, has a disturbing aura of irrationality about it? That a narrowing of the scope of the subject should be preferred to the abandonment of the paradigm is not unusual, nor is it irrational. The means of solution and the type of solution appear more important than the range.

Inevitably, the criteria employed in the existing paradigm have been used in judging the new; and on these criteria behavioural theory comes out rather badly. It has no answer to the questions of efficiency or stability as those questions are conventionally posed. It has no use for traditional basic concepts: optimisation has no usable meaning; economists' heavy investment in calculus becomes redundant (though the set-theoretic emphasis of modern general equilibrium theory may remove that particular disadvantage); equilibrium is not defined; and there are no general analytical solutions.

A comparison of paradigms

But the characteristics of one paradigm are not the only criteria by which a rival can be judged. It is more helpful to compare the abstractions and the methods of analysis which are legitimised by each, the kinds of answer which each can give, and the questions which each permits to be asked. Such a comparison has occupied much of this book. No simple analytical summary can be adequate; a paradigm must be experienced to be appreciated. Nevertheless it is worth emphasising that the quintessence of behavioural theory is its recognition of complexity and partial ignorance. As Shackle has long maintained, traditional economics evades the problems of ignorance; the theory of decision-making under uncertainty implies a very high degree of specific knowledge. It is the lack of such knowledge which leads to the behaviour which Cyert and March (1963) call uncertainty-avoidance, and which was discussed in some detail in Chapter 4, to the desire for liquidity, to the need to create a customer, and to the emphasis on flexibility in corporate strategy.

It is the lack of knowledge which makes satisficing rational. Satisficing is not equivalent to what Baumol and Quandt (1964, p. 23) call 'optimally imperfect decision-making'; for the requirement that 'the marginal cost of additional information gathering or more refined calculation be equal to its (expected) gross yield' is an example of precisely the kind of fiction which satisficing models reject. In this new paradigm, optimisation may be a device – often a useful device – used by the decision-maker; it cannot serve as the basis for the analysis of his behaviour. Remember: one can often optimise a model; one can never optimise a situation.

Economists' aversion from the effects of ignorance is probably largely responsible for the general belief that behavioural theory can apply only to situations in which there are significant elements of monopoly. But all the characteristics of that theory which are seen as consequences of monopoly are perfectly explicable by partial ignorance. That is not to say that elements of monopoly may not be important; but if we are to think clearly we must recognise that they are not formally necessary.

Behavioural theory tries to come to terms with the problems of choice. The decision-maker is faced with a situation which he cannot fully comprehend, and in which tomorrow's information will usually be better than today's: it will almost certainly be different, and it may well be different in ways which he does not expect. In these circumstances, the notion of entering into a complete series of contracts, however contingent, which will determine, in his present state of ignorance, the decision-maker's behaviour in any conceivable future circumstance, is wildly irrational. Even if this web of contracts required no time or effort to make, its cost would be high; the decision-maker would find himself, not the spider, but the fly in his own web, totally unable to break free in response to new threats and new opportunities.

This is the true crisis of the equilibrium method in economics. The theory of choice cannot cope with the problems of choice; it cannot even admit their existence. The new paradigm proposes to resolve the crisis by a bold redefinition of the problem space, and by adopting a programme which, though much more loosely-defined, involves the abandonment of the interconnected central notions of optimality, equilibrium, and determinacy. Instead of the definition of positions of rest, we are offered the means of investigating an ongoing process. Instead of a defined goal, we have a defined origin. Thus, for example, a firm's history and financial position become elements of the analysis, whereas in micro-equilibrium theory they are quite properly excluded as irrelevant.

Such a shift of focus, from destination to origin, has been a central feature of some major paradigm changes in other fields. It was, indeed, precisely such a shift, in the study of falling bodies, which gave rise to the concept of instantaneous, as distinct from average, speed, and thus in due course led to the development of differential calculus, which the equivalent shift discussed here now threatens to dethrone. It was precisely such a shift in the study of evolution which made Darwin's ideas so disturbing; and it is apparently this absence of finality which most disturbs some critics of behavioural theory – not surprisingly, because it leaves us exposed forever to the 'mystery and doubt' from which, as Shackle observes, we seek protection in theory – and, above all, in a theory which emphasises the uniqueness and stability of equilibrium.

Conclusion

One of the principal objects of this book has been to demonstrate how different is the behavioural paradigm from any of the varieties of microequilibrium theory. The intention was not to demonstrate its superiority – indeed an important part of the argument of this chapter has been that it is hard to find criteria for judging between paradigms that are not coloured by the paradigms themselves: rationality for example, apparently so objective, is in fact very heavily paradigm-dependent. Indeed, observant readers will have noticed that, like Kuhn's view of scientific progress, the historical development of the theory of the firm, as presented in this chapter, falls entirely within the behavioural paradigm: problemistic search is evoked by a disparity between aspiration and the apparent performance of existing theories – a disparity which may define a false problem – and neither equilibrium nor optimality are required to explain the theoretical developments of the last fifty years.

If the new paradigm were to replace the old, much would be lost. But if it were to be finally rejected by economists, perhaps even more would be lost. Fortunately, there is no reason why either should be rejected: once the effort has been made to view both of them with equal bias, there is nothing but an excessive and unscientific regard for consistency to prevent both being used, either separately or together as convenient, until the emergence of a new crisis and the rise of a new challenger. Perhaps next time, given a rather better appreciation of what is happening, the process will be rather less wasteful of time and energy; though it can never be either easy or comfortable.

12

The economics of certainty and the economics of ignorance

> The Theory of Economics does not furnish a body of settled conclusions immediately applicable to a policy. It is a method rather than a doctrine, an apparatus of the mind, a technique of thinking, which helps its possessor to draw correct conclusions.
>
> J. M. Keynes (1922)

The conception of economic theory employed in this book is that of a method – or rather, series of methods – of analysis. To treat economic theory as a doctrine is misleading, and may be dangerous. The truth of a doctrine depends on the validity of its initial assumptions, and the assumptions of economic theory are chosen for their convenience in relation to particular purposes, not for their truth. It is, of course, sometimes convenient to be truthful. Theories provide ways of organising data; they are paradigms to guide the generation of hypotheses. They select, and, therefore, necessarily exclude.

The exclusions of equilibrium theory

Some of the major exclusions of equilibrium theory have been examined in previous chapters. Its axiomatic treatment of preferences allows the existence of groups only if they are teams: with this very special exception, it is a theory of individuals, not of households, or of organisations. Joint decision-making is permitted only for objects fully shared: joint purposes, which are the cement of almost every organisation, must be served only through the market. Money as a unit of account is dispensed with by casting the whole analysis in terms of relative quantities; and those versions of the theory which ignore transactions costs have no place for money as a store of value. They also provide a second reason for the non-existence of firms.

Even if transactions costs are included, the analytical method requires a complete specification of all relevant possible outcomes and, in addition, a subjective probability distribution which is fully defined for each transactor over all relevant outcomes. If the universe is indeed queerer than we can suppose, then this is a requirement for a strictly inconceivable listing. If transactions have costs, the requirement is also illogical, since it cannot be optimal to incur all the costs which would be necessary to produce a complete listing of possibilities. But without such a listing, the strict logic of the theory – and it is a theory which prides itself above all on its strict logic – collapses. No optimum can be defined for an incomplete choice set. Thus the admission of transactions costs is a threat to the whole edifice. But if they are not admitted, not only do the firm and money disappear; the whole of macro-economics vanishes too. Involuntary unemployment – or any involuntary outcome of any kind – is logically impossible in a general equilibrium system with perfect knowledge. Macro-economics must then be a study of irrational behaviour, and can have no place in a discipline whose theme is the logic of choice.

When one recalls that the establishment of equilibrium solutions requires the denial of economies of scale, at least beyond a relatively small output, one must conclude that in terms of its breadth of coverage formal economics is back to the nineteen-twenties; the problems which led to the development of imperfect competition theory and Keynesian economics are defined out of existence. When compared with Marshall, it has retrogressed even further. Arrow (1962, p. 609) defines as 'the classic question of welfare economics...to what extent does perfect competition lead to an optimal allocation of resources'. That is a rash definition, for, as Richardson (1960) has demonstrated, general equilibrium theory has no means of showing to what perfect competition may lead. Even if it should reach an equilibrium, there is no particular reason why it should stop there. Indeed, if the question is to be treated with the rigour which the theory seems to demand, it cannot even be posed: perfect competition cannot exist outside equilibrium, and therefore cannot lead anywhere. General equi-librium theorists have not 'formulated a two-hundred-year-old tradition', as Hahn (1973a, p. 324) claims; they have invented a new question about the properties of a solution set, already deemed to have been discovered, in a very special system. The relevance of this invented question they have never attempted to make clear. To Adam Smith's problem of how to organise an economy in order to find desirable solutions they have, formally, nothing to say.

Of course, the narrow range of topics now included is argued at a far higher level of formal sophistication; but that has its own dangers, since improving the quality and depth of sophistication can so easily absorb – and has so easily absorbed – attention which might otherwise be directed towards more practical problems. Sufficiency is forgotten; abstraction is all. The double weakness of general equilibrium theory is that it excludes consideration of the consequences of ignorance, and leaves one in ignorance of the effects of what is excluded. Indeed, the power of the dominant paradigm is such that it becomes difficult to convince its adherents that anything not within its scope can be a proper subject of economic enquiry.

This difficulty may be illustrated by considering the use of the terms 'competition' and 'rationality'. The notion of a competitive market remained for very many years rather loosely defined: it was a market with many suppliers and many customers, none possessing a large market share, and concerned with similar, but not necessarily identical, products. This notion was eventually converted into a mathematically precise concept, which was given the name of perfect competition. The perfection is a perfection of mathematical form; but the sense of the term was very easily extended to imply that the model represented an ideal state of the world – rather as if a physicist should suggest removing the earth's atmosphere in order to create a perfect vacuum. A world of perfect competition is a world of perfect liquidity and perfect knowledge: it is therefore a world without problems. Since perfect competition can exist only in equilibrium, it is also a world without decisions. But man is a problem-solving animal: therefore a world of perfect competition offers man an environment which is implacably inhuman.

A similar confusion between desirable properties of a model and desirable properties of the world can be seen in the changing connotations of 'rationality'. Originally, rational behaviour was the behaviour of a reasonable man. But the formalisations have become steadily more and more specific and more and more demanding. Rationality nowadays denotes a fully-specified programme for action; and the logical properties of such a programme are too readily assumed to imply a strictly corresponding prescription for reasonable behaviour. But a rational model may well not be a model of rational behaviour: to rely entirely on a model which misrepresents the real situation, as all models must, though rational in the technical sense of following a logical programme, is liable to prove irrational in the original sense of being a reasonable response to that situation. The double sense of 'rational' denies us the right to question the adequacy of the model as a guide to behaviour. Whenever 'rational' can be replaced by 'programmed' without change of meaning, its use assumes knowledge and excludes all questions about the sources and adequacy of knowledge. Thus it is not surprising that, just as unity has been called the most divisive word in Irish politics, so rationality has become the most emotive word in economics.

The analytical method, favoured by mathematicians, of assuming a problem solved and enquiring into the conditions that the solution must fulfil has left no place for consideration of possible paths to that solution. The decision-makers within the system have no need of enquiry. Inquiring minds are dangerous, for they may discover something new. If the rationality of Simon's problem-solvers is bounded, the rationality of the decision-makers in equilibrium theory is tightly constricted. As Shackle (1972, p. 85) observes, 'If we refuse to examine their problems of choice, save on the assumption that they know everything relevant, plainly the question of what they can or cannot know is transformed into the question of what situations we shall or shall not allow to be part of the economic field of study.'

The economic field of study, thus defined, includes only choices that are fully informed, at least in a probabilistic sense. Not only does it therefore refuse to recognise the impossibility of a complete definition of any situation; it also debars time, the neglect of which has aggravated (if not caused) many of the theoretical troubles of the last fifty years. The requisite initial data may indeed include knowledge of future events, but can make no provision for the unexpected. The search for genuinely new information is not allowed; and the expectations included must be thoroughly cleansed of any taint of imagination, for only so can expectation be reconciled with determinacy. In Shackle's (1961, p. 272) words, 'Conventional economics is not about choice, but about acting according to necessity'. Every paradigm permits only certain kinds of questions; but it is rather unusual for a paradigm, strictly interpreted, to exclude what would be widely regarded as the central concerns of the subject – the problems of effective choice and the response to change.

Knowledge must be selective, and conditioned by the models that we use; and this, while allowing us to conceive of a decision-maker possessing all the knowledge which his interpretative framework suggests is relevant, also makes it quite inconceivable that any such framework can guarantee the completeness – or even relevance – of any set of knowledge. Though an equilibrium solution may be consistent with conflicting expectations, or generally erroneous expectations, not only does it then lose any connotations of optimality, however perfectly competitive and free from externalities it may be; it is also inevitable that with the passage of time some expectations must be disappointed. When this is perceived, the equilibrium solutions for all future dates will be changed without any change in the underlying data, and the economy will embark on an adjustment process about which formal theory can tell us nothing – except that we needn't worry about income effects if they are sufficiently unimportant to be neglected. A theory which takes serious account of time and ignorance must be a theory of processes, not of states – not even of dynamic states. The apparatus of equilibrium theory serves to conceal our ignorance, and thereby accentuates our ignorance.

The economics of ignorance

The type of model that is known, not too accurately, as behavioural, exists precisely to deal with ignorance. In its specific application to the problem of oligopoly price and output, this is very clear, since it is partial ignorance – the inadequacy of the data for producing pre-reconciled choices – which poses insuperable problems for the equilibrium theorist. The decision-makers in behavioural models lack some of the relevant knowledge; they may, in addition, fail to make use of some of the knowledge which they do have, or to which they at least have access. Their problems are incompletely structured, and the variables of interest are incompletely specified. Their actions therefore depend on what they define as their problem and on the way that they handle it; both sets of factors are likely to be significantly influenced by external events, but not entirely determined by them. Decision-makers have discretion; but it is possible for the analyst, given certain information, to suggest the directions in which that discretion is likely to be exercised. Indications of direction, it will be recalled, are all that Machlup (1967) has claimed for traditional price theory.

The decision-maker's situation is one in which resources may reasonably be devoted to search, and thus behavioural models include search activities, both informal and formal: the purpose of search is not simply to improve probability estimates, but also to generate new courses of action and reveal possible outcomes. But decision-makers may use other means of reducing uncertainty, for example by concentrating on short-run decisions, by negotiating with their environment, and by taking care not to act in ways which might disturb the stability of existing coalitions. (The latter may rule out some attempts to 'optimise'.) They will be prepared, through the design of the organisation and its information and control systems, to receive and respond to certain kinds, and only certain kinds, of information.

Once we allow for the possibility of new knowledge, about hitherto unsuspected courses of action, or hitherto unconsidered states of nature, it is logically impossible to be confident of predicting the course of events very far ahead. But predicting the course of human history is a matter for theologians, not economists. This approach warns us rather to expect the unexpected; to be prepared for changes, sometimes drastic, in plans and expectations, and to be wary of long-range plans or forecasts which depend upon present knowledge; that means all long-range plans and forecasts. It is often more useful to investigate, and prepare for, the consequences of possible future events than to refine estimates of their probability. For in considering the ways by which we attempt to deal with ignorance our theory demonstrates that success must be partial and incomplete.

Such an approach provides a relevant underpinning to Keynes' macrotheory. As Shackle (1972, p. 268) has argued,

In any other world [than a timeless one] prices are *convention*. They depend upon expectation, which is *originative*. When public prices must be agreed amongst those who are in some respects free to invent the suppositions on which those prices must rest, and who are indeed obliged to invent them since they are not supplied by observation of what is actual, the prices which are agreed are one set out of infinitely many possibilities.

Our discussion of reference standards suggests how these prices may be agreed, and supports Keynes' argument that long-range expectations are much less secure than short, so that the conventions governing the prices of durable goods are especially unstable. If we insist on our formal general equilibrium logic in these circumstances we cannot explain any prices, since all are interdependent; but a partial equilibrium approach may leave us rather more confident of the objectivity of some prices, and suggest that the phenomena discussed by Keynes may be confined to a particular set of prices. However, we shall also realise just why the effects are normally confined to durables, and recognise in what circumstances similar effects may be seen among other classes of goods. We may even produce a rational explanation of the otherwise irrational phenomena of wage rigidity and a money illusion.

A reclassification of economic theories

It may well be convenient to reorganise economic theory into two broad categories. One category would cover analysis of well-defined situations, or, more precisely, of situations which we are prepared to treat as well-defined. This category would include those situations of partial ignorance on which the analyst is prepared to impose a set of probabilities, or to assume such a set on the part of the decision-maker under study. Such situations would permit the full deployment of general equilibrium methods, and provide scope for all the rigour and elegance that anyone could desire. It would offer strong attractions to theorists. But it would not be simply an intellectual game. It would even be more than a training of the mind.

In the suggested context, general equilibrium theory would have two major kinds of practical usefulness. First, it would often have as much sufficiency as a laboratory experiment for making predictions about the behaviour of complex systems; for, as Simon (1969, p. 8) has emphasised, 'we can often predict behaviour from knowledge of the system's goals and its outer environment, with only minimal assumptions about the inner enviroment'. It may be a paradox that the conventional theory of the firm rests on the assumption that firms do not exist; but since it produces some useful results very simply, it is a paradox to be exploited. The danger in such uses of this kind of theory is that, as pointed out in Chapter 3, its practitioners may not appreciate that the necessary inferences can only be drawn by abandoning the criteria of formal rigour by which the theory is judged; but if there are other kinds of theory flourishing along-side, this danger should be reduced.

The danger is likely to be least if these other kinds of theory are explicitly based on the denial of some of the assumptions under-lying general equilibrium theory. That is why an attempt has been made in this book to examine these assumptions in some detail. For this is the second great practical value of general equilibrium theory: it draws attention to the fact that, once the logic has been sorted out, conclusions depend on assumptions, and the sufficiency of conclusions on the sufficiency (*not* the realism) of assumptions. The results of a constrained maximisation analysis depend on what are perceived to be the constraints when defining the solution space. An optimising model does not guarantee the best choice; it does guarantee that the choice is consistent with the assumptions on which it is based. What is called optimality is in fact usually consistency. In this way general equilibrium theory emphasises the importance both of the assump-tions which form the basis of our models, and of the information which we use for our practical analyses. These are enormously valuable contributions. That they are rather different from the contributions claimed for their theory by general equilibrium theorists themselves is no reason for disregarding them, or for decrying the theory.

The second kind of economic theory is the study of partial ignorance. At the level of the individual and of the organisa-tion, this theory would be concerned with topics discussed in earlier chapters, such as the effects of organisational design and experience on the perception of problems and the choice of solutions – including the use by decision-makers of the kind of theories belonging to the first category. But decision-making under uncertainty, as usually defined, belongs firmly in the first category. Whether a particular optimising model is regarded as good enough is often a very relevant question. W. H. Smith's consultants used a very simple type of gravity model to arrive at an 'ideal' location for the new warehouse, and thus provided a confirmatory check on the suitability of particular sites discovered by physical search. The model would not have been very good as the sole method of locational choice; as a simple method of checking the results of a quite different type of incomplete analysis it served very well (Loasby, 1973, pp. 5–6).

General equilibrium theory analyses a system without intermediate levels. It is a theory constructed like the watches made by Tempus. It has no use for subassemblies, no use for such categories as food or fuel. But these subassemblies are a necessary part of a theoretical structure assuming partial ignorance; because incomplete knowledge is likely to be organised around subassemblies. However, these subassemblies may not be uniquely defined. According to the analyst's, or the subject's, perception of the problem, for example, an industry may be defined by material, skill (and principal unions involved), product, or some other category; and even when the category is agreed there is room for difference of opinion. Such ambiguities, far from needing to be resolved by clear definitions, are part of the subject-matter of analysis. Imperfect specification, of both organisational and analytical structure, is necessary for progress in the face of complexity and ignorance.

In its short-run versions, a theory of the industry may look something like the theory of monopolistic competition, in a more Marshallian framework. Falling demand curves and falling cost curves may both be incorporated, as indications of potential movements through time. Such curves may be a projection of the expectations of the decision-makers at the organisational level of analysis, and decisions at that level may influence the shape of the curves. But industrial analysis will also attempt to explain industrial structure, particularly those aspects of structure to which Richardson (1960, 1972) has drawn attention, and in doing so will use concepts and methods similar to those used to explain the structure of organisations – for these are indeed often alternative systems for coping with particular kinds of problem.

The consequences of ignorance, notably the desire to limit ignorance, which show up in organisation and in industry, also affect both the type and the content of decisions. Such effects provide a micro-foundation for Shackle's interpretation of Keynes: the deferment of commitment in response to high levels of ignorance, seen at the level of the individual consumer, the individual enterprise, and the industry, produces an overall deficiency of demand. Thus the economics of organisational behaviour, imperfect competition, and macroeconomics represent three different levels of aggregation in the analysis of the consequences of ignorance.

Such a division of economic theory between the categories of certainty and ignorance was foreshadowed by Keynes (1936, pp. 293–4).

We can consider what distribution of resources between different uses will be consistent with equilibrium under the influence of normal economic motives in a world in which our views concerning the future are fixed and reliable in all respects. . .Or we can pass from this simplified propaedeutic to the problems of the real world in which our previous expectations are liable to disappointment and expectations concerning the future affect what we do today. . . Money. . .is, above all, a subtle device for linking the present to the future; and we cannot even begin to discuss the effect of changing expectations on current activities except in monetary terms.

His emphasis on psychological variables, and on the need for observation rather than axioms (1936, p. 149), even give Keynes a claim to be regarded as the founder of behavioural economics; though Marshall may have a better claim.

Both categories of theory deal with problems of choice within interdependent systems (even though general equilibrium analysis formally studies systems at the points of reconciliation, when interdependencies are not relevant), and with problems of system design and control. Theories of partial ignorance operate at a lower level of abstraction; and thus, inevitably, at a lower level of generality. Some very wide generalisations, including those made

by Keynes, about the consequences of certain kinds of expectations may be possible; another such is that, in an inward-looking
industry, standards of performance may be self-perpetuating
because of the interaction of firms' external standards derived
exclusively from that industry. But, on the whole, models and
conclusions are likely to be restricted to rather narrow ranges of
applications – and can therefore be more informative about those
particular instances. General equilibrium theorists, like mathematical theorists, are looking for great unifying principles; industrial and organisational economists are much more like industrial
scientists attempting to understand and predict the behaviour of
particular constellations of atoms in particular sorts of surround-
ings. Generalisations may emerge, but that is not the primary
purpose. Thus the development of these kinds of theory involves a
shift from equilibrium and generality to ongoing processes and
the particular.

If such a programme is to be pushed forward, there is certainly
need for a reallocation of effort within the profession; and we
have Hahn's (1970, p. 1) admission, in an article which seems to
recognise many of the difficulties which three years later he
ignored, that 'there is something scandalous in the spectacle of so
many people refining the analysis of economic states which they
have no reason to believe will ever, or have ever, come about'.
It is however a reallocation, not a complete redeployment. It is
clear that some of the pretensions of general equilibrium theorists
as to the uses of their theory will have to be abandoned – but that
is bound to happen eventually anyhow; and as has been argued
above, some additional uses are on offer. For what is proposed is
primarily an addition to the range of techniques to be used by
economists, in an attempt to extend their usefulness.

Conclusion

The proposals just put forward, and the argument of the book,
rest on two related beliefs. One is a belief in radical conservatism.
We understand so little of ourselves and our world that we
surely cannot afford to discard established knowledge and wisdom
because it does not fit into our new schemes of ordering. (It is a
serious indictment of formal economics that it has done just that.)

We must conserve what is helpful in our intellectual heritage – and our emotional and imaginative heritage too. But we need to look at our heritage with a fresh eye, to reassess and adapt it; nor must we allow what is established to deny a hearing to the new. A fair hearing it can hardly be, because of the impossibility of judgements free from the criteria embodied in existing paradigms; but the unfairness can be mitigated.

The second belief is a melioristic pessimism. Because it is impossible to produce a full description of any phenomenon, and because of our limited ability to understand, it seems inconceivable that we can ever attain a fully-comprehensive body of knowledge. However, we can surely do far better. The impossibility of final knowledge, and the possibilities of improvement, both argue against any authoritarian judgement about the nature, scope, or content of economics, or any authoritarian judgement in decision-making. Competition is a proper response to ignorance. None are so dangerous as those who are quite certain that they have the right answer, whether to the organisation of economic theory or to the organisation of the economy, because of the damage which they may do before being proved wrong. As Will Rogers lamented, 'It's not so much what folks don't know, as what they do know that ain't so.' That is why it is dangerous for economists to rely so heavily on fictitious perfection. Popper, Kuhn, and Shackle provide logical grounds for accepting the evidence of experience and upholding a belief so well expressed by J. S. Mill (1859).

That mankind are not infallible; that their truths, for the most part, are only half-truths; that unity of opinion, unless resulting from the fullest and freest comparison of opposite opinions, is not desirable, and diversity not an evil, but a good, until mankind are much more capable than at present of recognising all sides of the truth, are principles applicable to men's modes of action, not less than to their opinions.

References

Andrews, P. W. S. (1949) *Manufacturing Business*. London: Macmillan.

Andrews, P. W. S. (1964) *On Competition in Economic Theory*. London: Macmillan.

Ansoff, H. I. (1965) *Corporate Strategy*. New York: McGraw-Hill.

Ansoff, H. I. & Brandenburg, R. G. (1971) A language for organization. *Management Science*, 17 (Application): 705–31.

Archibald, G. C. (1971) Introduction. In *The Theory of the Firm*, ed. G. C. Archibald. Harmondsworth: Penguin.

Arrow, K. J. (1962) Economic welfare and the allocation of resources for invention. In *The Rate and Direction of Inventive Activity: Economic and Social Factors*, National Bureau of Economic and Social Research, pp. 609–26. Princeton: Princeton University Press. Reprinted in *The Economics of Information and Knowledge*, ed. D. M. Lamberton, pp. 141–59. Harmondsworth: Penguin, 1971; and in *Readings in Industrial Economics, Volume 2*, ed. C. K. Rowley, pp. 219–36. London: Macmillan, 1972.

Arrow, K. J. (1971) Political and economic evaluation of social effects and externalities. In *Frontiers of Quantitative Economics*, ed. M. D. Intriligator, pp. 3–25. Amsterdam: North Holland.

Arrow, K. J. (1972) Exposition of the theory of choice under uncertainty. In *Decision and Organization: A Volume in Honor of Jacob Marschak*, ed. C. B. McGuire & R. Radner, pp. 19–55. Amsterdam: North Holland.

Barnard, C. I. (1938) *The Functions of the Executive*. Cambridge, Mass.: Harvard University Press.

Baumol, W. J. (1959) *Business Behavior, Value and Growth*. New York: Harcourt, Brace and World.

Baumol, W. J. & Quandt, R. E. (1964) Rules of thumb and optimally imperfect decisions. *American Economic Review*, LIV: 23–46.

Boulding, K. E. (1966) The ethics of rational decision. *Management Science*, 12 (Series B): 161–9.

Bradbury, F. R. (1973) Scale-up in practice. *Chemtech*, pp. 532–6.

Bradbury, F. R. & Dutton, B. G. (1972) *Chemical Industry: Social and Economic Aspects*. London: Butterworth.

Bradbury, F. R., Gallagher, W. M. & Suckling, C. W. (1973) Qualitative aspects of the evaluation and control of research and development projects. *R & D Management*, 3: 49–57.

Bradbury, F. R., McCarthy, M. C. & Suckling, C. W. (1972a) Patterns of innovation: part II – the anaesthetic halothane. *Chemistry and Industry*, pp. 105–10.

Bradbury, F. R., McCarthy, M. C. & Suckling, C. W. (1972b) Patterns of innovation: part III – the bipyridyl herbicides. *Chemistry and Industry*, pp. 195–200.

Bruner, J. S. & Postman, L. (1949) On the perception of incongruity: a paradigm. *Journal of Personality*, XVIII: 206–23.

Burns, T. & Stalker, G. M. (1961) *The Management of Innovation*. London: Tavistock.

Chamberlain, N. W. (1968) *Enterprise and Environment*. New York: McGraw-Hill.

Chamberlin, E. H. (1933) *The Theory of Monopolistic Competition*. Cambridge, Mass.: Harvard University Press.

Churchman, C. W. (1965) Reliability of models in the social sciences. In *Models, Measurements and Marketing*, ed. P. Langhoff, pp. 23–38. Englewood Cliffs, N.J.: Prentice-Hall.

Clower, R. W. (1965) The Keynesian counter-revolution: a theoretical appraisal. In *The Theory of Interest Rates*, ed. F. H. Hahn & F. P. R. Brechling, pp. 103–25. London: Macmillan. Reprinted in *Monetary Theory*, ed. R. W. Clower, pp. 270–97. Harmondsworth: Penguin, 1969.

Clower, R. W. (1969) Introduction. In *Monetary Theory*, ed. R. W. Clower, pp. 7–21. Harmondsworth: Penguin.

Coase, R. H. (1937) The nature of the firm. *Economica* (N.S.), IV: 386–405. Reprinted in *Readings in Price Theory*, ed. G. J. Stigler & K. E. Boulding, pp. 331–51. London: Allen & Unwin, 1953.

Coddington, A. (1972) Positive economics. *Canadian Journal of Economics*, V: 1–15.

Cohen, K. J. & Cyert, R. M. (1965) *Theory of the Firm: Resource Allocation in a Market Economy*. Englewood Cliffs, N.J.: Prentice-Hall.

Cyert, R. M. & March, J. G. (1963) *A Behavioral Theory of the Firm*. Englewood Cliffs, N.J.: Prentice-Hall.

Davis, O. H. O. A. (1971) Comments (on Arrow, K. J., Political and economic evaluation of social effects and externalities). In *Frontiers of Quantitative Economics*, ed. M. D. Intriligator, pp. 25–9. Amsterdam: North Holland.

Dell, E. (1973) *Political Responsibility and Industry*. London: Allen & Unwin.

Demsetz, H. (1969) Information and efficiency: another viewpoint. *Journal of Law and Economics*, 12: 1–22. Reprinted in *The Economics of Information and Knowledge*, ed. D. M. Lamberton, pp. 160–86. Harmondsworth: Penguin, 1971; and in *Readings in Industrial Economics, Volume 2*, ed. C. K. Rowley, pp. 237–64. London: Macmillan, 1972.

Dewey, D. (1969) *The Theory of Imperfect Competition: A Radical Reconstruction*. New York: Columbia University Press.

Diamond, P. A. (1971) Comments (on Arrow, K. J., Political and economic evaluation of social effects and externalities). In *Frontiers of Quantitative Economics*, ed. M. D. Intriligator, pp. 29–31. Amsterdam: North Holland.

Drucker, P. F. (1955) *The Practice of Management*. London: Heinemann.

Drucker, P. F. (1964) *Managing for Results*. London: Heinemann.

Drucker, P. F. (1969) *The Age of Discontinuity*. London: Heinemann.

Dubos, R. (1961) *The Dreams of Reason*. New York: Columbia University Press.

Economic Development Committee for Mechanical Engineering (1970) *Ventilating, Air Conditioning and Refrigeration Equipment*. London: N.E.D.O.

Feyerabend, P. K. (1970) Consolation for the specialist. In *Criticism and the Growth of Knowledge*, ed. I. Lakatos & A. Musgrave, pp. 199–230. Cambridge: Cambridge University Press.

Fisher, N. (1973) *Iain Macleod*. London: André Deutsch.

Fishlock, D. (1973) How to read the warning signals. *Financial Times*, 6 November, p. 15.

Flanders, A. (1966) *The Fawley Productivity Agreements*. London: Faber.

Friedman, M. (1953) *Essays in Positive Economics*. Chicago: University of Chicago Press.

Frisch, R. (1950) Alfred Marshall's theory of value. *Quarterly Journal of Economics*, 64: 495–524. Reprinted in *Price Theory*, ed. H. Townsend, pp. 59–92. Harmondsworth: Penguin.

Gallagher, W. M. (1971) The Evaluation and Control of Research and Development Projects. (Ph.D. Thesis, University of Stirling.)

Hahn, F. H. (1970) Some adjustment problems. *Econometrica*, 38: 1–17.

Hahn, F. H. (1973a) The winter of our discontent. *Economica* (N.S.), XL: 322–30.

Hahn, F. H. (1973b) *On the Notion of Equilibrium in Economics.* Cambridge: Cambridge University Press.

Haldane, J. B. S. (1927) *Possible Worlds.* London: Chatto & Windus.

Hall, R. L. & Hitch, C. J. (1939) Price theory and business behaviour. *Oxford Economic Papers,* No. 2: 12–45.

Hanlon, J. (1973) Do routine tests guarantee fire safety? *New Scientist,* 25 January, pp. 176–8.

Harrod, R. F. (1972) Imperfect competition, aggregate demand and inflation. *Economic Journal (Supplement),* 82: 392–401.

Hart, A. G. (1948) Keynes' analysis of expectations and uncertainty. In *The New Economics,* ed. S. E. Harris, pp. 415–24. London: Dennis Dobson.

Herzberg, F. (1968) *Work and the Nature of Man.* London: Staples Press.

Hicks, J. R. (1939) *Value and Capital.* Oxford: Oxford University Press.

Hurwicz, L. (1972) On informationally decentralised systems. In *Decision and Organization: A Volume in Honor of Jacob Marschak,* ed. C. B. McGuire & R. Radner, pp. 297–336. Amsterdam: North Holland.

Kaldor, N. (1934a) A classificatory note on the determinateness of static equilibrium. *Review of Economic Studies,* 1: 122–36.

Kaldor, N. (1934b) The equilibrium of the firm. *Economic Journal,* XLIV: 60–76.

Kaldor, N. (1935) Market imperfection and excess capacity. *Economica* (N.S.), II: 33–50.

Keynes, J. M. (1922) Editor's introduction. *Cambridge Economic Handbooks.* Cambridge: Cambridge University Press.

Keynes, J. M. (1936) *The General Theory of Employment, Interest and Money.* London: Macmillan.

Keynes, J. M. (1937) The general theory of employment. *Quarterly Journal of Economics,* 51: 209–23.

Kuhn, T. S. (1962, 1970a) *The Structure of Scientific Revolutions.* Chicago: University of Chicago Press.

Kuhn, T. S. (1970b) Reflections on my critics. In *Criticism and the Growth of Knowledge,* ed. I. Lakatos & A. Musgrave, pp. 231–78. Cambridge: Cambridge University Press.

Lakatos, I. (1970) Falsification and the methodology of scientific research programmes. In *Criticism and the Growth of Knowledge,* ed. I. Lakatos & A. Musgrave, pp. 91–195. Cambridge: Cambridge University Press.

Lancaster, K. J. (1966) A new approach to consumer theory. *Journal of Political Economy,* 174: 132–57. Reprinted in *Consumer*

Behaviour, ed. A. S. C. Ehrenberg & F. G. Pyatt, pp. 340–70. Harmondsworth: Penguin.

Lancaster, K. J. (1969) *Introduction to Modern Microeconomics.* Chicago: Rand McNally.

Lange, O. (1936–7) On the economics of socialism. *Review of Economic Studies*, IV: 53–71, 123–42.

Latsis, S. J. (1972) Situational determinism in economics. *British Journal for the Philosophy of Science*, 25: 207–45.

Lawrence, P. R. & Lorsch, J. W. (1967) *Organization and Environment.* Boston: Division of Research, Harvard Graduate School of Business Administration.

Leibenstein, H. (1966) Allocative efficiency vs. x-efficiency. *American Economic Review*, LVI: 392–415.

Leijonhufvud, A. (1968) *On Keynesian Economics and the Economics of Keynes.* New York and London: Oxford University Press.

Levitt, T. (1962) *Innovation in Marketing.* New York: McGraw-Hill.

Levitt, T. (1969) *The Marketing Mode.* New York: McGraw-Hill.

Lindley, D. V. (1971) *Making Decisions.* London: Wiley Interscience.

Lipsey, R. G. (1971) *An Introduction to Positive Economics*, 3rd edition. London: Weidenfeld & Nicolson.

Little, Arthur D., Inc. (1966) *Transportation Planning in the District of Columbia, 1955–65*, a report by Arthur D. Little, Inc., to the Policy Advisory Committee to the District of Columbia Commissioners, 22 March 1966, printed by the U.S. Government Printing Office, Washington, D.C. (HR 11487).

Loasby, B. J. (1971) Hypothesis and paradigm in the theory of the firm. *Economic Journal*, 81: 863–85.

Loasby, B. J. (1973) *The Swindon Project.* London: Pitman.

Lorenz, K. (1971) *Studies in Animal and Human Behaviour, Volume 2.* London: Methuen.

Lowe, A. E. & Shaw, R. W. (1968) An analysis of managerial biasing: evidence from a company's budgeting process. *Journal of Management Studies*, 5: 304–15.

McGregor, D. (1960) *The Human Side of Enterprise.* New York: McGraw-Hill.

Machlup, F. (1946) Marginal analysis and empirical research. *American Economic Review*, XXXVI: 519–54.

Machlup, F. (1967) Theories of the firm: marginalist, behavioral, managerial. *American Economic Review*, LVII: 1–33.

Machlup, F. (1974) Situational determinism in economics. *British Journal for the Philosophy of Science*, 25: 271–84.

Marris, R. L. (1964) *The Economics of 'Managerial' Capitalism.* London: Macmillan.

Marshall, A. (1890, 1920) *Principles of Economics,* 1st and 8th editions. London: Macmillan.

Maslow, A. H. (1954) *Motivation and Personality.* New York: Harper & Row.

Meade, J. E. (1937) *Economic Analysis and Policy.* Oxford: Oxford University Press.

Medawar, P. B. (1967) *The Art of the Soluble.* London: Methuen.

Mill, J. S. (1859) *On Liberty.* London: Parker & Son.

Miller, D. W. & Starr, M. K. (1967) *The Structure of Human Decisions.* Englewood Cliffs, N.J.: Prentice-Hall.

Miller, S. S. (1963) *The Management Problems of Diversification.* New York: Wiley.

Musgrave, A. (1974) Logical versus historical theories of confirmation. *British Journal for the Philosophy of Science,* 25: 1–23.

Newman, J. H. (1864) *Apologia Pro Vita Sua.* London: Longmans.

Penrose, E. T. (1959) *The Theory of the Growth of the Firm.* Oxford: Oxford University Press.

Polanyi, M. (1958) *Personal Knowledge.* London: Routledge & Kegan Paul.

Popper, K. R. (1957) *The Poverty of Historicism.* London: Routledge & Kegan Paul.

Popper, K. R. (1969) *Conjectures and Refutations,* 3rd edition. London: Routledge & Kegan Paul.

Popper, K. R. (1970) Normal science and its dangers. In *Criticism and the Growth of Knowledge,* ed. I. Lakatos & A. Musgrave, pp. 51–8. Cambridge: Cambridge University Press.

Popper, K. R. (1972) *The Logic of Scientific Discovery,* 6th impression. London: Hutchinson.

Pounds, W. F. (1969) The process of problem finding. *Industrial Management Review,* 11: 1–19.

Raiffa, H. (1968) *Decision Analysis.* Reading, Mass.: Addison-Wesley.

Richardson, G. B. (1960) *Information and Investment.* Oxford: Oxford University Press.

Richardson, G. B. (1972) The organisation of industry. *Economic Journal,* 82: 883–96.

Robertson, D. H. (1950) A revolutionist's handbook. *Quarterly Journal of Economics,* LXIV: 1–14.

Robertson, D. H. (1951) Utility and all that. *Manchester School,* XIX: 111–42. Reprinted in Robertson, D. H., *Utility and All That and other Essays.* London: Allen & Unwin, 1952.

Robinson, E. A. G. (1934) The problems of management and the size of firms. *Economic Journal*, XLIV: 240–54.

Robinson, Mrs J. (1933, 1969) *The Economics of Imperfect Competition*, 1st and 2nd editions. London: Macmillan.

Robinson, Mrs J. (1951) *Collected Economic Papers, Volume 1.* Oxford: Blackwell.

Robinson, Mrs J. (1953–4) The production function and the theory of capital. *Review of Economic Studies*, XXI: 81–106.

Robinson, Mrs J. & Eatwell, J. (1973) *An Introduction to Modern Economics.* London: McGraw-Hill.

Robinson, R. (1971) *Edward H. Chamberlin.* New York and London: Columbia University Press.

Sapolsky, H. M. (1972) *The Polaris System Development.* Cambridge, Mass.: Harvard University Press.

Schumpeter, J. A. (1943) *Capitalism, Socialism and Democracy.* London: Allen & Unwin.

Scitovsky, T. (1943) A note on profit maximization and its implications. *Review of Economic Studies*, XI: 57–60.

Shackle, G. L. S. (1961) *Decision, Order and Time in Human Affairs.* Cambridge: Cambridge University Press.

Shackle, G. L. S. (1967) *The Years of High Theory.* Cambridge: Cambridge University Press.

Shackle, G. L. S. (1972) *Epistemics and Economics.* Cambridge: Cambridge University Press.

Shackle, G. L. S. (1973) Keynes and today's establishment in economic theory: a view. *Journal of Economic Literature*, XI: 516–19.

Silberston, Z. A. (1970) Surveys of applied economics: price behaviour of firms. *Economic Journal*, 80: 511–82.

Simon, H. A. (1965) *The Shape of Automation for Men and Management.* New York: Harper & Row.

Simon, H. A. (1969) *The Sciences of the Artificial.* Cambridge, Mass.: M.I.T. Press.

Simon, H. A. (1972) Theories of bounded rationality. In *Decision and Organization: A Volume in Honor of Jacob Marschak*, ed. C. B. McGuire & R. Radner, pp. 161–76. Amsterdam: North Holland.

Slim, Viscount (1956) *Defeat into Victory.* London: Cassell.

Sraffa, P. (1926) The laws of returns under competitive conditions. *Economic Journal*, XXXVI: 535–50. Reprinted in *Readings in Price Theory*, ed. G. J. Stigler & K. E. Boulding, pp. 180–97. London: Allen & Unwin, 1953.

Whitehead, A. N. & Russell, B. (1910) *Principia Mathematica.* Cambridge: Cambridge University Press.

Williams, B. R. & Scott, W. P. (1965) *Investment Proposals and Decisions*. London: Allen & Unwin.

Williamson O. E. (1963) A model of rational managerial behavior. In *A Behavioral Theory of the Firm*, R. M. Cyert & J. G. March, pp. 237–52. Englewood Cliffs, N.J.: Prentice-Hall.

Williamson, O. E. (1964) *Economics of Discretionary Behavior Managerial Objectives in a Theory of the Firm*. Englewood Cliffs, N.J.: Prentice-Hall.

Williamson, O. E. (1967) Hierarchical control and optimum firm size. *Journal of Political Economy*, 75: 123–38.

Index

I. PEOPLE

2. GENERAL

optimality, Pareto, 22, 25, 46–50, 74, 106, 116, 131, 170, 179, 189, 191
optimisation, 42, 122–3, 212–13, 223
organisations, 35, 67, 100, 106–7, 109–10, 130–1, 137–9, 141, 145–6
  objectives in, 115–29, 143–4, 146
organisational behaviour, 2, 58, 96, 127–9, 130–52, 190, 211–12
organisational design, 68, 79–80, 81, 83–4, 130–52, 221, 223–4
organisational slack, 119, 141, 145–6

paradigms, 193–215, 218, 220
paraquat, 54, 151
Pareto optimality, *see* optimality
PERT, 147, 149
pesticides, screening of, 52
pharmaceuticals, screening of, 52
pharmacologists, use of theory and experiment by, 38, 39
Polaris, development of, 146–51, 192
positive economics, 1, 6, 14–21, 22, 23, 26–8
potatoes, 16–17, 55
precision, error and ignorance, 36–7, 40, 50–1, 92, 99, 104, 113, 135, 152
prediction, 5, 8, 15–16, 36, 41, 51, 117, 221, 223
preferences
  consumers' and theory of value, 14–15, 22–3, 115–16, 156, 157, 169, 176–85, 216
  producers', 115–18, 125–8, 140–1, 145
Pressed Steel Co. Ltd, 91–2, 98, 158
prices, 58–65, 133–5, 163–4, 174, 184, 188, 222
probability, 7–10, 42, 138, 159, 171, 217, 221
problems
  and organisational design, 83–4, 131, 133–5, 143
  and paradigms, 9–10, 130, 176, 193–4, 197–8, 200–1, 206
  recognition and definition of, 4, 85–8, 96–107, 134–5, 144
  solution of, 50–2, 107–10, 145–6
  see also decision processes; reference standards
product divisions, 68, 133

profit
  as objective, 105, 120–1, 124
  in value theory, 6, 115–17, 119–22, 125–6, 153–4, 177, 178, 180–1, 183, 197, 210
  source of, 65–6, 161–2, 185–6
programming of decisions, 81, 83–6, 90–2, 96–9, 101, 109, 134, 152, 191, 200, 219
project development, 37, 43
purpose and choice, 6–7

rationality, 30, 124, 155, 157, 201, 213, 215, 218–19
  bounded, 3, 39–41, 50, 123, 141, 219
  consumer, 179–81
  of individual and organisation, 123–5, 142–3, 163
realism, 22, 24–6, 37–8
recontracting in economic theory, 60, 62, 165
reference standards, 95–114, 123, 142–3, 153–5, 189, 222
research programmes in economics, 13–14, 47, 62, 193–215
rigour, 21–2, 26, 43–50, 55–6, 125, 152, 196, 207, 210–11, 217, 222
risk, analysis of, 7–10

satisficing, 122–3, 129, 145–6, 213
scale, economies of, 64, 69–70, 174–8, 181, 183, 203–4, 217
scale-up problems, 37
science, natural, 3–5, 13, 16–17, 18–19, 27–8, 29, 82, 107, 194–201
science, philosophers of, 5–6, 130
screening, 50–5
search, 50–2, 64, 77, 88–9, 93, 107–9, 141, 151–2, 221
  and theory of value, 58–64, 184–5, 188
  sequential, 51–2, 93, 108–9, 145, 199
  short period, 61, 80, 195
Smith, W. H., & Son Ltd, 86–8, 93, 110–14, 199, 224
statistics, use of, 17–18
stock exchanges, Keynes on, 162
structure, need for, 4, 29, 64, 163, 194–6
subassemblies, importance of, 31–2, 70–2, 224